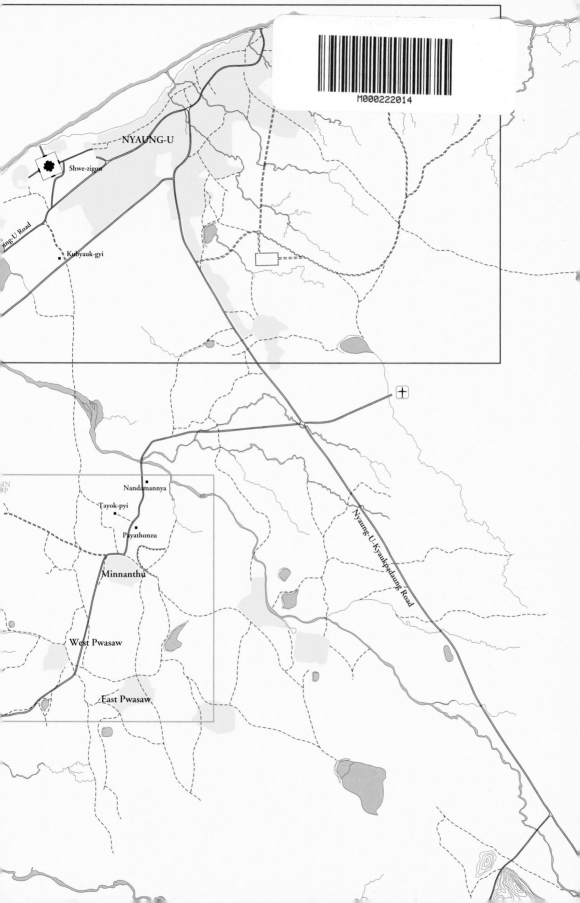

NYAUNG-U

Shwe-zigon

Kubyauk-gyi

Nyaung-U Road

Nandamannya

Tayok-pyi

Payathonzu

Minnanthu

West Pwasaw

East Pwasaw

Nyaung-U–Kyaukpadaung Road

ANCIENT PAGAN

ANCIENT PAGAN

Buddhist Plain of Merit

DONALD M. STADTNER

PHOTOGRAPHY MICHAEL FREEMAN AND DONALD M. STADTNER

First published and distributed in 2005 by River Books
396 Maharaj Road, Tatien, Bangkok 10200
Tel. 66 2 222-1290, 225-0139, 224-6686
Fax. 66 2 225-3861
E-mail: riverps@ksc.th.com
www.riverbooksbk.com

ISBN 974 9863 02 X

Editor: Narisa Chakrabongse
Production Supervision: Paisarn Piemmettawat
Design: NaPaHa

Print and bound in Thailand by Sirivatana Interprint Public Co., Ltd.

Previous pages: *The glistening Shwe-zigon stupa near a bend of the Irrawaddy river.*

CONTENTS

ACKNOWLEDGEMENTS

The Department of Archaeology in Burma provided invaluable assistance, from beginning to end. The first task was to organize a team to assist Michael Freeman with the scaffolding, vehicles and local crew required for photographing the mural painting. This fell to my friend U Thein Lwin. He and his colleague, U Nyein Lwin, were always there to help. I have benefited from conversations over the years with U Nyut Han, U Aung Kyaing, U Myint Aung, U Thaw Kaung, U Win Than Tun, U Myo Thant Tyn, U Aung Bo and U Win Maung (Tanpawady). In Yangon, Jacques Leider reviewed my painting and sculpture chapter. I turned to U Tun Aung Chain, also in Yangon, when no one else knew the answers to my questions. His erudition is matched by his modesty.

Colleagues worldwide lent direct help during the preparation of the book, while others provided indirect assistance through conversations and correspondence over the years. In Australia Pamela Gutman reviewed several of the introductory chapters and a number of the entries. Charlotte Galloway and Don Hein also shared their insights, covering sculpture and ceramics, respectively. Bob Hudson reviewed the historical chapter and guided me through the early archaeological data. In England, Patricia Herbert helped select the watercolours by Colesworthy Grant in the British Library. In France Bénédicte Brac de la Perrière reviewed my references to the *nats*. In the United States Patrick Pranke made suggestions on my religion chapter. Alexandra Green reviewed the entries for two 18th-century monuments. Robert Brown reviewed the entire introduction and many of the entries and contributed his customary insightful comments. Victor Lieberman reviewed my history chapter. I have also profited over the years with occasional but lively correspondence with a number of scholars, notably Michael Aung-Thwin (USA), Lilian Handlin (USA), Catherine Raymond (USA), Tilman Frasch (Germany), Paul Strachan (Spain) and Sunait Chutintaranond (Thailand).

In Bangok Pierre Pichard was helpful at every stage, beginning with opening up his exhaustive archive of photographs and architectural plans. He also made suggestions on my chapters covering architecture, sculpture and painting. Françoise Boudignon, also in Bangkok, reviewed my remarks on *jataka* painting.

Narisa Chakrabongse and Paisarn Piammattawat at River Books readily appreciated the need for a guide book to Pagan and provided a sharp editorial eye. Finally, special thanks go to Michael Freeman whose indefatigable energy was unfortunately not infectious; it left me weak in its wake. He really gave it his all.

SPELLINGS AND PROPER NAMES

Burmese proper names are often confusing, because there are
a number of ways of transliterating Burmese into English. For
example, the Kubyauk-gyi temple can be found in some books as
Gubyauk-gyi. Or the Htilominlo temple can come out looking like
Hti-lo-min-lo. We have adopted the most standard spellings that
have grown up in the writings about Pagan and those truest to
English phonetics whenever possible. The overarching aim has been
to present the visitor with names that flow from page to tongue with
least difficulty, although obvious inconsistencies are unavoidable.

Burma was the name given to the country during the English
period (1886-1947), but the country was traditionally named
Myanmar. The name was changed from Burma to Myanmar in
1989, but it is still known by its former name to many people
abroad. Moreover, the decision by the government to revert to the
former name has never been widely popular within the country. This
is why Burmese groups opposed to the government deliberately use
the name Burma and not Myanmar. Many place names throughout
the country were also changed by the government, using a uniform
system of transliteration. Thus, Pagan became Bagan, Pegu is Bago,
and the Irrawaddy River is now the Ayeyarwady. Again, we have
opted for ease of pronunciation and generally for the older, more
familiar spellings, such as Pagan and Irrawaddy.

The original names of Pagan kings used in stone inscriptions
differ from those in later Burmese chronicles. The names adopted
in the chronicles are far more well-known to Burmese and foreigners
alike, so these names are used in the guide. For example, the king
named Aniruddha in ancient days is known as Anawrahta in the
later chronicles; in the same way, the famous king known today
as Kyanzittha was named Thiluin Man in the ancient inscriptions.
Names from both original historical sources and the chronicles are
provided in the history section for comparison.

Each of the nearly three thousand monuments has been assigned
a number in an invaluable eight-volume survey of the site entitled
Inventory of Monuments at Pagan, compiled during the 1980s and
1990s. These numbers are now in general use by the Department of
Archaeology and are often found outside temples, usually in Burmese
numerals. The numbers associated with the thirty-three monuments
selected for this guide are found in the index, beside the name of the
temple, monastery or stupa. Numbers of other monuments are
provided in parenthesis within the guide, for ready reference to the
Inventory of Monuments at Pagan.

INTRODUCTION

Pagan's archaeological zone encompasses close to 3,000 recorded brick monuments in an area measuring roughly 13 by 7 square kilometers. Temples, stupas and monasteries stretch as far as the eye can see, up and down the Irrawaddy river and deep into the surrounding plain. Scarcely a week passed without new temple ground breaking during the city's peak. Indeed, Pagan's immensity has no close rival in the ancient Buddhist world. Friends in the Department of Archaeology have confessed to me that they never expect to visit even half the temples. The majority of the monuments belong to a period when Pagan was home to Burma's kings, and the centre of the country's religious life, between the 11th and 13th centuries.

Inasmuch as the thousands of brick monuments resemble one another superficially, it is tempting to jest that "if you've seen one, then you've seen them all." This would be a mistake. Each temple comes alive after appreciating its uniqueness. Like children in a schoolyard who at first glance appear alike, it takes but a moment to recognize that each sparkles with individuality.

The reasons for selecting these thirty-three monuments vary greatly, since each tells a different part of Pagan's larger story. The Ananda, for example, is included for its modern religious significance, its ancient stone sculpture and glazed tiles. Its spectacular murals, however, were lost long ago to successive whitewashing. For painting, we must turn to other monuments, such as the Loka-hteikpan which escaped refurbishment. The selection, therefore, is somewhat shaped by what centuries of neglect have left us.

Other monuments were chosen for their distinctiveness, such as the So-min-gyi, ornamented with unique glazed ceramics, or the Nanpaya, with its outer surface made up of carved stone. The emphasis is on the ancient period, but a few gems from Pagan's later period are included too. The aim is to provide a general framework for understanding the development of the city's monuments, painting and sculpture.

The thrill of exploring and making our own discoveries draw us back to Pagan, again and again. My fondest moments are visiting remote temples and finding traces of unusual painting or bicycling amidst the temples at dusk. It is these private encounters with the past that will likely stick with you too. The city's ancient residents no longer can speak to us, but their monuments echo their aspirations and most cherished beliefs. It is up to us to listen.

Devotee applying gold leaf, Sulamani.

HISTORY

Parched Earth

An ancient inscription speaks of Pagan as located within Tattadesa, or the 'Country of Parched Earth.' The extent and boundaries of Tattadesa (Pali) are unknown, but this name perhaps reflects an early distinction between the dry expanse of Upper Burma and the wet coastal lands making up Lower Burma. Indeed, the arid nature of the landscape surrounding the temples is the first thing to strike visitors. The rich monsoon that drenches Yangon annually does not sweep up from the coast to reach Pagan. Yangon can expect 466 cm during the rainy season (June-October), whereas Pagan receives a mere 143 cm during the same period. The brutal hot season in Upper Burma begins in April and only subsides when the rains begin in June. Pagan's airport recently recorded a temperature of 49 C. (120 F.), ranking it as the hottest spot in all of Southeast Asia on that day. The landscape is also inhospitable, "sparsely shadowed by low, straining, thorny trees", as one old time observer phrased it (Luce, I, 4). However, the surroundings may have been more inviting in the ancient period, since Upper Burma was possibly somewhat wetter at the beginning of the second millennium. In fact, a more benign ancient climate permitted extensive rice cultivation, adding another causal factor in the rise of Pagan civilization (Lieberman, 2003, 103). Rice growing areas were developed north and south of Pagan where there are indications of ancient dams and irrigation, specifically around modern Kyaukse and Minbu. The climate today in Upper Burma is now too dry for large-scale rice production, and the region imports its rice from the south.

A greater ancient annual rainfall may also have resulted in more abundant local trees. A stable flow of wood fuel was required for the many kilns that produced the staggering amount of brick needed for Pagan's expansion started in the eleventh century. For example, the Dhamma-yazika stupa alone consumed roughly 6 million bricks, based on estimates of its volume. Even assuming more trees in antiquity, a shortage of local wood was entirely possible. Supply problems at Pagan itself are suggested by the fact that bricks were brought to the city from other areas. In later Burmese history, insufficient fuel for kilns is documented in at least one case. This shortage was connected to the massive Mingun monument which prompted a royal flotilla to gather bamboo and wood up river in 1797 (Cox, 229). Future studies focusing on pollen and dendrological evidence may resolve

India, China, and Southeast Asia.

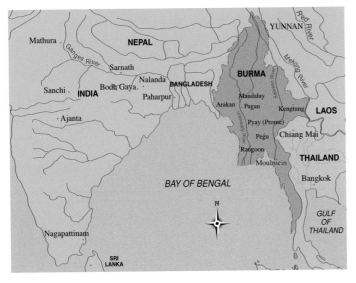

the question of ancient rainfall, but the issue is subject largely to guess work and debate for the moment.

The country we now call Myanmar, or former Burma, was on the eastern edge of ancient India, separated by mountains bordering Bangladesh. Other more distant ranges divide Burma from neighbouring Thailand, on the opposite side. Early civilization evolved up and down the Irrawaddy valley, while so-called tribal peoples inhabited the highlands. For visitors to Pagan in the winter the Irrawaddy is a quiet companion in the distance, but during the monsoon this placid river laps dangerously close to the tops of river cliffs. Burma and other countries in mainland Southeast Asia were on the receiving end of Indian civilization, starting even before the first millennium. This contact prompted technological changes and new religious beliefs combining Buddhism, Hinduism and indigenous thought.

Pagan is fated to be located in a notorious earthquake zone. The most well-known jolt occurred on July 8, 1975, when a number of prominent temples were heavily damaged. This quake measured about 6.0 on the Richter scale, and its epicenter was a mere 38 kilometers from the city walls. The Department of Archaeology and Unesco collaborated and sensitively repaired the worst damage. Macro-seismic studies were conducted at Pagan in the 1980s to determine how monuments could be strengthened and which monuments were under greatest threat. Many of these tests simulated earthquakes and measured the stresses and strains. It was also discovered that the transversal seismic waves wrecked their worst havoc closest to the Irrawaddy, since the alluvial sandy terrace upon which Pagan sits is most unstable bordering the river. This fact accounted for relatively little damage to the monuments three kilometres or so inland, in the area around the modern village of Minnanthu. Pagan will always be subject to quakes, since it is situated west of the Sagaing fault that extends over 1,000 kilometres in a north-south direction (*Pagan Newsletter*, 1983). The fault line runs just west of Mandalay, borders the Shan Plateau and ends near Pegu, or modern Bago, northeast of Yangon a short distance. Movement along the fault results from a northward motion of the Indian plate centred in the Himalayas. Ample historical records attest to a long history of earthquakes at Pagan, but the Mandalay area is more prone to severe shocks, since it is closer to the fault. The huge fissures in the Mingun Pagoda, near Mandalay, provide

Left: Compound walls of two neigh-bouring temples. Minnanthu village.

Above: Dedication of metal fi ial for the Shwe-zigon stupa, 1768. Detail of inscription in courtyard of Shwe-zigon.

Stone inscription recording donation of 295 palm-leaf manuscripts in 1442. U Thein Lwin from the Department of Archaeology. (DS)

Detail of the stone inscription shown above. (DS)

Kinnara, Kubyauk-gyi (Wetkyi-in).

tangible proof of a quake that struck in 1839. The last major jolt in Upper Burma occurred on September 21, 2003, and measured 6.6 on the Richter scale, centred 345 kms north of Yangon. The temples at Pagan rocked, but only minor damage was recorded.

Painted ink inscriptions on the walls of the temples testify to repairs made following quakes, beginning as early as the 14th century when a monk restored a head of a Buddha destroyed by a quake on April 4, 1380 (Than Tun, 1996). The Burmese chronicles refer to quakes also at Pagan, in the reign of Narapatisithu (1174-1211), and then in 1286, 1298, 1644, 1768, 1174 and 1838. Even as recently as 1956 a quake destroyed a portion of the Ananda temple, revealing an inscribed silver plate placed there following a repair from earthquake damage on March 22, 1839. This is not to say that earthquakes are all bad, since certain early Buddhist literature associates quakes with major events in the Buddha's life, such as his birth and enlightenment. If you find yourself inside a temple at Pagan with the ground shaking, you must quickly decide between kneeling in prayer or relying on your own two fast feet.

"Even Poor Women Selling Pots Shall Become Rich"
Kyanzittha's Palace Inscription

Pagan symbolizes a remarkable mobilization of resources and peoples that saw few parallels in the ancient world. Religious aspirations fueled this building boom, but a powerful state organization was required to transform millions of bricks into thousands of monuments. Kings and commoners alike were linked together in a fervid construction campaign producing over two thousand monuments between the 11th and 13th centuries. These three creative centuries are often referred to as the Pagan period, but much of importance occurred at Pagan before and after.

Estimating the city's population is difficult, since homes were of perishable materials, and there was, of course, no ancient census. One early English scholar put the figure as high as two million, but this is a guess. Daily life in old Pagan is witnessed only by millions of ceramic shards littering the fields now. However, the landscape today probably shares similarities with ancient times, with temples scattered amidst villages and cultivated fields. Habitation was likely dense in certain areas, but sparse in others, like today. Some religious buildings may have been close to a market or a village, since one

The 1975 earthquake toppled the Gawdaw-palin's tower, restored as a hollow concrete structure in 1991-1992. (DS)

Right: Shwe-zigon compound, bells.

An early 19th-century folding-book map of Pagan. City walls in centre. Irrawaddy river in wavy lines on bottom. Temples and royal donors indicated in Burmese captions. (Courtesy The Oriental and India Office Collection, British Library)

13th-century inscription refers to a monastery's compound wall as protection against fire.

Why certain areas attracted construction and others were relatively neglected is unknown. What is certain, however, is that monumental architecture first commenced close to the river and within the Walled City in the 11th and early 12th centuries. Many shrines sprang up well inland by the end of the 12th century, but building close to the river never ceased. One major wave of patronage occurred during the Konbaung Period (1752-1885) which saw the creation of new monuments and the refurbishing of others. Temples from this era were often clustered around the city's two most venerated shrines, the Ananda and the Shwe-zigon, and within the Walled City.

The village called Pagan in the Konbaung era was traditionally centred in the Walled City and its immediate environs, but today the name has expanded to include the entire archaeological zone. During this period various English spellings for the city were in use, such as Pakghong and Pegaam. The bustling jetty town of Nyaung-U to the north overshadowed the surrounding villages, at least by the 18th century. A settlement called New Pagan in the southern part of the archaeological zone was formed by families who were forced out of their homes within the city walls by the military government in the early 1990s.

Pagan's Decline

The majority of the ancient monuments at Pagan began an inexorable decline after the capital shifted from Pagan to Ava in the 14th century. One English envoy observed in 1797 that numberless temples, "have sunk into indistinguishable masses of rubbish, overgrown with weeds . . . . and the plain is every where covered

with fragments of their materials" (Cox, 414). The situation was no better by the mid-19th century when, "the greater number [of monuments] have been abandoned to the owls and bats and some have been desecrated into cow-houses by the villagers." (Yule, 36). Before the massive rebuilding campaign in the 1990s, the landscape largely resembled what visitors encountered many centuries ago.

The complex reasons for the pervasive neglect and consequent deterioration of the monuments are unknown, but loss of patronage was the crux of the problem. Temples and monasteries required constant repair, and once the flow of funds for maintenance was interrupted, then the shrines fell to the mercy of the elements. The upkeep of large monuments was generally in the hands of 'temple servants' who saw to the daily affairs of the establishment, paid for by revenue generated by grants of land made by wealthy individuals or royal elites. The shift of the capital from Pagan to Ava by the mid-14th century may have fractured the relationship donors had with their benefactions. When a patron resided in Pagan, he or she likely provided immediate supervision of the grant and the upkeep for the temple, stupa or monastery, but this vital personal link may have been severed, or at least attenuated, once the capital moved. Moreover, donors probably focused their patronage in and around the new capital of Ava, although little has survived from these early centuries in that region. Pagan continued to attract donors after the move to Ava, but it appears these funds went largely to the creation of new shrines and not to the repair or upkeep of temples. Also, dilapidated monuments were likely considered the property of others whose ownership was theoretically enjoyed in perpetuity. Creating a new temple accrued more merit than rebuilding an old one, or so it would appear. This neglect of monuments is scarcely unique to the Pagan period, since the Burmese countryside today is littered with monuments in total decay, many of which were built less than fifty years ago and which often stand side by side with new ones. In these modern cases, no provision was made for the upkeep of these monuments, and therefore the shrines found themselves crumbling within a short span of time. No longer maintained, vegetation lodged in walls and roof terraces wrecked havoc, as can be seen today throughout Burma. This age-old problem was recognized by a 17th -century monk who was likely recording folk lore when he concluded, "A stupa stands fine until a banyan tree destroys it" (Than Tun, 1996).

There is no evidence of destruction brought on by an invasion, pestilence, climatic change, a massive earthquake or a peasant revolt. Loss of patronage was almost certainly the chief culprit in explaining why Pagan's monuments fell inexorably into ruin, but the reasons for the loss of support remain conjectural.

Temples, Kingship and Merit
At the apex of society was the king who ruled by virtue of merit accumulated over previous lives. For example, an inscription records the response of village women upon spotting the king at a crossroads: "such grandeur and magnificence as this derives from his pious deeds in the past" (E. B. I, pt. II, 120). Progressive rebirths

G.H. Luce (1889-1979), the doyen of Pagan research. Photo by U Tin Oo in the late 1950s, when Luce was directing photography for Old Burma – Early Pagan.

Opposite: Ancient temples remain a focus of worship. The entrance hall of the Nagayon with a restored standing brick figure and sculpture replica in niche. The wall surface was once entirely painted, concealing rows of header and stretcher bricks.

Mahabodhi temple and Irrawaddy river.

rested on accumulating merit, and donations to religious institutions in this lifetime were considered essential. The concept of storing merit for furture rebirths derived from India, but it was a powerful factor in ancient Pagan and indeed in modern Burma. The ruler was also expected to ensure prosperity and justice. The same inscription, for example, claims that during the reign of King Kyanzittha (1084-1113), "even poor old women selling pots shall become rich", implying that the king's rule equated with good times, if not opulence (E.B., I, pt. II, 123). This hyperbolic vision was of course tempered by usurpations and pernicious land disputes, but this idealized view reflected the cherished ideals of the elite. Members of society outside that narrow circle were consigned to silence, because they were too poor to commission monuments and leave inscriptions. Their lives can be pieced together, however, since tradesmen, agriculturists and artisans are referred to regularly in epigraphs sponsored by the elites.

Human habitation at Pagan started early in the first millennium A.D., if not before, but evidence for extensive monumental architecture begins only in the 11th century. Construction accelerated during the 12th and 13th centuries and only slowed by the 14th century when the capital shifted from Pagan to Ava. Pagan never lost a central role in the religious life of Burma, which explains why ancient temples today stand beside others only two or three centuries old and ones built even last month. As recently as 1806 a king organized a special flotilla to Pagan from Upper Burma in order to raise a new metal finial atop the centuries-old Shwe-zigon stupa. Over the same few days the monarch took possession of a white elephant conveyed in a special barge from Lower Burma. Such a state ceremony, coupled with the capping of the Shwe-zigon, highlights the religious and cultural symbolism attached to Pagan, even centuries following its eclipse as the capital of Burma. Pagan remains a potent symbol for the people of Burma, and this is one reason why the government has rebuilt the city.

Royal elephant, c. 1855, watercolour, Colesworthy Grant.
(Courtesy The Oriental and India Office Collection, British Library)

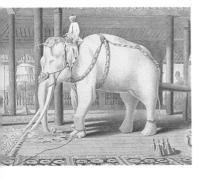

Unravelling Pagan's History

Pagan's history is reconstructed from diverse sources. The most reliable and informative are the four hundred or so stone inscriptions found throughout Pagan over the last century and augmented by new discoveries made each year. The majority were associated with specific monuments, such as temples and monasteries, and describe the circumstances of the donation and the provisions for their construction and upkeep. Even the type of payment for artisans is sometimes included. These inscriptions are far richer in detail than their counterparts in India. The inscribed stones were usually set up inside or outside temples, resembling the modern dedications established in front of rebuilt monuments today. The donation was also likely recorded more offically in palm-leaf manuscripts, or folded paper-books (*parabaik*, Burmese), but the stone version was for public view. These epigraphs are generally dated to the Burma Era whose starting point was 638 AD. For example, a temple inscription dated to 630 in the Burma Era would equate to 1268. Rarely used was the Buddhist Era, reckoned from the Buddha's death. A monument associated with an inscription can fix the temple's date, but most inscriptions are missing altogether or have shifted from their original locations. Even the celebrated Ananda has no surviving inscriptions describing its founding. Of the thirty or so monuments highlighted in this guide, only a handful can be associated with dated inscriptions.

Some historical information can also be gleaned from ink inscriptions on the interior. Many of these are horoscopes, usually placed there by individuals after the the temple was long since completed. Dated horoscopes often provide valuable clues about the various stages in a temple's history. Horoscopes painted on walls can be recognized easily, since they are circular diagrams divided into twelve segments, each containing numbers representing the signs of the zodiac and the planets (Eade).

The first European to take an active interest in Pagan was G. H. Luce, an English scholar who taught at Rangoon University, beginning in the 1920s. He produced the first major study of Pagan in the late 1960s, *Old Burma – Early Pagan*, based in part on thousands of ink inscriptions that he and his Burmese colleagues labourously deciphered over decades in dimly lit temple interiors. Other pioneers include Charles Duroiselle and Taw Sein Ko, Director-Generals of the Department of Archaeology, before the Japanese occupation in 1942.

Inscriptions within the old Pagan Museum. (DS)

Walled City and moat near the Tharaba Gate. Today water is pumped into the moat. Restored stupa in distance.

Pagan Kings

Chronicles	Inscriptions	Dates
Anawrahta	Aniruddha	1044-1077
Sawlu	Maṅ Lulaṅ	1077-1084
Kyansittha	Thiluiṅ Man	1084-1113
Alaungsithu	Cañsū I	1113-1169
Narathu	Imtausyaṅ	1169-1170
Naratheinhka	Narasiṅgha	1170-1174
Narapatisithu	Cañsū II	1174-1211
Zeyatheinhka	Natoṁmyā	1211-1235
Kyaswa	Klacwā	1235-1249
Uzana	Uccanā	1249-1256
Narathihapate	Tarukpliy Maṅ	1256-1287
Kyawswa	Klawcwā	1288-1298

The Glass Palace Chronicle

The single most influential source shaping our interpretations of Pagan is a Burmese chronicle compiled by court officials in 1829 inside a 'mirrored hall' within the palace at Ava. This work therefore came to be known as the *Glass Palace Chronicle*. Much of it was drawn from a chronicle compiled in the preceding century that relied upon even earlier material. This comprehensive 'history' begins with the origins of Buddhism in India and traces the descent of kings in Burma and their principal accomplishments, from military campaigns to raising monuments. The Chronicle is remarkably accurate for later periods, but its veracity dwindles progressively, especially for events before about 1200 (Lieberman, 1986). The 'facts' in the Chronicle, therefore, must be corroborated by other sources before they can be accepted.

The English translation of a portion of the *Glass Palace Chronicle* in 1923 coincided with increased interest in Pagan, and it soon became the funnel through which interpretations of the city were forced. The compilers of the Chronicle, however, reflected the beliefs and legends about the monuments current in the 18th-19th centuries, but its relevance for the ancient period must always be in doubt. For example, the Ananda temple in the Chronicle is referred to by the name of Nanda and its foundation linked to a legend about a cave-temple named Nanda-mula in the Himalayas used as a model by the temple's patron. This colourful story surely surrounded the Ananda in the later period, but there is no proof that this legend was current when the monument was built. The tales attached to other temples in the Chronicle have also been misleading for similar reasons. The Chronicle naturally focused on temples that were under worship at the time and overlooked the thousands that had fallen into disuse. Certain information in the Chronicle and other Burmese texts contains a kernel of truth from the ancient period, but the material has been greatly embellished over the centuries and must be weighed cautiously. The same caution applies to the occasional notices about Pagan appearing in Chinese, Khmer and Sinhalese records.

Before the Rise of Pagan

The founders of Pagan were Burman who moved into the central Irrawaddy river area from southern China in the 9th and 10th centuries. Prior to their arrival two separate ethnic and linguistic groups occupied most of Burma. These people are the Pyu and Mon. Both contributed to the formation of Pagan's culture, but in ways yet to be determined.

The Bupaya stupa facing the Irrawaddy was rebuilt with reinforced concrete after the 1975 quake. The courtyard has a small nat shrine.

The Pyu

The Pyu emerged at the beginning of the first millennium A.D. in centres up and down the Irrawaddy. By the 5th century these peoples participated in an imported culture from India, adopting Sanskrit royal titles and engraving Buddhist scriptures in Pali on gold sheets. A major Pyu centre was a brick walled city known as Shri Kshetra, located near Pyay, formerly Prome. This Pyu city was much later included within the Pagan realm and from that time considered a sacred city in the national mythology of Burma, even into the 19th century.

Pagan itself was likely a Pyu settlement for much of the first millennium, since thousands of Pyu style bricks bearing impressed seals and finger-markings are found there. These bricks are sometimes found beneath later structures, suggesting that the Burmese built directly upon some earlier Pyu monuments (Hudson, Nyein Lwin, Win Maung). No complete monuments of definite Pyu date have been found, except possibly for one ruinous temple preserving some unusual stucco ornament [no. 996]. The Pyu were weakened in the first half of the 9th century by an invading group from the Nanchao kingdom, originating in Yunnan, China. Following the short-lived occupation by these invading peoples from Yunnan, the Burmans moved into centres bordering the Irrawaddy during the 9th and 10th centuries. Evidence for much of this history relies on Chinese and Burmese chronicles, so it must be treated with some caution until it can be supplemented with archaeological finds or epigraphy.

A ruined, vaulted gateway in the compound wall of Tayok-pyi. The tilled field is a reminder of ancient Pagan's agricultural base. Cattle are mentioned in ancient inscriptions also.

The Mons of Lower Burma

The Mon occupied the southeastern portion of the country and like the Pyu shared the Buddhist civilization acquired from India. These peoples may have been ethnically and linguistically related to the Dvaravati Mon in Thailand, but their art is quite distinct. The Mon were spared the invasion from Yunnan but were brought into the sphere of the Pagan kingdom in the 11th century. The Mon contribution to Pagan's art is hard to access, since only a handful of Mon monuments and sculpture has survived for comparison, and these are also without firm dates. However, the Mon cultural influence at Pagan was strong, judging from the adoption of Mon language in the early Pagan inscriptions and the fact that Mon priests officiated at the consecration of a palace. The *Glass Palace Chronicle* claims that the Mon were conquered by the Pagan King Anawrahta (1044-1077) who also introduced Theravada Buddhism to Pagan from the Mon. Few 'facts' of this story can be sustained, except that political influence from Pagan probably extended into Mon territory during his reign. The undeniable Mon influence at Pagan may also have derived from a number of Mon-speaking peoples possibly present in Upper Burma during the early phases of Burmese occupation. The Mon were perhaps accorded special religious and cultural status, despite their relatively low numbers.

The Founding of Pagan

The *Glass Palace Chronicle* records that the Pagan region was settled as early 107 A.D., moulded together out of 19 adjacent Pyu villages. One of its early rulers was Pyusawhti who was a product of a sun spirit and a snake princess. This ficticious character has been revived recently, and his enormous bronze effigy now dominates the fountain outside the Pagan musuem. The Burmese-speaking peoples moved into centres along the Irrawaddy in the 9th century, according to the *Glass Palace Chronicle*, and perhaps dominated the Pyu. However, there are no reliable historical records for Pagan until the 11th century. There is, therefore, a long gap between the legendary arrival of the Burmans to Pagan in the 9th century and the city's first historical records.

By the 11th and 12th century Pagan's formal name was Aridamaddanapura, a Pali word meaning 'City of the Crusher of Enemies.' This official name was probably used alongside the local name, Pokam or Pukam, also known from inscriptions. It is from these ancient local names that our modern Pagan derives. This name was originally probably only used for the Walled City and its close surroundings but soon came to include a wide area, as it does today. We call the entire area Pagan for convenience, but local inhabitants still think of the region in terms of a number of small, widely scattered villages, such as Wetkyi-in, Taungbi, Myinkaba, and Minnanthu. Since the 1990s the city is often spelled Bagan, adopting the government's system of transliterating Burmese into English. The jetty town of Nyaung-U is referred to in ancient inscriptions, but its growth into a sizable town occurred much later when it became a centre for lacquer production by the 18th century.

A stone window from an ancient monastery incorporated into 19th-century Pitakat-taik.

Consolidation of Empire: Anawrahta and Kyanzittha

The first ruler at Pagan for which there is concrete evidence is Anawrahta (1044-1077). His power derived partially from controlling the rice producing regions in Kyaukse, 150 kilometres northeast of Pagan and Minbu, 110 kilometres south of Pagan. He also opened up maritime trade after taking control of the coastal Mon country. His only records are numerous small Buddhist terracotta votive plaques found throughout much of Burma. He is credited in the chronicles with founding numerous famous monuments, but no claims can be confirmed. One structure possibly connected to his reign is a large stupa near Yangon, near Twante, associated with large terracotta tablets bearing his name. Anawrahta was also said to have seized the Mon capital of Thaton and the entire Buddhist canon for his introduction of Theravada Buddhism to Pagan. This colourful story was disputed long ago by historians, but this unsubstantiated view entered the national mythology and persists. This very legend unfolds over modern painted panels inside the east corridor of the Shwe-zigon stupa, reinforcing the national myths. Anawrahta's fame is now perpetuated by a new palace bearing his name, begun by the government late in 2003 within the Walled City and planned for completion in 2004. There is, however, no evidence that this king even had his own separate palace, and its original location, dimensions, and appearance are matters of complete conjecture.

Anawrahta's son, named Sawlu (1077-1084), enjoyed a brief reign before the accession of Kyanzittha who consolidated the empire. He was likely an usurper, since inscriptions makes no reference to his

predecessors. Kyanzittha was reincarnated from the Hindu god Vishnu, and his birth was foretold at the ancient Pyu city of Shri Kshetra by the Buddha. Another stone inscription describes the consecration of his palace, with Mon priests invoking Vishnu and Buddhist monks reciting Pali prayers. The location of this palace can perhaps be identified with the ruinous brick foundations in front of the Shwegu-gyi within the city walls. Another stone record is located just outside the compound of the Shwe-zigon. He also likely dispatched a mission to Bodh Gaya in India to restore the temple commemorating the enlightenment of the Buddha. The Chronicle associates Kyanzittha with other benefactions, not the least of which is the celebrated Ananda, but no firm evidence corroborates these claims.

In about 1112 A.D. Kyanzittha fell gravely ill, and his son dedicated a golden Buddha image and a temple for his recovery. This information appears on two slabs with an incised text repeated nearly identically in four languages: Pyu, Old Mon, Pali and Old Burmese. It is dated to 1112 A.D. It marks the earliest written appearance of the Burmese language, since many of the written records up until that time were composed in Mon. One original stone can be seen in the museum, and the other is in the compound of the Myazedi stupa, adjacent to the Kubyauk-gyi temple in Myinkaba village. The slabs were discovered in the late 19th century and expanded our understanding of the still enigmatic Pyu language. To this degree, it has been dubbed Burma's Rosetta Stone.

After Kyanzittha's death, his grandson, Alaungsithu (1113-1169), ascended the throne. His long reign saw a dedication of lands to the Shwe-zigon stupa and the construction of the Shwegu-gyi temple. The tallest temple at Pagan, the Thatbyinnyu, is attributed to him in the Chronicle, but it cannot be proved. He is said to have sailed to Sri Lanka where the king presented him with an image of a former Buddha. He came back to Pagan but not before trying to climb Mount Meru, centre of the Buddhist universe.

Early 20th-century architecture blending Burmese and European traditions. South corridor of Ananda, donated by a family in 1929.

Alaungsithu was succeeded by Narathu (1169-1170), and other kings, notably Narapatisithu (1174-1211). Important 13th-century kings include Kyaswa (1235-1249), and Narathihapate (1256-1287). Fewer larger monuments were created in this later period, but the number expanded greatly. It was also during the 13th century that other centres arose, distant from Pagan, such as Sale, Hsale, Kyuntaw and others.

Excavations of a possible ancient palace area within the city walls, viewed from the Shwegu-gyi. The Mahabodhi temple can be seen in the distance. (DS)

Social Organization

The king, his court, ranking nobles, and heads of monasteries formed Pagan's elites. These individuals scarcely could have numbered even ten percent of society, but it was this group that sponsored the thousands of monuments, to judge from inscriptions. The remainder of society was bonded to these elites in various formal ways or were 'free agents' living along side this system. The king stood at the centre of a bureaucracy whose officers organized peasants who tilled crown land. Bonded labour attached to monasteries worked monastic farmland, prepared offerings for the rituals and saw to the general upkeep of the grounds. Others attached to monasteries were artisans, such as plasterers and wood carvers, or even musicians and dancers used for special occasions. Those holding bonded labour could donate individuals to other elites or to monasteries. Bonded status was generally hereditary. Disputes over the ownership or transfer of certain bonded labourers were the subject of legal cases throughout Burma's history.

Non-bonded commoners were free-agents, and this group included farmers who paid their taxes in kind. Some artisans were also non-bonded and therefore free to move from project to project. They were usually paid in silver, rice paddy, or select items, such as cloth or metal utensils. There is even a case of a sculptor receiving a horse. This basic division of labour between bonded and non-bonded groups appears in Burma first at Pagan but remained in place until British colonial times. The nobility during the Pagan period did not pose a threat to the crown, unlike European feudalism where a strong landed gentry formed pockets of resistance to the centre.

There were no minted coins, but from stone inscriptions we know that people were often paid in silver measured in standard units called *klay* or *klyap* (the modern *kyat*), corresponding to the 'tical' in later Burmese history when it equaled 16.33 grams. Units of *kyat* in gold are mentioned but much less commonly than silver. None of these objects has survived, but they were likely small slabs of metal certified to conform to the same purity and weight, as we know from later Burmese records. The largest unit of measurement was the *viss*, followed by the *buih*. For example, a copper spire for a monument was said in an inscription to weigh forty-seven *viss*, eight *buih* and four *kyat*. A *viss* in colonial times measured 1.63 kg and has remained a standard unit.

The Eclipse of Pagan

By the early 14th century the capital shifted north from Pagan, first to Pinya and then finally to Ava where it remained for centuries (the Ava period, c. 1365-1557). Ava is just south of Mandalay, founded only in 1857. The shift was perhaps occasioned by disturbances created by Mongol incursions in the late 13th century that breached Burma from Yunnan. It was formerly believed that the Mongols actually seized Pagan in the late 1280s, but no evidence suggests that they reached that far or that there was any widespread destruction at any time (Aung-Thwin, 1998).

The reasons motivating the shift from Pagan to the Ava region are still unknown. The Pagan state may have suffered internal weakness due to an ever growing power of the monastic institutions whose extensive land holdings were tax exempt, a theory proposed by Michael Aung-Thwin but which has been questioned. That the move from Pagan was necessitated by a decline or crises is one that is taken for granted, but perhaps this conventional approach has steered us to look for answers in the wrong places. Perhaps Ava was selected as a new capital because the court felt it needed a military buffer further north, since the Mongols attacked from that direction and moved south. Or, perhaps the rulers felt that the capital needed to be closer to the rice-producing area of Kyaukse.

Once the centre of political gravity shifted from Pagan to Ava at the beginning of the 14th century, the city entered a new phase. This period is marked by a decline in the use and maintenance of temples, prompted by a drop in patronage on the part of the society's elites. This is suggested by 14th-century religious painting intrusively added to many temple interiors. The larger and more important temples were therefore never abandoned, but the majority of monuments fell into complete disuse. Also, the pace of building slowed dramatically and the temples were more modest. For example, over two thousand monuments sprang up between the 11th and 14th centuries, but slightly less than 200 were created between the 15th and 20th centuries. Architectural traditions from the classic period continued and are reflected in numerous later monuments.

Pagan's last flourish occurred during the Konbaung period (1752-1885) where it served as a regional centre. Certain key temples were extensively renovated, such as the Ananda and Sulamani. New monuments were also created, such as the Upali Thein ordination hall and the Ananda Temple Monastery. A handful of European accounts describe the renovations in this period. Also, Pagan was the site of an important military defeat during the first Burmese War in 1824 when Burma lost some of its coastal tracts to English forces. Pagan was included in the British Empire after the last Burmese War in 1885 when Mandalay was taken and the monarch exiled to the Bombay Presidency. Formal annexation of Burma occurred in the following year, and soon Pagan fell under the protection of the Department of Archaeology, responsible to British administration in Calcutta. Modest building took place during the colonial period and a number of temples were repaired, generally with sensitivity. Much of Burma's religious architecture was also heavily influenced by European conventions, witnessed in the blended styles among the long corridors fronting the Ananda.

Burma achieved its independence in 1948, and the newly formed Department of Archaeology continued the work interrupted during the war years. Following Pagan's devasting earthquake in July, 1975, the government joined with Unesco to repair and strengthen the monuments most severely at risk. This fruitful union has also led to the restoration of Pagan's mural paintings in an ongoing programme. The earthquake also prompted the publication of an invaluable documentation of the temples, an eight-volume work entitled *Inventory of Monuments at Pagan*, produced by a French architect, Pierre Pichard. One aim of the *Inventory* was to provide a record of the monuments that could be used in any reconstruction of temples in the event of future tremors. In view of the extensive rebuilding at Pagan, however, the *Inventory* has assumed new importance, since it is our only record for the majority of the monuments before their reconstruction in the 1990s.

Pagan continues to play a central role in the cultural and religious life of the country, and it was this very prominence that led to a far reaching rebuilding campaign in the early 1990s which is still unfinished. Unfortunately, its planning is fundamentally misguided and has sparked international condemnation from archaeologists, art historians, presevationists and unofficial disapproval from Unesco. The thrust of the criticism is that the reconstruction of monuments and the restoration of sculpture is too often inaccurate, left to complete conjecture, if not to fancy. The rebuilding is no less controversial inside the country for the same reasons. Inasmuch as Pagan is the country's chief tourist attraction, the government runs the risk of "killing the goose that laid the golden egg."

Hundreds of temples have been rebuilt at Pagan, beginning in the 1990s. The rebuilding has been controversial, inside Burma and abroad. Temple no. 331 (DS).

Overleaf:
A late 18th-fresco of the ascetic Sumedha forming a human bridge for Dipankara Buddha who prophesized that Sumedha will be reborn as the Buddha Gotama. Ananda Brick Monastery. Outer wall of shrine, east side. (PP)

RELIGION

Rabbit, a symbol of the moon. Painted stucco ornament within a 20th-century pavilion in the courtyard of Shwe-zigon.

Transforming Bricks Into Merit

The thousands of monuments at Pagan absorbed incalculable resources and touched the lives of countless people, from the king to the poor women selling pots we met in the first chapter. What motivated Pagan's elites to invest so much and make such sacrifices? In what ways did this building boom in Burma relate to the remarkable life of a prince in India who discovered a radical way of looking at the human condition five hundred years before Christ? The dramatic story of the Buddha's relentless search for meaning is vividly portrayed in the sculpture and painting at Pagan.

Buddhism

There is no single definitive biography of the Buddha, since the legends surrounding his life were compiled centuries later and often differed from one another in various ancient texts. One important source for the Buddha's life at Pagan was a biography from Sri Lanka, known as the *Nidanakatha*, dating to the 5th or 6th century. This text in the Pali language covers only the period from his birth to shortly after his enlightenment, and other Pali texts were used to supplement the life history. Despite numerous differences recorded in the biography of the Buddha in various texts, the basic outline of the Buddha's life is remarkably similar.

From a White Elephant to a Tainted Repast

The Buddha was born in a royal family in northeastern India. His full name was Siddhartha Gautama, and the term Buddha is a title meaning the Enlightened One. His mother dreamed that a white elephant entered her side. Ten months later she grasped the branch of the *shala* tree (*Shorea robusta*), and the infant Buddha emerged from her right side.

A sage predicted that the child would evolve into a spiritual leader or a world emperor. To thwart his son's pursuit of a religious career, the youth was surrounded by untold luxury, including a lovely wife. One day, however, the Buddha journeyed beyond the palace walls and encountered the Four Sights: a sick man, an old man, a corpse, and a wandering holy man.

This first exposure to suffering disquieted him deeply, and the birth of his son later only heightened his malaise, since it underscored the suffering inherent in all attachments. To seek the

The Buddha's Great Departure from the Palace. 19th- and 20th -century wood carvings are found throughout Burma. Part of an open pavilion named after its donor, U Tun Sein, facing the Shwe-zigon. Refurbished in the 1940s.

solution to suffering he secretly abandoned the palace for the forest.
After bidding farewell to his horse and groom, he removed his
jewelled headdress, severed his hair and clad himself in rags

For six years he practiced austerities until he realized that he was
heaping only more suffering upon himself without getting any closer
to finding the causes of suffering. He came to a village today known
as Bodh Gaya, in Bihar state, and entered into deep meditation
seated beneath *a pipal* tree (*Ficus religiosa*). This tree is commonly
referred to as a Bodhi tree and symbolizes the Buddha's
enlightenment. Here the Buddha was attacked by the demon Mara
who symbolized worldly attachments. Mara created tornadoes, floods
and sandstorms, and together with his army threw himself at the
Buddha. The Buddha then called upon the Earth Goddesss to help
him defeat Mara, since the goddess had witnessed his meritorious
deeds during the last of his former lives, when as Vessantara he
donated his kingdom as alms. "The great earth [the goddess]
resounded with a hundred, a thousand, or a hundred thousand
echoes as though to overwhelm the forces of Mara, and saying,
'I was your witness.' "(*Nidanakatha*, 98).

The Buddha spent seven weeks near the Bodhi tree and then
began forty-five years of teaching in northeastern India, delivering
his first sermon near Varanasi, at Sarnath. His wanderings never
went beyond India, but legends assert that the Buddha visited
Southeast Asia. The most important for Burma was the story of two
travelling merchants who made food offerings to the Buddha on the
last day of that seven-week period at Bodh Gaya. The Buddha
rewarded them by giving him strands of his hair that are now

*Left: A mural painting of Queen
Maya grasping the flowering* shala
*tree and supported by her sister.
The infant Buddha emerges from
her right side. Nandamannya.*

*Above: Worshipping pilgrims inside
the north entrance hall of the
Dhammayan-gyi. The tan wash of the
walls is original. The stone inscription
protected by metal cage. (DS)*

*Below: Two of the Four Sights, an old
man, right, and a sick man, left,
compound of Shwe-zigon, wood, 20th
century.*

The Buddha severs his hair and becomes an ascetic, after abandoning the palace. One of scores of sculptures depicting the life of the Buddha inside the Ananda Temple.

The shaven head, the simple robe and the alms bowl emulate the life of the Buddha. Novitiate in Mandalay. (DS)

believed to be interred within the Shwedagon Pagoda in Yangon. This story was known in Pagan but only achieved its special importance in the 15th century when the merchants were identified as Mon. This story and many others reveal that relics played a major role in Buddhism from a very early stage.

The Buddha's death at the age of eighty was occasioned by a tainted meal fed to him inadvertently by a well-meaning metal worker in a small village. If it was pork, truffles or even something else is still debated. His distressed disciples urged him not to expire in this little wattle-and-daub town but to die in one of India's great cities where his remains would be honoured by the wealthy who inhabited brick and wooden homes. The Buddha declined and died between two *shala* trees on the outskirts of the poor village. Cremation followed but before his death the Buddha instructed his disciples to honour his ashes like those of a world emperor, to enshrine the remains in a mound, or stupa, placed at four crossroads. And the Buddha added, "Those who there offer a garland, or scent, or paint, or make a salutation, or feel serene joy in their heart, that will be to their benefit and well being for a long time." [Trainor, 49] This famous passage prefigures the enduring tradition of stupa worship.

The Aftermath: the Pali Canon

The Buddha's teachings and even the story of his life were not put into writing until centuries later, encouraging accretions that further distorted the facts of the Buddha's life. Disparate traditions coalesced into what we call now the Pali canon, or the Tipitika, literally the "Three Baskets". The canon divisions are the *Vinaya* (everyday rules for monks), the *Sutta* (the sayings of the Buddha), and *Abhidamma* (philosophy).

Early Buddhism's sacred language grew up in India and is known as Pali. It is closely related to Sanskrit. For example, the Sanskrit word for the Buddha is Gautama, but in Pali it is Gotama. Or the well-known Sanskrit word nirvana is *nibbana* in Pali. The Pali canon became the basis of Buddhism in Sri Lanka and Southeast Asia where it is still revered. Pali can be heard today at Pagan over loudspeakers set up at key monuments, the sacred syllables rolling across the countryside. The actual texts available in ancient Pagan probably did not differ too greatly from the canon that has come down to us, judging by the captions painted beneath the Buddhist murals.

The monks spoke an early form of Burmese, called Old Burmese, but the learned knew Pali and some understood Sanskrit also. Mon at Pagan spoke what we call Old Mon and numerous inscriptions are in this language. Pali also may have served as a lingua franca for communication between monks from Sri Lanka and Burma, similar to Latin's role in the West. Pali texts from Sri Lanka were also known at Pagan, notably the *Mahavamsa*, a chronicle detailing the history of the faith on that island. Pali is still taught throughout Southeast Asia, and translations of the Pali canon into Burmese, Thai and Khmer guide the lives of millions of people today. Southeast Asian Buddhism based on the Pali canon is often labelled by scholars Theravada Buddhism, despite numerous divisions and diverse practices. The term Theravada, however, never appears in Pagan inscriptions.

Why the Bump on the Buddha's Head

The Buddha is never considered a mere mortal in the Pali canon. Indeed, his supranormal status is reaffirmed by his frequent performance of miracles and the special circumstances of his birth. His divine status is marked by thirty-two special physical markings distinguishing him from birth. For example, all his toes and fingers are of equal length, and he has symbols on the soles of his feet. All of the attributes are rarely found on Buddha images, but one constant characteristic is a cranial protuberance, or the bump on top of the Buddha's head. The hair we see on the Buddha is meant to resemble a closely cropped tonsured monk. The small dot in the middle of the forehead, just above the eyes, signifies a special tuft of hair and is considered one of the thirty-two signs. The Buddha's robes are modelled on those of a monk.

Monk kneeling before the Shwe-zigon stupa.

Hand gestures

The Buddha's hand gestures, or *mudras* (Sanskrit), symbolize special episodes in the Buddha's life and different modes of his character and mission. The most common is the Buddha at the moment of enlightenment where he is shown seated. His lowered right hand, palm inward, signifies the moment when he called the Earth Goddess to witness his selfless deeds over past lives. His left hand rests in his lap. In some depictions the demons are shown attacking and the Buddha is seated beneath the Bodhi tree. The key feature is the lowered right hand and seated position. This representation was by far the most common among the central images inside temple sanctums at Pagan.

A seated Buddha with both hands folded one upon the other signifies meditation. If both hands touch one another at chest level this refers to his first sermon at Sarnath. Standing Buddhas often feature the right hand raised, palm outward, believed to offer reassurance to the devotee. Other hand postures are only found in later Burmese art, such as the standing Buddha, with both arms by his sides.

Buddha gazing at the Bodhi tree without blinking in the second week after his enlightenment at Bodh Gaya. Corridor wall, Pahto-thamya. (DS)

The Seven Weeks at Bodh Gaya

One popular theme at Pagan is the seven-week period the Buddha spent at Bodh Gaya. In the earliest literature only four weeks are known, but it was expanded to seven, such as in the *Nidanakatha*. Many incidents occur during these forty-nine days, but below are listed the most popularly represented events. Depictions of these Seven Weeks can be found at Pagan among the

The lowered right hand signifies the "call to witness" to the Earth Goddess prior to the Enlightenment. Partially restored brick and stucco, inside roof terrace shrine, Pahto-thamya. (DS)

murals throughout the city's history. An early painted example occurs inside the Pahto-thamya, while an 18th century series is at the Sulamani.

- Obtains Enlightenment beneath the Bodhi tree and defeats Mara.
- Stands gazing at the Bodhi tree for a week without blinking.
- Walks to and fro on a jewelled walkway gifted by the gods.
- Formulates philosophical conceptions (*abhidamma*) in a jewelled house presented by the gods.
- Is tempted by Mara's three beautiful daughters in the vicinity of a banyan tree (*Ficus bengalensis*).
- Is shielded by the snake-king Muchalinda who protects the Buddha with his snake hoods from a storm sent by the god named Sakka.
- Receives food offerings on the last day by two travelling merchants who receive strands of the Buddha's hair which are enshrined as relics inside a *stupa*; he is also presented with four bowls by four world guardians.

The Eight Great Events

Another theme of wide currency at Pagan focused on eight events in the Buddha's life. Each is also associated with important pilgrimage locations in northeastern India. Sculptures presenting most of these themes are seen in the entrance halls of the Ananda temple and throughout Pagan. The Eight Great Events was also a popular theme in Pala art, and there is little doubt that Pagan's sculptors and painters drew heavily on Pala models.

- Nativity. Queen Maya grasps a flowering *shala* tree, and the Buddha emerges from her right side.
- Enlightenment. The Buddha sits beneath the Bodhi tree, his right hand touching the earth.
- First Sermon. The Buddha's two hands touch together at chest level. Two deer and a discus, symbolizing his teachings, often appear at the base.
- Twin Miracles. The Buddha replicates himself to defeat heretics by performing a miracle.

Buddha departing from his sleeping wife and son, a poignant moment in his spiritual quest. Painted stucco on a 20th-century pavilion facing the Shwedagon Pagoda, Yangon. (DS)

- Descent from the Heaven of the 33 Gods. The Buddha descends on steps, accompanied by Sakka and Brahma.
- Parileyyaka Retreat. A monkey presents honey to the Buddha, seated with a bowl in his lap.
- Nalagiri Elephant. An elephant sent to attack the Buddha by his evil cousin, Devadatta, is shown defeated, kneeling at the Buddha's feet.
- Parinirvana. The death of the Buddha at Kushinagara, who is shown lying on his right side between two *shala* trees.

The Twenty Eight Buddhas

The Buddha was preceded by a number of legendary Buddhas whose lives were spiritually connected in a continuous lineage. The number

of these Buddhas varies in different Buddhist traditions, but in Burma beginning with the Pagan period the number totaled 28, the historical Buddha Gotama being the 28th. The lives of the other Buddhas are modeled on the life of Gotama. For example, each defeats the demon Mara and obtains enlightenment beneath a tree. These trees are of different species, and many times each is distinguished in the paintings and sometimes individually labelled in Pali. These Buddhas stretch back into legendary time. The theme of the 28 Buddhas was popular at Pagan, from the ancient period to the 19th century. Pali texts important at Pagan describing the 28 Buddhas included the *Nidanakatha* and an earlier text, the *Buddhavamsa*.

Procession of monks. Pahto-thamya in distance. (DS)

The Four Buddhas and Metteyya

The last four Buddhas in the sequence of 28 belong to our present age, or the *bhadrakalpa* (Sanskrit). They can be shown seated or standing. The four huge wooden figures enshrined in the Ananda temple are the most well known examples at Pagan. There is also in Buddhism a Buddha of the Future, Metteyya (Pali), or Maitreya (Sanskrit). Starting from the Pagan period in Burma Metteyya was thought to appear 5,000 years following the historical Buddha. Other Asian traditions recognize different time frames and conditions. In later Burmese history Metteyya's entry into the world was only guaranteed if the Buddhist community was thriving, without schisms and adherents drifting from the rules. The Buddha of the Future was important at Pagan, but no temple was solely devoted to him. He was significant in Burma from the Pagan peirod until the 19th century but is no longer worshipped today. Metteyya can be represented as a Buddha or in princely attire. Pagan developed the pentagonal *stupa* to honour Metteyya and the last four Buddhas, a unique contribution to Buddhist architecture worldwide.

Metteyya and the bodhisattva Lokanatha (Pali) (Avalokiteshvara, Sanskrit) appear paired in clay votive tablets, flanking a seated Buddha. They also are painted within niches in the side walls of sanctums whose centre is occupied by a brick Buddha facing east.

The historical Buddha was preceded by 27 legendary Buddhas whose lives are modelled on the Buddha's. This Buddha abandons the palace on an elephant, encountering Mara, his hand raised, far right. 18th-century fresco, Upali Thein.

Multi-armed bodhisattva. Such Mahayana imagery coexisted at Pagan with Theravada themes. Inner corridor, Kubyauk-gyi, Myinkaba village, 1113. (DS)

Bhuridatta jataka in which the Buddha-to-be assumes the form of a snake. Unglazed tile incised with the name of the jataka and its number (547) in the sequence at the West Hpetleik. The tale is numbered 543 in the Pali canon.

Two examples are labelled with ink captions inside a 13th-century temple at Hsale (no. 13), proving the identifications. Lokanatha is in the north niche, on the right, and Metteyya is in the south, or on the left (*Pagan Newsletter*, 1986). These same deities are possibly the two standing figures encountered frequently in the entrance halls of many temples, dressed in fine attire and stationed on either side of the doorway leading to the shrine. Most have been horribly restored, such as in the Ananda. These are sometimes called guardian figures, but they are likely Metteyya and Lokanatha. In Mahayana art from India Maitreya is often represented with a *stupa* in his headdress, while a small seated Buddha is found in the headdress of Avalokiteshvara. These two attributes are not found at Pagan, even when the figures are clearly bodhisattvas.

The Jatakas

Early in Indian Buddhist literature stories arose highlighting the hundreds of previous former births of the historical Buddha. These tales are called *jatakas*, or birth-tales. Each story showcases a pious act on the part of the Buddha in which he appears in animal or human form. The collection numbered 547 and belongs to the Pali canon. Different *jatakas* illustrated specific moral virtues, such as charity, loyalty, and patience, and came to be evoked in legal proceedings or royal proclamations in later Burmese history, much like Biblical parables. The popular tales even gave rise to maxims in Burma, such as "You can get rich selling even a mouse".

The *jatakas* were often painted on the walls of Pagan temples, usually with one tale assigned to a single frame and labelled below with ink inscriptions in Mon and later in Burmese. The *jatakas* also appear on ceramic tiles placed in exterior niches of monuments. The traditional collection of stories found at Pagan probably derived from Sri Lanka. Variations from the standard 547 Pali collection do occur at Pagan, however, notably at the East and West Hpetleik stupas, where three extra *jatakas* were added to raise the total to 550.

The last ten *jatakas*, called the Mahanipata, were especially revered at Pagan and throughout Southeast Asia. At Pagan the sequence of the last ten differs somewhat from that found in the Pali canon, and this unusual order has been officially adopted in modern Burma. The *jatakas* are also performed on stage, and the government has recently sponsored competitions among troupes from different parts of the country. They are also performed in the puppet theatre.

Burmese Spirits or *Nats*

The *nats*, or indigenous Burmese spirits, are also part of the religious backdrop at Pagan. They are countless in number but the most important were grouped together long ago and collectively called the Thirty-Seven Nats. Many are semi-historical figures who often met unsavoury deaths. Others are drawn from India and resemble Hindu gods, such as Durga on a tiger and Sarasvati (Thuraberi, Burmese) upon a swan and even the elephant-faced Ganesha (Mahapeine, Burmese). The *nats* are headed by Thagyamin (Sakka, Pali; Indra, Sanskrit), a Hindu deity who also plays an important role in Buddhism as a supporter of the faith.

The *nats* are worshiped at the major Buddhist monuments at Pagan and throughout Burma. An important *nat* centre is located sixty kilometres to the southeast of Pagan at Mount Popa, an extinct volcano where modern *nat* images are a major pilgrimage focus. Most households in the country have modest *nat* shrines to which daily offerings are made, together with donations to the Buddha.

The most visible *nats* at Pagan are enshrined in two large chapels guarding the entrance to the walled city at the Tharaba gate. These were installed in the 19th century and obscure the appearance of the ancient gateway. Inside are brother and sister *nats*. Young novitiates at Pagan begin the day they take the Buddhist tonsure at the Tharaba gate, with their families making offerings to the nats, an indication of how the two faiths co-exist in Burma.

However, firm evidence for *nat* worship at Pagan during the 11th, 12th and 13th centuries is nowhere to be found, either in inscriptions or among the art work. One gilded wooden figure now in the modern *nat* shrine at the Shwe-zigon stupa is said to represent the *nat* identified with Sakka but this is conjectural. In contrast, evidence for *nat* worship following the Pagan period is abundant.

There were never *nat* temples at Pagan, but there are a number of *nat* shrines attached to the Buddhist monuments today. Prominent examples are located within the compounds of the Shwe-zigon and the Manuha. Two *nat* shrines are also found outside the compound wall of the Ananda, on the west and north sides.

Some of the nats *are drawn from Hindu mythology, such as the elephant-faced Ganesha, known in Burmese as Mahapeine. Mount Popa, 20th century. (DS)*

The Hindu Contribution

Hinduism played a profound role in the civilization of Burma, spilling into areas where Buddhism provided little direction, such as coronations and palace consecrations. Hinduism was likely active in the Pyu period, but it became firmly established at Pagan by the 11th century. A stone inscription recording the construction of a palace invokes the Hindu god Vishnu and the tone of the rituals recalls Sanskrit architectural texts. King Kyanzittha traced his descent from

Modern nat *shrine, compound of Manuha temple. Thuraberi, left, and Medaw flanked by her sons, the Taungbyon brother.*

Brahma, a Hindu god, was incorporated into Buddhism at a very early stage. Stone sculpture, Pagan museum. (DS)

Vishnu and in one inscription is even associated with the family of Rama, another major Hindu deity. The only surviving Hindu temple is within the Walled City, the Nat-hlaung-kyaung, where a small number of Hindu sculptures are preserved. One ancient inscription proves that Tamil traders were at Pagan, but the Hindu presence at court was probably independent of commercial connections.

Hindu influence accelerated following the shift of the capital to Ava and continued until annexation by the British in 1886. A 19th-century king even requested from the British a brahmin astrologer, together with his wife, so that offspring could be available for court service. Royal patronage of Hinduism ended abruptly with colonial rule, and Hindu influence rapidly declined. Its last vestige in Burma are Indian astrologers found along one of the corridors of the Mahamuni temple, in Mandalay. In neighbouring Thailand, where foreign rule never interrupted court traditions, Hindu rites are still practiced. Thai brahmins also officiate for specific rituals at certain Buddhist temples, such as Wat Suthat in Bangkok.

Two important Hindu gods, Indra (Sakka, Pali) and Brahma, were incorporated very early into Buddhism and played subordinate roles to the Buddha. At Pagan Brahma is usually shown three-headed and holding an umbrella, while Sakka is depicted often holding a conch.

The Hindu epics so important to other Southeast Asian countries, the *Mahabharata* and the *Ramayana*, are not in evidence in ancient Pagan. The *Ramayana* became somewhat popular by the Konbaung period (1752-1885), perhaps influenced by Thailand, but it never attained the popularity it still enjoys in other countries. Adorning the inverted U-shaped metal supports of later bronze bells, occasionally one may see the heroine of the epic, Sita, seated in a heavenly chariot with the demon Ravana. One such example is in the Shwe-zigon compound.

Some of the nats *are modelled on Hindu gods, such as Thuraberi, based on the Hindu goddess Sarasvati. Manuha compound.*

Who Built Pagan Temples and Why

The motivations fueling this fervid patronage of religious monuments can be glimpsed by examining hundreds of stone inscriptions and votive tablets left by lay devotees, religious leaders and members of the court. Their aspirations are usually couched in formulaic declarations but their words are a key to their most cherished beliefs. Donating temples, *stupas*, or monasteries were considered good works that accumulated merit for specific religious aims that hinged on the concept of future rebirths.

One often stated goal was to achieve Buddhahood, or nirvana, or the end of the cycle of rebirths. Another goal was to be reborn in order to witness Metteyya, the Buddha of the Future, thought to appear 5,000 years after the Buddha's death. Devotion to Metteyya is noted first on the votive tablets of Anawrahta where the King declares in Sanskrit that by making this tablet "May I obtain the path to nirvana when Maitreya is fully enlightened" (Luce, II, 3).

The rewards for donors were in the future, but patronage of monuments also enhanced one's social and political status.

Religion at Pagan

A wide variety of sources informed the spiritual beliefs of Pagan's elites during the ancient and pre-modern period. The most deep and enduring stemmed from the Pali canon, proved by thousands of ink captions drawn directly from Pali texts. These inscriptions are generally placed immediately below the pictorial scenes which they describe. Pagan also maintained contact with the Theravada community of Sri Lanka, notably with the revered Mahavihara division.

Newly uncovered terracotta votive tablets embedded between bricks in flooring outside of temple no. 1515. Thousands of such tablets have been recovered at Pagan, many on view at the museum.

The influence of Mahayana Buddhism at Pagan is uncertain, since evidence for full Mahayana worship is nowhere recorded in any inscriptions. However, the subject matter reflected in the murals of a number of temples has led some observers to claim that there was an extensive Mahayana presence at Pagan. Mahayana subjects, such as multi-armed bodhisattvas appear among the earliest temples, such as the Kubyauk-gyi (Myinkaba). Such Mahayana imagery was borrowed from Pala India but was likely worshipped in a Theravada context where patrons and artists made little distinction between these broad divisions in Buddhism emphasized by 20th-century scholars.

Hindu traditions from India were also part of the mix, but these mainly governed secular court rituals. In these largely Hindu ceremonies, Buddhist rites and monks were also included, proved by King Kyanzittha's Palace Inscription. Indigenous spirits, or *nats*, may have also played a role, but no positve evidence for their worship has yet come to light before the 14th century. One example suggesting the eclectic and fluid flavour of religious life at Pagan centres on the deity Gavampati.

Gavampati – Mon or Burmese Deity?

Gavampati is known in Pali literature as a minor disciple of the Buddha, but he played a major role at Pagan, at least during the time of Kyanzittha. In this king's palace inscription, over four thousand monks paid homage to a "golden statue of Buddha, a statue of Gavampati and the *Vinaya*, *Sutta* and *Abhidamma* [the three divisions of the Pali canon]." (E. B., III, pt. 1, 37-38). The reasons for his remarkable status are unknown, and he is nowhere found in the early records of the Pyu or Mon prior to the Pagan period. He was also not important in India or Sri Lanka. No images of this deity can be postively identified, although Luce tentatively took small, rather crudely modeled, corpulent seated monks sculpted in stone as Gavampati.

After the collapse of the Pagan dynasty in the early 14th century the same Gavampati came to play a pivotal role in Mon inscriptions from Lower Burma in the late 15th century. For the later Mon, Gavampati interceded with the Buddha and brought relics from India to the Mon capital of Pegu, or modern Bago. Indeed, he

Terracotta votive tablet. The hand-gesture signifies the Enlightenment, Department of Archaeology, Pagan. (DS)

An enduring symbol of the Buddha himself are his footprints. The most famous set at Pagan is within the west entrance hall at the Ananda Temple. Painted examples often occur in the ceilings of entrance halls, such as the Loka-hteikpan. (DS)

Monks play a special role in Theravada societies. Monk delivering a sermon inside a pavilion surrounding the Shwedagon Pagoda, Yangon. (DS)

became a type of tutelary deity for the later Mon. We must ask why did the Burmese in early Pagan elevate this deity? Was the worship of Gavampati at Pagan borrowed from the Mon, though there is no evidence that the Mon knew of this deity until the 15th century? Or did the later Mon absorb a much earlier Pagan tradition highlighting Gavampati? Or was Gavampati the centre of a long-standing cult in Burma that only happened to manifest itself in the Pagan period and then independently among the Mon much later (Pranke, 189). No ready answers to these vital questions exist, since the historical sources are skimpy and plagued by gaps. This simple case of Gavampati illustrates the complex nature of religious life at Pagan.

Pagan's Legacy

Pagan's name is linked with various learned monks who contributed to many areas of Buddhist knowledge. Among the more prominent were Aggavamsa, Vimalabuddhi, and Uttarjiva. These figures and many others are mentioned only in much later chronicles, such as the *Sasanavamsa*, so we cannot be sure if they really lived at Pagan in the ancient period, but their association with Pagan underscores the ancient city's importance throughout the later history of Burma.

One stone inscription at Pagan dated to 1442 provides a record of the wide ranging learning that probably also characterized the earlier period. It records a specific donation by a governor and his wife, comprising a monastery endowed with rice fields and servants, together with 295 palm-leaf manuscripts. From the titles of the books, we know that they included commentaries on the Pali canon, chronicles from Sri Lanka, and treatises on Hindu statecraft, medicine, astronomy and astrology.

Buddhist Divisions At Pagan

One vexing question at Pagan concerns possible formal divisions with the Buddhist community, or *sangha* (Pali, Sanskrit). Chronicles compiled after the Pagan period refer to two branches, or fraternities, the earliest known as the Arahanta Sangha, later superceded in importance by the Sihala Sangha, associated with Sri Lanka. The first was said to have descended from the Mon monk named Arahan who came from Lower Burma and who converted Anawrahta in the eleventh century. We cannot be sure of Pagan's true spiritual connections with the Mon in Lower Burma, if any, but this division, or another, was an important force at Pagan, at least during the reign of Anawrahta and Kyanzittha.

The second division is linked with a wave of influence from Sri Lanka beginning after Kyanzittha's reign, during the

time of Alaungsithu in the late 12th century. Such influence is confirmed by an inscription recording the founding of the royal Dhamma-yazika stupa where relics presented by the Sri Lankans were revered. Monks from Pagan, most notably Chapada, paid a visit to Sri Lanka. During the 13th century another influential group arose, called the 'forest dwellers' (*arannavasi*, Pali), which seems to have been independent of this Sinhalese line. It was headed for some time by the monk Mahakassapa, and their monuments were clustered in the Minnanthu area in east Pagan. The 'forest monks' were heavily patronized at Pagan, but the relative strength and following of the indigenous division and the one inspired by Sri Lanka cannot yet be determined. However, when the capital shifted from Pagan to Ava in the fourteenth century, the indigenous division grew in importance at Ava, while the group affiliated with Sri Lankan influence flourished among the Mon in Lower Burma (Pranke).

It is difficult to associate any possible religious divisions with a style of architecture or with preferences for certain themes in sculpture and painting at Pagan. It is noteworthy, however, that the apparent rise of the Sinhala division is accompanied by a continuation, if not increase, in Mahayana imagery that ultimately stemmed from Pala India. This paradox is one more reason to suppose that Mahayana subject matter had little to do with Mahayana religious influence as such. That there are no records of Mahayana monks from India at Pagan is another indication that this broad division of Buddhism played only a minor role at Pagan, if any.

The Women of Pagan

Women played a vital role at Pagan, from the mothers of kings to the poor sellers of pots. Their contribution is shadowy, however, since women appear far less frequently than men in the inscriptions. This imbalance reflects an ambivalent view toward women in traditional Buddhism. On the one hand, women played pivotal roles in the early life of the Buddha, namely, his mother, a young woman named Sujata who sustained him with a meal before his enlightenment and, finally, the Earth Goddess who defeated the demon Mara. These are model women. On the other hand, women were at the top of the list of the most dangerous and enticing worldly attachments. Women were often viewed as temptresses, a view also common to the Hindu tradition.

Worshipping nun facing the Shwedagon Pagoda, Yangon. (DS)

Even women's beauty illustrated the transitory nature of reality and delusion. For example, when the Buddha tiptoed out of the palace, he spotted the charming courtesans deep in slumber, "some of them with saliva pouring out of their mouths, some with their bodies wet with saliva..., some grinding their teeth, some talking in their sleep, some groaning." Their once splendid quarters turned in his eyes to, "a charnel ground full of corpses scattered here and there" (*Nidanakatha*, 172).

Mara's daughters. Nandamannya.

Selling flowers and paper umbrellas to pilgrims, Shwe-zigon, Pagan. (DS)

Mara's Daughters

When Mara failed to defeat the Buddha his three lovely daughters vowed, "...dear father, we are women, we will ensnare him in such bonds as the passions and bring him to you" (*Nidanakatha*, 105). The daughters, whose names allegorically translate as Craving, Discontent and Lust, shrewdly reasoned that men's tastes varied, that "some are attracted to virgins, some by women in the prime of youth, some by women in middle age, and some others by older women. Let us then entice him in all possible ways" (*Nidanakatha*, 106). Each daughter multiplied herself three-hundred fold, and they all flirted with the Buddha six times. The Buddha naturally spurned them, but the same ancient Pali text refers to a tradition where the Buddha punished the older women : "Let these women remain like that forever, with their broken teeth and grey hair" (*Nidanakatha*, 106). These older daughters, described as hags, are rarely seen in Buddhist art but are depicted at Pagan, at least in one temple, the Nandamannya.

Buddhist Nuns

Buddhist nuns also shared the landscape at Pagan, but too few inscriptions make it difficult to calculate if they formed a large part of the community or even which monasteries belonged to them. Their numbers were probably relatively few. The Pali word for nun, *bhikkhuni*, is nowhere in the inscriptions but other words were used. However, some nuns may have been rather senior in the hierarchy, since one inscription refers to seven monks and one woman chanting a sacred prayer together, implying a certain level of equality. Women outside the order, such as queens and wives of noblemen, often made religious donations, from entire monuments to the smallest clay votive tablets.

The order of nuns was begun by Prajapati, Buddha's aunt, who effectively became the Buddha's mother following the death of his real mother seven days after his birth. She collected 500 like-minded women and requested the Buddha to allow women to renounce their family life and enter the forest. The Buddha refused, whereupon Prajapati cut her hair. Disconsolate, covered with dust and weeping, she had one of the Buddha's disciples intercede on her behalf. The Buddha relented, and an order of nuns soon grew up. Such ambivalence about women in Buddhism informs this story and still colours the status of women Nevertheless, nunneries exist in Burma today and the head-shaven residents dress in light pink robes.

The lives of some seventy of the earliest female Buddhists are recounted in a Pali text known as the *Therigatha and its Commentary* (Murcott). In these moving accounts, women defied tradition by abandoning the traditional roles of wife and mother. Some were in unhappy marriages, while some chose the spiritual life after the loss of their children.

Youngster at the time of his tonsure, at the hands of a senior monk in Pagan.

Pilgrims placing donations into a giant alms bowl, Manuha compound

Religion at Pagan Today

Today Pagan remains a major pilgrimage focus in Burma. Visitors stroll down the modern outer corridors and bargain for souvenirs or purchase items to be donated to monks, such as bowls, fans, and robes. Often pilgrims light candles and incense at special places. Many buy thin pieces of gold leaf that they will personally afix to especially auspicious images whilst reciting Buddhist prayers. Temples also have modern shrines enabling devotees to make offerings to the planetary deities associated with the day on which they were born in the lunar calender. The week is divided into eight days (with two divisions on Wednesday) and specific animals are associated with each day, such the Garuda bird, or Galon (Burmese), linked with Sunday. There are also eight planets connected with each of the days. These are most clearly seen at the Shwedagon in Yangon encircling the base of the stupa.

Affixing gold leaf to the famous Mahamuni Buddha, Amarapura. (DS)

One newer challenging pilgrimage rite involves visiting four distant shrines before noon. The first is the Shwe-zigon, followed by a hill shrine across the Irrawaddy, known as Tant Kyi Taung. After crossing the river once again, one must go to the Lokananda stupa, south of New Pagan, and then finally scoot to Tuwyin Taung Pagoda, on the mountain range visible east of Pagan. This is most likely an effective pilgrimage, since a close friend confided that he was able to sell his motorcycle for a nice profit after completing this arduous Tour-de-Pagan.

Two young novitiates. (DS)

In addition, the *nats* are worshipped at a number of major Pagan shrines, principally the Shwe-zigon. *Nat* worship also takes place within the Walled City at nine separate places, such as at the Bupaya stupa, in a linked ritual recently under investigation by Bénédicte Brac de la Perrière.

MATERIALS

Ancient stamped brick, Pagan Museum, 45x24x9.5 cm. (DS)

Previous pages: Carting bricks at a present-day kiln, Pagan.

Building site, Minnanthu.

Pagan is the story of brick transformed into religious merit. Indeed, if brick were a measure of merit, then Pagan would be the epicenter of virtue. One donor in the 18th century even boasted that his monastery had consumed close to a half million bricks, as if each signalled a level of sacrifice and devotion. The number needed for a single day's construction at Pagan was surely staggering. The immense Dhamma-yazika required a mere six million, based on estimates of the stupa's volume. Although this versatile medium was also used throughout Southeast Asia, only in Burma did it so dominate religious architecture, even up to the present day.

Bricks were fired locally at Pagan, but many were also manufactured up and down the Irrawaddy and shipped to Pagan in boats, often stamped with the names of villages and towns where they were produced. Others bore the names and titles of individuals, presumably those who donated them. The proportion of bricks used at Pagan from other places would be difficult to determine, but it may have been substantial. Some stamped and incised examples can be seen in the museum, while others can be spotted inserted randomly into the walkway at the Mingalazedi.

The capacity of the ancient kilns is also unknown, but a single labourer in the 18th century was responsible for producing three hundred bricks per day, according to a document concerning the Mingun monument in the Mandalay region. Younger men stomped the clay to achieve the correct consistency, while older workers pressed it into moulds before firing. This same record refers to 7,000 labourers assembled on the bank of the Irrawaddy to fabricate brick, an output resulting in slightly over two million bricks per day. One ancient Pagan inscription speaks of payment going to two brick kilns, and for transportation to the building site in carts.

No ancient brick kiln sites have been located at Pagan, but the old techniques are probably similar to production methods in pratice today. The bricks are not fired in vaulted chambers but are made in large solid stacks. Wide openings at the bottom on the ground are for fuel which today include palm trunks, bamboo, and driftwood collected in the river. Dried palm seed is scattered throughout the stack to help evenly distribute the heat; the seed ignites from the heat issuing from below. The baking lasts days and once the pile has cooled, it is completely disassembled. These temporary kilns can be established quickly and easily where water and suitable materials are at hand. The largest modern kilns at Pagan are located near the Irrawaddy, close to the Shwe-zigon, but smaller operations are seen all over Pagan. Since these temporary kilns leave no traces over time, no ancient brick making sites have been found.

Before the arrival of the Burmese at Pagan in the 9th century, the Pyu people produced bricks with simple stamped designs and wide finger-markings. No brick structures survive intact from this Pyu phase, but thousands of these early bricks are found at Pagan, often used by later builders. In at least one example, a brick structure of probable Pyu date was concealed by a later temple (no. 996).

The bricks at Pagan are well baked and larger than modern equivalents. The average size is 36 x 18 x 6 cm, with much variation. Bricks with different dimensions were used even within the same temple, and ancient brick was forever being re-used. The brick facing of monuments was carefully executed, but the inner fabric was somewhat haphazard, often made up of broken brick and debris. Some auxiliary buildings associated with monasteries were built solely of broken bricks.

Binding the brick facing to the inner wall was of little concern in most cases, and this partially explains the weakness of the walls. In many temples, however, rows of header bricks penetrating the wall deeper than the stretcher brick courses laid end to end helped bind the exterior face to the inner core.

Nevertheless, the thin clay mortar binding the bricks has proved to be the Achilles Heel of Pagan. Mixed with sand and possibly organic materials that have disintegrated long ago, this binding agent inexorably loses its holding power. Moreover, the layer of mortar between the bricks on the facing is extremely thin. As the mortar is exposed to water it expands and eventually washes out, with disastrous repercussions. For example, after 18 cm of rainfall in October, 1983, 13 monuments were severely damaged.

Stone

Sandstone was used sparingly at Pagan, but its role was important for the structural soundness of walls and arches. Long and thin dressed stone blocks were set into the exterior walls at regular intervals to help bind the outer surface to the inner fabric. In some cases, these stones penetrated the walls a full metre. In other cases, the stones were bulky and crudely shaped and rather randomly placed into the walls. Examples can be seen in the north entrance of the Sein-nyet-ama where the fresco has peeled off. Large arches were sometimes reinforced by alternating brick and stucco voussoirs, seen for example inside the Ananda and the Nagayon. Stone also sometimes formed entire courses, normally running along the tops of walls, such as at the Sulamani and Htilominlo. It must be remembered, however, that the stone was never visible, always concealed by stucco or fresco.

Stone was also used for floor paving, doorway thresholds and sometimes for lintels and jambs. Stone bases for supporting wooden posts occur in the compound of the Lemyathna temple (no. 450) and in the conjecturally restored ordination hall at the Hsin-byu-sin complex (no. 700). Others of a slightly different nature were found in the

Modern brick production likely reflects many ancient practices, however, no ancient kilns have been found at Pagan. The stack of fired brick is completely dismantled once firing is finished. Openings at the bottom are for wood fuel. (DS)

Brick fragments from the Pyu period with stamped designs and finger markings on edges. Pagan. (DS)

Chipped off stucco reveals rows of header bricks and stones set within the base, devices designed to bind the wall surface to the inner brick fabric. Green and yellow ceramic insets accent basement mouldings.

excavations within the city walls where they supported large circular wooden posts, and more have been uncovered in the nearby excavations begun in 2003.

Small stone blocks emulating the size of bricks were used for the facing of two brick temples, the Nanpaya and the Kyauk-ku-umin. This technique was likely more costly, and this probably explains its rarity. The only stupa made entirely of stone is the celebrated Shwe-zigon, again suggesting that stone was reserved for significant projects. Stone retained its status even as late as the 18th century, judging from documents surrounding a still standing stone stupa built in Sagaing by King Bodawpaya (1782-1819).

Stucco

A temple without its coating of stucco was unthinkable to Pagan's residents, like a wedding cake without frosting. Each centimetre of every temple exterior was covered by stucco. This coating provided protection against the elements, and at the same time gave scope to the most inventive artistry in all of Asia. Most of the exterior stucco is now lost, but enough remains to form generalizations.

Stucco was applied in two separate stages. First, the exterior wall was completely covered in an even layer. Then, additional stucco was applied directly over this first layer in the areas where raised ornamentation was desired. Moulds were used for many basic designs, but much of the work was hand-fashioned with a variety of metal or wooden implements. The stucco of some temples has weathered poorly, becoming blackened and weakened by lichen and algae. Elsewhere stucco survives in near pristine condition. A few exteriors have been cleaned and treated with an invisible protective coating, such as the Kubyauk-gyi (Myinkaba) (*Pagan Newsletter*, 1985).

Two successive styles of ancient stucco work can be distinguished readily. The earliest dated example is found on the exterior of the Kubyauk-gyi (Myinkaba), finished in 1113. The decoration is bold and well-proportioned, with much in high relief. The Kubyauk-gyi stucco is fragmentary, but entire walls of early ornament survive at the Myebontha (no. 1512).

The second phase of stucco work arose by the second half of the 12th and continued into the 13th century. Its style is lace-like and far more intricate than the earlier work. These new stylistic developments can begin to be traced at the Sulamani (1183), the Dhamma-yazika (1197-1198) and the Kubyauk-gne (1198). In addition, new motifs were introduced alongside older ones. Later period stucco, such as at the Tayok-pyi, can be compared with the earlier work at the Kubyauk-gyi (Myinkaba) to appreciate the differing approaches. This evolution went through numerous stages, which can be charted only after further study. Also, making value judgements about these two phases is highly subjective, since they are so dissimilar as to be somewhat akin to comparing Piranesi with Picasso. Nevertheless, if you ramble around Pagan for a few days your eye will begin to detect the basic differences.

One distinctive and ubiquitous motif throughout Pagan's history is a continuous frieze of faces, each spewing forth vegetation. This motif was borrowed probably from Pala sources, but it is also known in Orissa and other parts of India, including Sri Lanka. The fanciful face is known as a *kirtimukha* (Sanskrit), often translated as 'face of glory'. It is sometimes said to be the face of an ogre, but it has positive, auspicious associations.

Stucco continued to be used from the 14th century onward, but the various twists and turns in style have not yet been worked out. Examples from the 18th and 19th centuries are found at the Pitakat-taik and the Ananda Temple Monastery and in numerous temples and stupas. Modern stucco can be seen among the restorations of the Ananda gateways.

Motifs from ancient Pagan survived into the modern period or were consciously revived. For example, compare the row of bold *kirtimukhas* at the Kubyauk-gyi temple, (Myinkaba), with the same motif at the adjacent Myazedi stupa (no. 1320), from the 19th century. Also, *kirtimukhas* from the Konbaung period often have extended arms, sometimes holding linked vegetation. These can be seen on the rear of the Manuha and among numerous Konbaung buildings throughout Burma.

The composition of Pagan's stucco has never been studied, but the principal ingredients were likely lime mixed with sand and water to form a thick paste. One traditional Burmese recipe also includes molasses made from palm sugar and a gelatinous glue produced from boiling buffalo hide. A reference to 1,500 units of lime, and the same number of units of molasses and 100 skins of buffalo is found in the 18th-century inscription at the Ananda Temple Monastery. The exteriors of new and restored temples at Pagan are not given a stucco covering, and this explains why they clash so violently with the ancient temples.

Two phases of stucco work. The bold, three-dimensional treatment at the Kubyauk-gyi (Myinaka), 1113, (top) contrasts with the restrained 13th-century Tayok-pyi (bottom). In both examples kirtimukha faces spew forth pearl-shaped ornaments.

Jars from Upper Burma are sold near the Ananda Temple (DS).

Brick kiln under construction, with bamboo centring, Kyaukmyaung, Upper Burma. Enclosed brick kilns ensure high temperatures required for glazed ceramics. No ancient kilns have been found, despite extensive glazing at Pagan. (DS)

Stucco and ceramic insets, Htilominlo.

Ceramics

Objects of fired clay played a vital role at Pagan, beginning from the Pyu period. Even today the fields are littered with millions of unglazed shards belonging to diverse periods. Utilitarian earthenware was probably fired at low temperatures directly upon the ground, a technique in use throughout central Burma, such as in the village of Taunggon, about 25 kilometres east of Nyaung-U, or upriver at Yandabo. The best ancient earthenware sites at Pagan are the Otein Taung mounds, near the Sulamani (Hudson, Nyein Lwin, Win Maung).

Ceramics were even used in court ceremonies, as recorded in one inscription revealing that over 4,000 participants held clay pots as they chanted Pali prayers at the consecration of Kyanzittha's palace. One terracotta lamp made in two sections was found while clearing perhaps a 14th-century structure (no. 2814). It measures half a meter high and is on view at the museum. Ceramic roof tiles must have been widely used, but little is known about this tradition.

Glazed ceramics require a higher firing point in order for the glaze to fuse with the surface, and proper kilns with brick walls were probably used to create and sustain this degree of heat. Glazed ware was produced in vast quantities at Pagan, but not a single kiln has been found, despite decades of searching and more recent exploration by the Myanmar Ceramic Society, headed by Dr. Myo Thant Tyn. A few small brick-lined kilns at Pagan once thought to be for ceramics appear to be for making glass beads, according to the researches of Don Hein. One can be seen near the Nagoyan temple, on the opposite side of the paved road.

Brightly coloured, glazed architectural pieces accented the exterior surface of many monuments, usually placed at regular intervals in the base moldings and within the roof terraces. The shapes varied but were generally rounded, square, or circular. They contrast today with the aged brick but were surrounded originally by stucco. Square green panels alternating with stucco patterns can be appreciated up close on the first terrace of the Shwegu-gyi, a temple finished in 1131 and the earliest dated monument with glazed work. Glazed ceramics certainly started earlier, probably in the 11th century.

Long glazed green coloured strips were sometimes placed within the flame-like projections over doorways, creating a spectacular effect as the surface catches sunlight at an angle. Unique continuous panels of glazed ornament are found at the So-min-gyi stupa, featuring fanciful animals and dancing figures set within thick foliage. Rare green plaques featuring a female dancer and male drummer are found in the Museum für Indische Kunst, Berlin, removed over a hundred years ago from exterior niches of the Manaung temple (no. 1479). Other unusual glazed work appears on the large corner stupas on the top terrace of the Mingalazedi. Much of the colouring appears to be a pale white, but it would originally have been green which has now weathered.

Entrance to the Sulamani, 1183. Glazed insets glisten in the sun.

Ceramic head. So-min-gyi. The lower portion of the face is missing its stucco.

Glazed tile, jataka no. 13, roof terrace, Ananda Temple.

Boar, So-min-gyi.

Pagan's artisans also experimented with glazing sandstone a green colour. Even *jataka* plaques of carved sandstone were coated with a green glaze. Examples appear to be limited to the Shwe-zigon stupa, according to the unpublished research of Dr. Aung Bo. Glazed stone and brick were also used for flooring, and both are seen inside the Nagayon.

A yellow coloured glaze, perhaps of vanadium oxide, was later introduced and often used as an accent against a green background. These two-coloured pieces were not entirely successful, since the yellow portion did not adhere well in many cases, such at the Htilominlo temple. However, those at the Sulamani have stood up rather better.

Pagan's elite probably enjoyed glazed vessels, but none have survived. Those in the museum today are likely from the 15th-16th centuries and were imported from Lower Burma, according to Dr. Aung Bo.

Pagan's best known ceramics are its thousands of surviving *jataka* plaques. It is usually considered that the earliest were unglazed, limited to the series from the Shwe-san-daw, and the two Hpetleik stupas, both perhaps from the 11th century. Later, *jataka* plaques were glazed in a green colour, with a wide range of hues due to diverse

Unglazed tile. Incised with number 543. This tale is numbered 540 in the Pali canon West Hpetleik.

A musician on a remarkable ancient wooden doorway. It was 'discovered' in 1922 and is now in a pavilion facing the Shwe-zigon.

firing conditions and the composition of the copper oxide. The tiles were probably first formed in moulds. The figurative sculpture was fashioned by hand separately and then placed on the plaque before it was covered with glaze and fired. Making sure that the figures adhered properly to the plaque was likely a major concern. Green glazed *jataka* series continue long after the ancient Pagan period in Upper Burma, but the compositions were greatly simplified. The last great ceramic series in Burma was created for the Mingun monument, in 1791, near Mandalay. These were made in the same way as those at Pagan, but the tiles were covered in a range of single colours.

Wood

Pagan's flourishing wood sculpting traditions survive only in tantalizing bits and pieces. By far the best is a huge doorway displayed within the compound of the Shwe-zigon. It was found inside one of the temples facing the *stupa* in 1922. It stands over four meters high and is enlivened with dancers and musicians in low relief. Wood sculptures of Buddhist subjects are in the museum, but their exact original locations and how they were used are unknown. Some of the earliest should be dated to the 12th or 13th centuries. Stone inscriptions talk of Buddha images carved from the original Bodhi tree in India and sandalwood, but none have been found. Life-size standing wooden male figures have been located at Pagan in great numbers, but their identity and their date are still unknown. They are generally crowned and heavily adorned with jewellery.

An entire wooden throne miraculously survived from the ancient period and is now in the museum attached to the Yok-son Kyaung Monastery in Sale, about 46 km south of Pagan. It stands about three metres in height and likely accommodated a seated wooden figure. Comprised of many sections, once fastened together by metal clamps, it also bears traces of original painting.

Wood was employed for domestic structures and palaces, but nothing has survived. Timber was also used within brick monasteries, forming the first floors of residential buildings. Sculpted wooden lintels above doorways are now and then seen, such as at the Nagayon, but in other cases the lintels were concealed by brick and plaster, such as at the Pahto-thamya. Wood covers for palm-leaf manuscripts are referred to in inscriptions, but all have perished. Woodwork from the Konbaung period does survive at Pagan, notably in the enormous wooden doorways at the Ananda and the Shwegu-gyi temple. There are also Konbaung wooden monasteries at Pagan, studied by Fraser-Lu. One of the finest monasteries in the region is the late 19th-century Yok-son Kyaung in Sale. This was ably restored by the Department of Archaeology, with assistance from U Win Maung (Tanpawady).

A huge wooden throne is preserved in a museum at Yok-son Kyaung Monastery, Sale. c. 11th-13th century. The left hand side of the throne reveals motifs also occurring in ancient stucco. (DS)

Wooden Buddhas probably from the ancient period. Department of Archaeology, Pagan. (DS)

*Death of the Buddha. Ancient gilded repoussé from
temple no. 1554. Brahma and Sakka (?) on the left,
with Vishnu (?) on the far right. Pagan Museum. (DS)*

*Bronze Pyu period Buddha
from near Pyinmana.
Department of Archaeology,
Yangon. H. 20 cm. (DS)*

Lacquerware is famous at Pagan today, but when it first appeared in
Burma is controversial. Fragments of lacquer were excavated recently
that possibly belong to the 13th century (Blurton and Isaacs). The
small town of Nyaung-U was celebrated for its lacquer production by
the 18th century, but this is no longer true. The best place to witness
an active workshop demonstrating each of the complicated steps is at
Moe Moe Lacquer shop in New Pagan. There is also a government
lacquerware museum at Pagan.

Metal work

Religious objects in bronze, silver and gold rank among the
masterpieces at Pagan and can be seen at the local museum and
the national museum, Yangon. The most important techniques were
developed earlier during the Pyu period, such as the lost-wax method
and repoussé. Abundant inscriptions refer to silver and gold images
enshrined as relics within monuments. Metal work irrefutably from
the ancient Pagan period outside of Burma is extremely limited. One
example, a small, rather crude seated Buddha, is incised and is dated
to 1293 (Guy).

Metal sculptures were enshrined not only within stupas but also
inside the large central brick Buddha figures in temples. These were
probably placed in the head, the chest area, and beneath the image,
to judge from the countless number of images with crude holes cut
into the brick in these places by treasure seekers centuries ago.

Metal Buddha images were also enshrined as relics inside the walls
of temple towers. The most spectacular find occurred as recently as
1999 when a collapsed tower revealed a standing Buddha over a
meter in height, now in the museum. These finds suggest that some,
if not all, of Pagan's spectacular metal sculptures were never meant to
be seen or worshipped directly but interred only. One large standing
metal Buddha, however, was found in the sanctum of a small 12th-
century shrine (no. 2166), opposite the Ananda Temple Monastery.
It is now in the museum. If the original image was in the ancient
temple, or if it was removed there later, cannot be determined.

*The original bronze, 1.14 m high,
is now on display in the museum.
The inlaid glass background is modern.
It is unknown if this was the original
location of this masterpiece. (Ha)*

ARCHITECTURE

The first-time visitor to Pagan is often bewildered by the diversity of the monuments. Behind this complex variety, however, the city's architects knew only three major building types: the temple, the stupa, and the monastery. Less common were ordination halls, libraries for palm-leaf manuscripts and modest, single-room image-houses.

The city's zenith saw the creation of over 900 temples, 500 stupas and 400 monasteries between the 11th and 13th centuries. This burst of construction slowed only after the capital shifted from Pagan to Ava, near Mandalay, by the mid-14th century. The city was never abandoned and building continued, albeit at a much quieter pace, totaling a mere two hundred monuments or so between the 15th and 20th centuries. This explains how ancient shrines come to be side by side with those of recent origin.

The temples may appear somewhat similar at first glance, but Pagan's designers fashioned a vibrant "balance between uniformity and diversity", as the French architect Pierre Pichard observed (1996, 5, 225). No two monuments are exactly alike. Indeed, each expresses striking individuality.

Virtually all of the monuments were photographed and briefly described in Pichard's *Inventory of Monuments at Pagan*, including even indistinct brick mounds. The total number of monuments Pichard recorded was 2,834, ranging over eight thick volumes. This count also included numerous 18th- and 19th-century monuments. Thanks to this monumental survey that consumed over a decade,

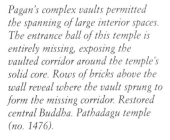

Pagan's complex vaults permitted the spanning of large interior spaces. The entrance hall of this temple is entirely missing, exposing the vaulted corridor around the temple's solid core. Rows of bricks above the wall reveal where the vault sprung to form the missing corridor. Restored central Buddha. Pathadagu temple (no. 1476).

many characteristics of Pagan's monuments can now be quantified with greater precision and certainty.

The earliest construction took place near the river's edge and within the Walled City during the 11th and early 12th centuries. No dated monuments survive from the 11th century at Pagan, but the earliest dated temple, the sophisticated Kubyauk-gyi (Myinkaba) of 1113, implies that the city's building traditions stretched deep into the preceding century. The city's brick walls are dated by radiocarbon tests to approximately 1100-1200, which is also confirmed by traces of stucco ornament adhering to the Tharaba Gate. The only firmly dated monument within the walls is the Shwegu-gyi, dedicated in 1131. At least one wooden palace may have stood inside the walls, but its ground plan has not yet been fully traced. By the late 12th century construction expanded inland, evinced by the Sulamani dated to 1183.

The 13th century saw an explosion of activity in areas around the modern villages of Western Pwasaw and Minnanthu in the east, but also throughout Pagan. More monuments sprouted up in this century than at any other time in Pagan's history. In the 13th century the number of monuments jumped to more than 1,300, compared to no more than 250 for the 11th and 12th centuries, according to Win Than Tun who based his analysis on Pichard's *Inventory*. The 13th-century monuments were all much smaller than some of the enormous temples of the two preceding centuries, such as the Ananda, but this century represented a construction boom.

The 13th century also saw the rise of other centres within the realm, mostly located to the south on the Irrawaddy. The closest was Sale, 46 km from Pagan, with 103 recorded monuments. Another was Hsale, 75 km south, with 41. Much further south was Myingun, 195 km, with 26 temples, and Kyuntaw, 240 km, with 26 buildings preserved on an island in the Irrawaddy (*Pagan Newsletter*, 1986). Up river from Pagan and inland from the west bank was another centre known as Pakkhanji, now with a site museum.

The eleven largest structures at Pagan number the well-known Ananda, Nagayon, Thatbyinnyu, Sulamani, and Dhamma-yazika, and all are traditionally dated to the late 11th and 12th centuries. Each is estimated to have consumed approximately fifty times as many bricks as the average size stupa or temple. The Dhamma-yazika alone took 6 million bricks, based on estimates of its volume. Taken together, these eleven Leviathans amounted to roughly one quarter of the entire building activity between the 11th and 13th centuries, according to Pichard's calculations. These were probably royal foundations but we cannot be certain, since few inscriptions survive. Court members and other elites also patronized more modest temples, such as the Kubyauk-gyi (Myinkaba) and the Shwegu-gyi.

The length of time taken to construct even the largest monuments was probably no more than three or four years. This estimate is based on starting and completion dates for two buildings recorded in inscriptions. One is the Shwegu-gyi temple, a medium-size temple that took seven and a half months. The second is the huge Dhamma-yazika stupa that required about two years. Construction time probably hinged on even flows of patronage and

Rich original stucco ornament in the roof terrace of the Pahto-thamya. (DS)

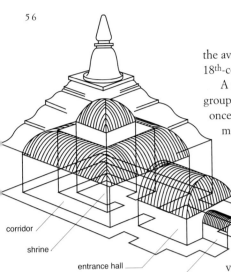

corridor

shrine

entrance hall

porch

Architectural drawing showing interior vaults of a hollow core temple, Abeyadana.

the availability of materials and labour. For example, the modest 18th-century Ananda Temple Monastery took nearly a full decade.

A team of professionals likely organized the diverse artisan groups and the supply of brick and other essential materials once permission was granted from the crown and the funding mechanisms were in place. Architects are rarely mentioned in inscriptions and nothing is known of their training. Indian architects may have been present at Pagan, but there is no direct evidence. Carefully drawn plans must have guided projects, but these are lost.

Pagan's Vaulting

Covering large interior spaces with brick vaults was the most challenging task faced by the ancient builders. The vaults needed to be lightweight but at the same time robust in order to support the heavy roof terraces and tower. That so many hundreds of vaults survived over the centuries is testimony to their design and durability.

The origins of vaulting in Burma are murky, but Pichard has suggested that the very notion of vaulting was perhaps borrowed from Buddhist centres in eastern India where the few surviving examples are rather small and simple, such as at Ratnagiri in Orissa (Pichard, 1999). The original impetus may have come from India or developed independently on Burmese soil, but it is universally agreed that Pagan's architects took vaulting to unprecedented levels in Asia.

The earliest vaulting at Pagan appears fully mature, without signs of slow and gradual development that surely occurred over decades, if not a century or more. More detailed research will no doubt reveal the progressive stages leading up to the first dated temple, the Kubyauk-gyi (Myinkaba), 1113. It is often said that the Pyu or the Mon contributed the knowledge of vaulting to Pagan, but there is no surviving evidence for this. The temples said to be of Pyu date at Shri Kshetra, for example, are likely of the Pagan period or later, and there are no extant vaulted shrines attributable to the Mon in Lower Burma before the rise of Pagan in the 11th century.

A number of different types of vaults were employed at Pagan, depending on the requirements. Cloister vaults usually appeared over square or rectangular sanctums, while corridors and entrance halls were covered with barrel vaults, whether full, three-quarter or half. Vaults of different heights sometimes intersected the corners of corridors to create diversity and subtlety. The corridors generally received a half or three-quarter barrel vault in temples of the 11th and 12th centuries, while a slightly pointed barrel vault was favoured in the 13th century.

The basic vaulting technique at Pagan differed greatly from Roman and European practices. In the West the individual building blocks of an arch or a vault, called voussoirs, were laid in horizontal courses, whereas at Pagan the bricks were set vertically, with their broad side perpendicular to the length of the vault. The fired brick voussoirs were cut on one side to form an irregular trapezium. In the West cumbersome temporary wooden scaffolding, or centring, supported the vault until it was completed, but at Pagan this was unnecessary. Also, Western vaults required durable mortar but this was less true at Pagan where clay was employed between bricks, combined with fine sand and possibly organic ingredients (that have disintegrated over time).

Vaulting permitted the covering of large internal spaces, both at Pagan and in the West, whether in brick or stone. This technology made the temples at Pagan distinctive, with encircling inner corridors and wide entrance halls. This type of vaulting differed in principle from the system used by the Khmer in Cambodia and Thailand which relied upon the corbelled arch. Corbelled vaulting was unsuitable for spanning large areas but was ideal for covering small sanctums and narrow corridors, two hallmarks of Khmer architecture. In the Khmer realm therefore there are no enclosed spaces that are as wide and as spacious as those encountered at Pagan. (Corbelled vaulting in the Mayan architecture of Meso-America produced similar results.) The Khmer probably borrowed corbelled vaulting from ancient India where it was also the principal system of construction. The corbelled system was known in Pagan but was used sparingly and only above small spaces, such as narrow doors and windows.

These contrasting construction systems should not be ranked one against the other, since each masterfully fulfilled the differing needs of these diverse civilizations. The incomparably simple post-and-lintel system of building, for example, produced the Parthenon in Athens. Each civilization perfected these diverse building modes to realize different religious aims.

Collapsed corridor vault showing outer wall of sanctum and a ruined recumbent Buddha (no. 1686). Rebuilt in 1991-1992. (DS)

Temples and Stupas

The English term 'pagoda' is often used in Burma for both a temple and a *stupa* and can therefore be somewhat confusing for the visitor. However, the Burmese word for *stupa* is *zedi*, derived from *cetiya* (Pali, Sanskrit). The term appears in ancient Pagan records as *ceti*, from *ceitya*, or *puthuiw* (Burmese). The modern Burmese word for temple is '*ku*', from '*guha*' (Pali, Sanskrit), literally meaning cave. In Indian mythology the gods reside in caves within mountain ranges, and the temple is therefore likened to a mountain and the inner sanctum to a cave. These symbolic associations were un-important in Burma, although the physical form of the Pagan monuments was greatly indebted to types developed in India. This word '*guha*' is rarely found in later Indian inscriptions to describe a temple, but it likely appears more often in Pali literature and this probably explains why the term was used at Pagan. The popular Burmese word today for either *stupa* and temple is *hpaya*, which can also used for a Buddha image and even for a king.

The difference between a temple and a stupa is generally a sharp one in most Buddhist countries, but the distinctions are often blurred at Pagan. For example, a circular shaped building crowned with a stupa-like dome can be fully entered via a single passage leading to a Buddha image intended for viewing (nos. 467, 474). Also, there were numerous temples topped with stupa-like domes, such as the Pahto-thamya and Abeyadana. In fact, temples with such domes became common in the 13th century, such as the Nandamannya.

Temples and stupas were rarely built in conjunction with each other, suggesting that patrons built one or the other but rarely both together. Even in cases where two stupas were built at the same time and close together, no attempt was made to align them, such as the East and West Hpetleik stupas which do not share the same axis. One exception is the Sein-nyet-ama temple and the Sein-nyet-nyima stupa that were laid out simultaneously and aligned with each other on an east-west axis. Stupas and temples were frequently accompanied by smaller ancillary monuments that could be added at any time, often placed between an inner and outer compound wall, such as at the Mingalazedi. Vaulted gateways in the centre of each compound wall were the sole entrances for many large stupas and temples.

The Stupa

In Burma and all the Buddhist world the stupa enshrined relics. The Buddhist concept of relics is elastic and includes any objects seen as valuable and auspicious. The most sacred were believed to be the corporal remains of the Buddha, such as his teeth or hair. Another class of relics were objects used by the Buddha, such as the alms bowl and even his tooth-brush, fashioned from a twig of a tree. Other relics are associated with the master's disciples or venerated monks. Several Pagan inscriptions include extensive lists of relics. One dated to 1227 records the following deposits: " . . . the bodily relics of the Buddha, images of the Buddha made from the branch of the sacred banyan tree, one cast in silver, one in crystal, one in ivory, and one in sandalwood. Beneath all of the relics and images are spread gold and silver cushions and placed above the images are gold and silver

Miniature stupa, Bodh Gaya, India. (Courtesy Forrest McGill)

umbrellas. Parched rice of gold and silver, and gold and silver lights are also offered. When these gems are enshrined the relic chamber is sealed with bricks. Then, magnificent figures of gods and various beings are made with stucco." (Than Tun, 1978, 129)

One major royal stupa at Pagan was the Dhamma-yazika enshrining relics presented from the king of Sri Lanka, recorded in an inscription and reaffirmed in the *Glass Palace Chronicle*. Such gifts not only underscore the religious stature of Sri Lanka in Burma but also the way in which kingdoms exchanged relics to promote regional goodwill. This is no less true today. The Chinese government, for example, lent a tooth relic of the Buddha to Burma in the 1990s from which two copies were made, one enshrined inside a stupa in Yangon and the other near Mandalay.

Few relics are recovered today at Pagan, since treasure-hunters have left virtually no monument untouched, beginning probably in the 14th century. By the start of the 20th century stupas not under active worship had been raided for relics long before. For example, all of Pagan's stupas had large gaping holes on their exteriors, discarded brick strewn about like piles of earth from an animal burrow. Most of these crude cavities were bricked up in the 1990s.

The earliest stupas in India were semi-hemispherical in shape and crowned with multiple stone umbrellas. An umbrella signified veneration for royalty, the Buddha or a sacred object. At Pagan the umbrellas are usually indicated by closely spaced brick rings within the spire of the stupa. These rings lack the outward appearance of umbrellas, but they represent this important concept. In some examples, the rings are quite distinct, and long narrow vertical elements link the rings from top to bottom, reflecting a feature found on miniature stone stupas from Pala India. This can be seen at the early Pahto-thamya within the Walled City, although it has been partially restored.

The crowning sections above the umbrellas have perished on all of Pagan's stupas, but their form can be conjectured on the basis of examples depicted in wall paintings and stucco ornament. Pristine examples in stucco are found on the façades of the Sulamani and Dhammayan-gyi temples, beside the major entrances. The summit

The most revered stupa at Pagan, the Shwe-zigon is believed to contain a tooth-relic from Sri Lanka and a forehead bone of the Buddha. Upper half of stupa is concealed by mats, in preparation for gilding. (DS)

Miniature stone stupas at Bodh Gaya, India, some with their original finials symbolically representing umbrellas. These finials were copied at Pagan, such as at the Pahto-thamya. (Courtesy Forrest McGill)

Depiction of stupa, stucco ornament on the façade of the Sulamani, 1183.

consists of a tapered bud-shaped object resting upon a single or double layer of lotus petals. This crowning element may have originally been metal, according to inscriptions. The shiny metal finials attached to the top of many stupas and temples today at Pagan are called *hti*s (Burmese), but their use in the ancient period is unknown.

Relics were never designed to be seen after they were deposited inside the stupa, only worshipped from outside. Ritual circumambulation of stupas occurs in some Buddhist traditions but finds no direct mention within the entire Pali canon or in Pagan inscriptions. Where circumambulation does occur in Buddhist societies, devotees proceed in a clockwise direction, presenting their auspicious right side toward the venerated object inside the stupa. Ritual circumambulation of stupas is not part of modern day Burmese worship, but it is commonplace in neighbouring Thailand where three passes are usually performed. Upon finishing the circumambulation, flowers and candles are placed at designated areas surrounding the stupa, especially on full-moon nights. It is true that thousands walk about the Shwe-zigon in Pagan and the Shwedagon in Yangon, but there is no specified required number of times nor is it part of a formal or informal ritual specifying circumambulation.

Devotees may have practiced circumambulation in ancient Pagan, but there is no direct evidence for it. The upper terraces of the larger stupas were unsuited for circumambulation, since access to each terrace walkway was impeded by the high walls of the median staircases. To enter the pathways on the terraces, one needs to climb rather awkwardly over the walls of the stairway. The arrangement at the Shwe-san-daw is an exception, but it probably reflects modern tampering. Some large stupas omitted stairways to any of the upper terraces, and this is one strong argument for believing that circumambulation was never intended, at least for the upper part. This is true for the Sein-nyet-nyima and the So-min-gyi. Worshippers may have encircled the bases of the monuments, but this cannot be yet established.

Stupas varied in design but the bell-shape was the most favoured for large examples, such as the Mingalazedi and the Shwe-zigon. This form dominated later Burmese architecture and we see it also at the Shwedagon in Yangon. Much less common were stupas of hemispherical shape. Bulbous shaped stupas such as the Lokananda (no. 1023) and Bupaya (no. 1657) are among the most revered at Pagan, but we cannot be sure of their date. Some stupas are thought to have borrowed their form from Sri Lanka but this needs more investigation. Perhaps one of the earliest stupas can be attributed to Anawrahta. This large example is located between Yangon and Twante and was associated with large votive plaques bearing this king's name. It has wide octagonal bases constructed in laterite, no median staircases, and is capped with a dome made of brick. This plan is not found at Pagan, suggesting that it may reflect lost Mon traditions in Lower Burma.

At the corners of the terraces were often imposing urns, square turrets, and miniature stupas, mostly restored in the 1990s. The most prominent stucco ornament on stupas was an encircling row of kirtimukhas (Sanskrit), a motif borrowed from India. The Shwe-zigon is the best place at Pagan to witness an ancient stupa still under active worship, here combined with devotion to *nat*s.

In some fifty examples at Pagan, a large stupa encased a smaller inner one. The inner example exhibited no sign of deterioration or repair, suggesting that the two were either built together at the same time, or, more likely, after a short span of time. In these examples, ancient grave robbers broke into both the outer and inner stupas!

Temples

In contrast with stupas built to enshrine relics, the temples at Pagan were built to worship Buddha images. They were designed for worshippers to enter a sanctum featuring one or more principal Buddhas made of brick, coated with stucco and painted. Temples also contained relics, often concealed within the central image inside the sanctum. This explains why all of the principal Buddhas at Pagan were violated by fortune seekers in search of objects of value, probably beginning as early as the 14th century.

Pagan's exact debt to Indian architecture is widely debated, but it is correctly assumed that the influence stemmed from ancient eastern India (modern Bihar, Bengal, Bangladesh and perhaps Orissa). For example, the basic ground plan at Pagan, a sanctum preceded by a covered porch, was also the standard plan for temples in India. Also found in India are temples with a central sanctum surrounded by a covered corridor, a typical plan at Pagan. Much of eastern India during this period was controlled by the Pala dynasty (c. 750-1200) in whose realm both Buddhist and Hindu temples were created, in stone and in brick. In as much as Pagan's painting and sculpture reveal extensive borrowings from Pala India, it is logical to think that the city's architecture looked in that direction too. Few temples within the Pala realm have survived intact, however, so it has been difficult to draw direct parallels with Pagan. That the characteristic design of the curvilinear tower of many Pagan temples is unequivocally borrowed from India is proof that deep and profound influences were transmitted from the sub-continent. Such towers are called *shikhara* (Sanskrit) in ancient Indian architectural manuals.

Numerous architectural motifs at Pagan are easily traced to Pala art, such as the frieze of *kirtimukhas* encircling the drum of most stupas and on the exterior walls of temples created in stucco. (It is also found in Orissa, at Lalitgiri, for example). Another Pala motif widely found at Pagan, especially in the early period, was a cusped arch placed against a background of thin horizontal

Encased stupa (no.1754). Such encased stupas were not unusual at Pagan, numbering over fifty. The photograph indicates ancient relic-seekers broke into the inner stupa. (Courtesy Pierre Pichard)

Cusped arch with flame-like vertical projections, and crocodiles, or makara *at ends. Stone inserts bond the outer surface to the inner fabric. Façade of Kubyauk-gne, 1198 (no. 1391). (DS)*

registers resembling terraces or stories. In Pala art a similar design is found in numerous palm-leaf manuscripts where it encloses seated deities. It is witnessed at Pagan in stucco above the windows of the Kubyauk-gyi (Myinkaba) and in numerous other examples, and is also found in wall paintings, above niches containing stone images.

Determining the degree to which Pagan temples resembled the largely lost building traditions of eastern India will require more research. Although Indian and Burmese architects almost certainly used different vaulting techniques to cover interior spaces, the exterior appearances of temples might have been similar. Indeed, researchers in the future might well find that the best place to study Pala architecture is in Pagan.

Pagan's Two Temple Plans

Pagan's architects worked within a framework of only two basic ground plans, but these types afforded limitless variation. One is based on a solid brick core encircled by a vaulted corridor, while the other has an open vaulted sanctum, usually also surrounded by a corridor. It is unknown if one plan developed before the other, but both were likely in use from the beginning. Surviving temples in northern and eastern India were not designed around a solid core, so perhaps this type was an innovation at Pagan where different vaulting techniques favoured different solutions. For example, a solid central core might have provided greater stability for supporting the weight of the tower. Ritual circumambulation within the corridors of both temple types may have occurred, but no evidence for it exists.

In temples with a solid central core the chief Buddha is placed against the wall facing the entrance hall. The earliest dated solid-core temple is the Shwegu-gyi, 1131, where a huge Buddha was placed in a niche within the core; a smaller one was on the rear wall of the core. In some cases a Buddha appears on all four walls. Less commonly figurative sculpture in brick depicting key events from the Buddha's life, such as his birth and death, is found on the side and rear walls. In all temples with a solid core, however, the principal Buddha facing the doorway is shown seated in the earth-touching gesture signifying his enlightenment, with his lowered right-hand touching the base. These large images can be within deep niches or project slightly from the core into the corridor. Temples fitting this description were built throughout Pagan's ancient period and include the Shwegu-gyi, Sein-nyet-ama and the Tayok-pyi.

The other major temple type consists of an inner chamber, covered by a cloister vault, encircled by a corridor. This can also be described as a hollow core temple. A prominent seated Buddha image inside the sanctum faces the entrance, resembling temples based on a central core. The earliest dated temple conforming to this basic plan is the Kubyauk-gyi (Myinkaba), from 1113, but monuments with this basic design continued to the end of the Pagan period. In occasional examples, a single Buddha is flanked by two large seated Buddhas, such as the Pahto-thamya, or small kneeling disciples, like the Abeyadana. Another variation consists of a square vaulted sanctum with no surrounding corridor. In these examples, the Buddha image is placed against the rear wall, or on a brick base within the sanctum, such as the Loka-hteikpan.

Imposing entrance halls provided a transition from the outside world to the sanctum for both types of temples. The roof is somewhat lower than the temple itself, accenting the sense of progression. The hall itself is usually fronted by a small vaulted porch and a narrow vestibule. The entrance halls and corridors are always painted with frescos, often *jatakas*, and many have niches for stone sculpture.

Pagan's designers brilliantly juxtaposed large areas of plain wall surfaces with stucco ornament in high and low relief. The exterior stucco was unpainted, and much of it has remarkably retained its original shape and natural light colour. The high base mouldings are sometimes accented with small flat green and yellow glazed ceramic inserts. Framing the walls at the top was a frieze of *kirtimukhas*, with bands of foliage descending from their mouths.

An ubiquitous feature at Pagan above doorways and windows is a double-pediment made up of a cusped section surmounted by high, vertical flame-like shafts filled with vegetation. At the two ends of the pediment are usually fanciful aquatic creatures resembling crocodiles, *makara* (Sanskrit), from whose gaping mouths often spew forth a rampant lion or other figures. In some cases, the tails of these creatures form the cusped ornament. This type of arch and the *makaras* were borrowed elements, probably from Pala India, but they are also found in early Sri Lanka. The vertical flame-like elements may be adaptations of floral designs surrounding cusped arches seen on Pala sculpture. A seated male or female figure, usually holding lotuses in both hands, is found in the central flame-like section. A similar type of double-pediment is found within the Khmer realm, but there is no proof that one influenced the other or if both Southeast Asian civilization borrowed and adapted the motif from India.

Temple Towers

Pagan's skyline is marked by hundreds of dramatic temple towers, or superstructures. Each varies but most are designed with receding square terraces capped by a tall curvilinear tower, or *shikhara* (Sanskrit), or a *stupa*-like dome. For many early temples the terraces were made with sloping roofs surmounted by narrow recessed bands just beneath the tower, such as the Nagayon and the Kubyauk-gyi (Myinkaba). Sloping roofs gradually gave way to wide terraces with flat roofs, witnessed in the Shwegu-gyi dated to 1131. The Ananda temple, however, employed sloping roofs for the lower terraces and flat roofs for the upper ones. Median stairways connecting each of the terraces in many temples are generally ornamental in nature. In cases without stairways, large niches often appear in the centre of each terrace. At terrace corners were square turrets, urns, miniature stupas or small *shikharas*.

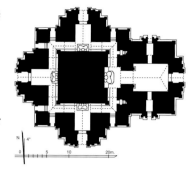

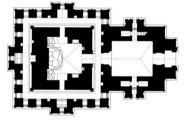

Solid-core temple, top: Tayok-pyi and hollow-core variety, bottom: Pahto-thamya. Both types were used throughout the ancient period.

Cusped arch with horizontel registers over window at Kubyauk-gyi (Myinkaba), 1113, resembles designs found in palm-leaf manuscripts from India in the Pala period.

The tall curvilinear portion of the tower is based directly on the *shikhara* form of superstructure known in northern and eastern India. The towers are generally of stone in the subcontinent but could also be of brick. The *shikhara* at Pagan is usually made up of multiple horizontal receding registers, with a wide flat vertical segment in the centre of each side. The five small shrines surrounding the Dhamma-yazika stupa are well-preserved examples that can be examined at close range. In many cases, each stage of the *shikhara* is ornamented with circle designs, sometimes filled with small figures or floral ornament. Many temples used stupa-like domes rather than *shikharas*, especially favoured in the 13th century. The most prominent temples had *shikharas*, however, such as the Thatbyinnyu and the Sulamani. The only large *shikhara* to have not been restored is the Dhammayan-gyi.

From Windows to Doorways

Perhaps the most far reaching architectural development at Pagan began with the gradual elimination of multiple windows on the side and rear walls of the outer sanctum and the substitution of doorways or single windows. The walls of the earliest temples were pierced only by windows, such as at the Nagayon, Pahto-thamya, the Kubyauk-gyi (Myinkaba) and others. These window openings were narrow and filled with perforated stone or brick insets, restricting light into the interior. The earliest dated temple to adopt doorways on the sides and rear was the Shwegu-gyi, 1131, built about twenty years after the Kubyauk-gyi (Myinkaba), 1113. Each doorway at the Shwegu-gyi projected only a short distance from the wall and was flanked by two windows, a concession to the older way of approaching the wall surface. The ambiance created by the increased light in the Shwegu-gyi's interior differs vastly from the earlier darker temples.

Two phases of temple design. The earlier is marked by a plain wall surface with multiple windows, such as the Kubyauk-gyi (Myinkaba), 1113 (below), while the later is dominated by massive side and rear doorways forming wide and deep entrance halls, 13th-century, Tayokpyi, above. This trend begins as early as the Shwegu-gyi, 1131.

The side and rear doorways gradually grew in importance until they dominated the exterior appearance of temples, forming deep and wide recessed projections defined by pilasters. Indeed, the doorway projections on the sides and rear grew so large and elaborate that these three sides competed in significance with the principal entrance hall. The main entrance hall therefore dwindled in importance and size, becoming only slightly longer than the other entrances, such as the Thatbyinnyu and the Sulamani. The result was nearly a symmetrical plan, such as the Nandamannya. In the largest temples, such as the Dhammayan-gyi and Htilominlo, windows continued to be used. In general, however, the multiple windows that characterized temple elevations in the 11th and early 12th centuries had disappeared by the 13th century.

If this transformation was tied to religious or liturgical concerns is unknown, but it had enormous practical consequences. For example, these side and rear entrances formed wide and deep vestibules, or mini-halls, within the temple, ideally suited to uninterrupted wall surfaces for Buddhist murals. A good example is the 13th-century Tayok-pyi. The largest temples, however, were designed with proper entrance halls on all four sides, such as at the Thatbyinnyu and Sulamani, but even here the principal entrance hall was never too much longer than the other three sides. This major change in design was also accompanied by a severe reduction in stone sculpture.

The summits of temple towers have not survived in any of Pagan's temples, and therefore their original appearance is conjectural. They may very likely have resembled the tops of the stupas, judging from depictions of temples in stucco ornament (no. 744). In these examples, the tops are capped with the same tapered bud-shaped object resting on one or two layers of lotuses that was true for stupas. This crowning segment may have been made entirely of gilded copper, based on inscriptions describing this finial (*athwat*, Burmese). For example, one inscription records that the donors "weighed and cut off into the hands of the coppersmith forty seven *viss*, eight *buih* and four *ticals* of copper; seven *viss* and nine ticals were lost in the course of the work and the net weight of the spire was forty *viss*, seven *buih* and five *ticals*. The sterling gold included was thirty nine *ticals* and three quarters and liquid quick silver one hundred and fifty nine *ticals* [for the gilding]. With all of these

The curvilinear design of the Indian temple tower inspired Pagan's architects. Lakshmana Temple, corner shrine, 954 A.D., Khajuraho, Uttar Pradesh, India. (DS)

Ordination hall (no. 450). Stone bases for wooden columns. Lemyathna. Small damaged 'boundary stones' are found around the edges of the platform. (DS)

precious things we caused the spire of the temple to shine." (Than Tun, 1978, 131-132). Another inscription records that the copper finial weighed 55 *viss* of copper and was gilded with 46 *ticals* of gold. None of this metal work can be traced today with any certainty. North Indian inscriptions often speak of glistening orbs crowning temples, but they are not described in detail, and it does not seem they were made of metal.

Two Storied Temples
The largest temples at Pagan follow the basic single storied solid core plan but are designed with a separate square storiey above. The function of this second storey is unclear, but one of its objectives was to house a large Buddha figure

Two-storied temples are based on a square, solid brick core encircled by an inner corridor. The upper storey contains a seated Buddha facing east. Double-storied temples probably begin in the second half of the 12th century. The earliest dated example is the Sulamani, 1183.

facing east. These temples include the Sulamani, Gawdaw-palin, Htilominlo and Thatbyinnyu. The principal entrance hall of these large temples faces east, suggesting that orientation to this cardinal direction was important, albeit with numerous important exceptions throughout Pagan. Inner corridors encircling the central core on both stories highlight the central image, placed in a niche on the eastern face. The exception is the Thatbyinnyu where there is no Buddha facing the entrance on the ground floor. These four major temples and others were refurbished over and over, and in the Konbaung period seated brick Buddhas were often added to the upper and lower corridors, set against the inner wall and sometimes recorded in ink inscriptions placed on the surrounding wall.

The origin of these double-storied temples is unknown but the placement of small Buddha shrines on the roofs of temples began very early. The earliest dated example appears at the Kubyauk-gyi (Myinkaba), 1113, where a miniature temple is found above the entrance hall. At the early Pahto-thamya a miniature shrine rests on each of the four sides of the superstructure, each with a damaged seated Buddha. Staircases lead to the roofs, but how these upper shrines were used in rituals is unknown.

Within the upper walls and towers of two of these large double-storied temples were vaulted inner corridors forming separate stories, or entresols. Some had easy access, while others were never designed to be entered. The Thatbyinnyu has two, while the Htilominlo has one. Even smaller temples had simple entresols (nos. 744, 1219). The purpose of these entresols is unknown, but they certainly reduced the mass of the entire building and a concomitant need for brick. They were not considered essential to the stability of the building, however, since none were used at the huge Sulamani, Gawdaw-palin and Dhammayan-gyi.

Monasteries

Restored monastery within compound wall of the Mingalazedi Stupa.

Monasteries are found throughout Pagan, beginning from the ancient period and continuing into the present. The total population of monks at any time at Pagan is difficult to estimate, but one inscription from the 12th century refers to 4,180 monks attending one service. If this sum represented the entire confraternity, a part of the total, or was hyperbole, is unknown. The city's zenith saw the creation of over 400 monasteries, representing roughly a quarter of all of the building during these three centuries (Pichard, 2003). These monastic buildings range from large complexes with numerous secondary structures to small, single-cell buildings standing alone. Some of the least restored and most impressive are in the eastern zone, in and around the village of Minnanthu.

Brick monasteries in India were generally designed with individual cells facing an open

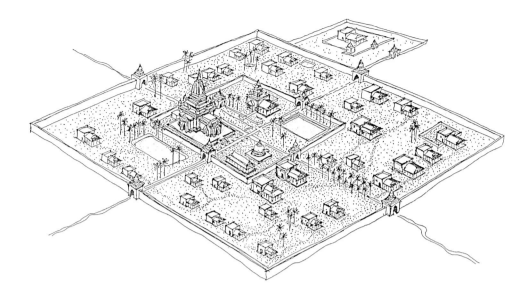

courtyard, with a shrine in the rear wall containing a seated Buddha, such as at Nalanda in Bihar or in Ratnagiri in Orissa. This form was rarely seen at Pagan, appearing in only two instances (nos. 1147, 1371). Also, the plan of the monastic complex at Paharpur, Bangladesh, with a temple in the centre of a compound surrounded by cells, was never used at Pagan.

Hsin-byu-shin monastic complex, reconstructed plan.

A large complete monastic unit contained a temple or stupa, an ordination hall (*sima*, Pali), a preaching hall, and one or more residences for monks and the chief abbot. All of the buildings were bound by a high compound wall pierced by gates and often inner and outer enclosure walls. Perhaps the best example is the Lemyathna complex situated in the eastern zone, a short distance southwest of the Payathonzu, and likely dated by an inscription to 1223. The Lemyathna temple (no. 447) faces an ordination hall, once constructed of wooden columns supported by circular stone bases that still survive (no. 450). This building is called "*dhammasa*" in an inscription, suggesting that it was used for preaching the Buddha's teachings ('*dhamma*'). It was likely used also as an ordination hall, since fragments of stone boundary pillars still surround it. On the opposite side of the compound are two prominent, restored double-storied residence buildings (nos. 448, 449). A wide wooden porch was attached to at least one of the two (no. 449), visible where the stucco ornament on the brick wall joined to the missing roof. This residence had an upper storey with wooden flooring supported by joists, the holes for which are still seen within the walls. Above the floor forming the ceiling is a barrel vaulted corridor encircling an inner core. The lower and upper stories were both covered with barrel vaulting, in some cases. A good example is found in the compound of the Dhammayan-gyi, left partially restored.

Some monastic residences were called 'pavilion monasteries' (*prasat klon*, Burmese), and these may have been rather grander than the flat-roofed examples, comprising elaborate two storied towers. (prasat derives from *prasada*, Sanskrit, meaning palace or pavilion). One example lies to the north east of Minnanthu where a 13th century inscription in the adjacent temple refers to a '*prasat klon*'. Another example (no. 73), now rebuilt, is near the Shwe-zigon.

Most large monasteries included temples in their original plans rather than stupas, and this is also supported by the surviving inscriptions. Some monasteries were later built in connection with stupas, however, such as at the Mingalzedi and the Shwe-zigon. Lesser structures associated with monasteries included libraries where palm-leaf manuscripts were stored. Inscriptions suggest that there were perhaps special walkways where monks practiced meditation, but none have survived. Other epigraphs refer to refectories, storehouses and perhaps teaching-monasteries.

There are scarcely more than a dozen surviving ancient ordination halls at Pagan (see nos. 450, 700, 909), suggesting that monasteries perhaps shared ordination halls. In many cases, residential units attached to temples or stupas were part of the original plan, such as at Lemyathna, or added later as the need arose. Within the compound of the Dhammayan-gyi temple, for example, there is a large unit that probably belonged to the chief monk. One or two residences were placed between the inner and outer compound wall at the Mingalazedi, while another large monastic complex (745) shares the northern compound wall with the Sulamani. Here, nearly 70 small vaulted cells are joined together to form the walls of an open courtyard. (These have not been yet

Monastic residence (no. 449), Lemyathna. Façade, on right, reveals where the timber porch was once affixed. (DS)

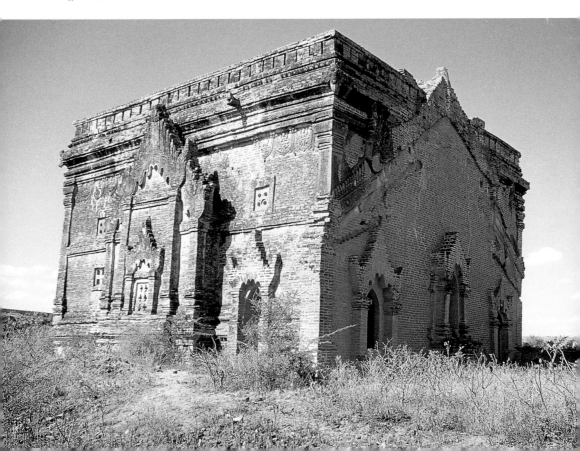

restored, and I highly recommend visiting this
abandoned monastery). In general, elaborate
fresco painting is unusual within
monastic living units, but the exterior
was highly adorned with the usual
stucco ornament.

The most common monastic
building was a simple single-celled
unit that accommodated a single monk
or perhaps a small number of individuals.
These were built either in isolation or more
frequently in conjunction with a stupa, temple or
monastery. Even where these units appear to be independent,
monks living there belonged to an organization providing for their
upkeep. These small rectangular structures would have a vaulted
room, with a simple flat roof. Two doorways were usually placed in
the centre of one of the long sides and a single door on each lateral
side. Most were faced with wooden porches, which consisted of
timber posts and a tiled roof. At the rear of the porch, against the
outer wall of the unit, was a brick niche, probably intended for a
Buddha image, most likely in wood. This type can be seen
throughout Pagan.

*Reconstructed sketch of monastic
residence, Lemyathna, (no. 449)
including timber porch.*

There were also cave-monasteries at Pagan, built partially
underground or cut into a cliff side. The two most well known
are the Kyanzittha-umin (no. 65) and the Kyauk-ku-umin, a temple
but with monastic cells deep within the ground. Other examples
exist throughout the plains at Pagan, such as the Kyanzittha-umin-
le (no. 56), near the Shwe-zigon, and the Taung-Kyanzittha-umin
(no. 297), southeast of the Kubyauk-gyi (Wetkyi-in). Small dark
cells are found within each of these monasteries, providing strong
evidence that at least some monks meditated alone in isolation.
Similar cliff side monastic units with solitary cells are now and
then seen in later Burma, such as the Tilakaguru cave-monastery,
in Sagaing.

The Later Architecture of Pagan

The first-time visitor to Pagan will likely find it hard to distinguish
between the ancient buildings dating to the 11th, 12th and 13th
centuries and temples and stupas belonging to subsequent periods.
This is largely because many of the basic architectural shapes and
motifs are similar, having been repeated, with changes, over the
centuries. Also, the exteriors of many temples, old and new, are
whitewashed, and this contributes to the sense of uniformity. But
once our eye becomes trained, then it will be easy to spot the
ancient temples from those created in more recent times. Also,
many later temples have wonderful interior murals, so they are
usually worth a peek inside.

The number of temples and stupas created after the 13th
century are quite few compared to the boon years between the 11th
and 14th centuries. Indeed, between the 15th and 19th centuries a
mere 192 went up, a trifle compared to over 2,000 that had been
built previously. This slow pace was probably a result of the capital

shifting to Upper Burma in the 14th century. This long period has been little studied compared to the ancient epoch, but Pagan traditions continued and slowly were modified. One large temple near the Dhamma-yazika, the large Thissa-wadi temple (no. 918), dated to 1334, illustrates the continuity but also certain innovations, such as the addition of a third storey.

Influences from India waned over the centuries, and indigenous forms become more pronounced. This was more the case for painting, while architecture adhered somewhat more conservatively to ancient conventions. By the 18th century, however, our knowledge fills out, since many dated monuments appear at Pagan and throughout Upper Burma. This era corresponded to the Konbaung dynasty (1752-1885), which was based in Upper Burma. Perhaps the most famous monument is the Mingun Pagoda, near Mandalay, but there are many 19th-century stupas and temples in the Ava region and surrounding the lake at Amarapura, such as the Pathodaw-gyi and the Kyauk-taw-gyi.

At Pagan itself the 18th and 19th centuries saw a tremendous rise in new building and refurbishing of earlier temples, many of which had never fallen out of worship, such as the Ananda and the Shwe-zigon. It was during this period that the gigantic wooden Buddhas at the Ananda were put into place, together with the huge wooden doorways. Pagan was also designated an administrative centre, sometimes ruled by princes sent from the capital. One great patron was King Bodawpaya (1782-1819), and it was during his reign that the Shwe-zigon was once more restored and the Thatbyinnyu refurbished. This king also visited Pagan to take possession of an auspicious white elephant, captured in Lower Burma. The most important Konbaung building at Pagan occurred during his reign,

19th-century temple (no. 1942), near Tharaba Gate. The symmetrical plan and the stupa-like crown resemble many of the later ancient temples at Pagan.

such as the Upali Thein, the Ananda Temple Monastery and the Pitikat-taik. Ink inscriptions prove that lay donors from the immediate Pagan area and from outside areas provided support. Few traces of the wooden monasteries have survived from this period, apart from their wide masonry stairways (Fraser-Lu).

Construction in the Konbaung era was broadly modelled on basic ancient types. For temples, the most common plan reflects the typical form developed by the 13th century, that is, a nearly symmetrical plan with four doorways and no windows. Temples are also generally crowned with a stupa-like dome but sometimes by a *shikhara*. The exterior stucco ornament shows little restraint when compared to ancient work.

It is decidedly more flamboyant, with parallels to the florid woodcarving found among contemporary wooden monasteries. Both temples and stupas are often crowned with tall tapering spires comprised of small umbrella rings, terminating in metal finials. These ringed spires are far greater in relative height to the basic structure than in the ancient period.

The scalloped pediment found above doorways in the ancient period is widely used, but it loses its integrity in a mass of stucco swirls. This can also be seen in wood, such as among the restored thrones of the Mandalay Palace, or an original one in the Yangon museum.

One motif repeated throughout Pagan and Burma in this later period is a peacock, represented only by its chest and head, depicted frontally. This can be fashioned in wood or made of cut brick and covered with stucco. It appears frequently in the centre of pediments over doorways or windows. The breast of the bird juts out and the face is highly stylized, with rarely a mouth or eyes. Examples are visible among the roof terraces of the Pitakat-taik, and at the Mi-ma-laung-kyaung (no. 1611), opposite the museum. Other motifs include tall fanciful lions, known as *chinte* (Burmese), often surrounding a base of a monument, reminiscent of their ancient counterparts still visible at the Shwe-san-daw and Mingalazedi stupas. Newer motifs include four legged lions with an adjoined male torso and crowned head, called *manokthiha* (Burmese). These are also found around the

Family members before their newly built stupa, over an ancient brick mound, an act of devotion recorded in the inscription. The degree to which the temple in the background is conjectural can be measured by the new pinkish brick. (DS)

The peacock, a later symbol of Burmese nationalism, supplants the British Lion and Unicorn. Powindaung caves, early 20th century. Painted brick and stucco. (DS)

72

Standing row of chinte, or fanciful couchant lions. 20th-century pavilion, Shwedagon Pagoda, Yangon. (DS)

Above right: A manokthiha, or half-man, half lion. Whitewashed brick and stucco. Kyauk-taw-gyi temple, Amarapura, c. 1850. (DS)

Rebuilding a temple. (DS)

bases of shrines but can appear within the roof terraces also. The frieze of kirtimukha-faces still appears but an adaptation includes faces with outstretched arms, seen for example on the rear side of the Manuha temple. Another common motif are rows of arrow-shaped crenellations, appearing in foundations or in roof terraces. Even European motifs now and then intrude into this architecture, witnessed by engaged, round pillars seen here and there (no. 1646). By the 20th century a true hybrid architectural style arose, seen most conveniently among the corridors facing the Ananda, from the 1920s and 1930s. There was even a brief Art Deco phase at Pagan, such as a small pavilion facing the Shwe-zigon.

The Rebuilding of Pagan in the 1990s

The entire Pagan plain was violently shaken by an earthquake in the summer of 1975. This jolt to the monuments, however, has proved benign compared to the shock waves inflicted on Pagan, beginning in the 1990s. The controversial rebuilding of Pagan is now largely finished, leaving in its wake a deeply scarred landscape. The rebuilding is controversial both inside and outside of Burma, largely because the evidence for the majority of the rebuilding is thin, at best. Reconstructions have been too often based on conjecture that many times borders on fantasy. Unesco has registered unofficial disapproval, but to no avail. Critics of the the rebuilding of course welcome the need to shore up and repair monuments, but these massive refurbishments go far beyond basic conservation. Burma's leading historian, Than Tun, has dubbed the rebuilding of Pagan, "Blitzkrieg archaeology." (1999, 37).

The problem has been made only worse by a programme where private donors, from Burma or abroad, are able to donate funds for the reconstuction or rebuilding of a monument.

New construction dots the landscape at Pagan. (PP)

Completely new *stupas* or temples are many times constructed directly upon ancient mounds, selected and sold for their auspiciousness. This 'adopt a pagoda' programme is also elitist, since the majority of Burmese can scarcely afford to donate a few hundred *kyat* at their local shrine. This programme began in 1996 and has attracted over 2,000 donors. Pagan has reverted to a 'field of merit', with spiritual rewards only open to the well-to-do, as in the past.

In addition, none of the new construction is covered in stucco, a major omission if the desire is to replicate ancient Pagan. (No ancient temples were without stucco covering.) The new brick work, therefore, clashes with the aged appearance of the surviving temples, the new monuments appearing like plucked, pink chickens amidst the ancient shrines.

Another problem concerns the thick modern cement used to bind the new brickwork. The ancient mortar was thin, so that individual bricks went their own way in the event of an earthquake. In future quakes, however, the brick will adhere in large, rigid block-like masses, causing greater destruction to any surviving original brickwork below. Also, the cement that is used "contains salts that migrate through the brick and damage the murals", as noted by Pichard (Covington).

PAINTING AND SCULPTURE

Painting and sculpture were the flesh and bones of the city's great houses of worship. Indeed, no temple was complete without mural painting and stone or brick images. Mural work and sculpture, however, did not follow the same course at Pagan between the 11th and 13th centuries. Fresco painting, for example, exhibits at least two major phases and retained its vitality to the end, while stone work grew somewhat mediocre, beginning probably by the the mid-12th century. More research and new discoveries may change this assessment, but it suggests that Pagan's diverse media were subject to different forces, for reasons yet to be known. These shifts and differences in style were probably of little importance for Pagan's residents, since these changes occurred slowly and over decades.

Pagan's ateliers drew upon a wide range of artistic sources from outside Burma. The nature of foreign influences and the inter-action between these forces and indigenous contributions are issues at the heart of Pagan civilization. It is widely agreed that Burmese artists depended heavily upon the art of the Pala realm in eastern India, between the 11th and 13th centuries. Pala Buddhist art was not only important for Burma, but it exerted an incalculable influence in Kashmir, Nepal, Tibet and throughout mainland Southeast Asia. For example, painted roundels with dancing figures at the Kubyauk-gyi temple (Myinkaba) bear an uncanny resemlance to roundels found among the 11th-century painting at Alchi in the Ladakh region of Kashmir. Such a similarity is more than coincidental, since both regions were eager recipients of Pala influence. The Palas even had connections with distant Indonesia where an inscription proves that the dynasty responsible for Borobudur in Java funded a monastery at the Pala centre of Nalanda. The Pala realm had fallen to Islamic dynasties by the middle of the 13th century, but Pala artistic influence had been securely established outside its borders.

The type of Buddhism practiced in the Pala realm was

Below: Pagan Museum. (DS)

Bottom: Queen Maya grasping the flowering tree and giving birth to the Buddha who emerges from her right side. Palm-leaf manuscript, detail, Bihar, India, c. 11-12th centuries. (Courtesy Detroit Institute of Art)

Mahayana and differed from the Theravada traditions dominant in Pagan and Burma, but such religious distinctions mattered little to Pagan's artists and residents. For example, *jatakas* were rarely depicted in the Mahayana art of eastern India, yet the style of Pagan's ubiquitous *jatakas* resemble Pala illustrated palm-leaf manuscripts.

The Pala realm itself stretched from Bihar state through modern Bangladesh bordering coastal Burma, or Arakan (modern Rakhine State). Arakan was never under Pagan domination, but it may have served as one of the many conduits of Pala influence. No important Pala works of art have been located at Pagan, but Pala influence is a strong undercurrent in the city's art. Perhaps Pagan artists and architects traveled to India, but no evidence exists for this type of direct exchange. It is known from local inscriptions that Indian craftsmen worked at Pagan, but we cannot be sure from which part of India they came, or if they played a leading role. Painters and sculptors were considered craftsmen, and their works are anonymous. Inscriptions reveal that they were paid more than unskilled labourers, but their status in society was likely rather modest.

Much Pala sculpture survives in eastern India, but only traces of mural painting are extant, and these are found at Nalanda. However, dozens of illustrated Buddhist palm-leaf manuscripts have come down to us from Pala India. Probably much of the Pala influence was transmitted by such manuscripts taken to Pagan, but none have yet surfaced in Burma. Other Pala influence may have derived from portable terracotta votive plaques or their metal moulds, and from small bronze sculptures. Another possible source was the Buddhist centre of Nagapattinam, on India's southeast coast. A handful of small bronze Buddhas probably produced in Nagapattinam are in the Pagan museum, but they seem to have had no impact on the local art. Sri Lanka was important for Burma religiously, but its artistic role at Pagan has yet to be adequately traced. It was likely rather restricted.

Why Can't We See the Sculpture and Painting?

One question arises immediately for visitors to Pagan: why did the ancients expend so much effort to create such beautiful frescos and sculptures, if the dark temple interiors made it virtually impossible to properly appreciate them? Even if the insides were illuminated by strong candles and flame torches, a goodly portion of the work was too high on the walls to be readable. The same can be said for the glazed *jatakas* tiles placed high among the roof terraces of the Ananda; like the murals, the plaques were never designed to be

Palm-leaf texts from India conveyed Buddhist teachings throughout Southeast Asia. The written text is often with coloured illustrations. The two holes in each leaf were for cords binding the multiple leaves together between two wooden covers. Bihar, India, c. 11th-12th century. (Courtesy Detroit Institute of Art)

A Buddha seated beneath a tree is painted over a late 12th-century wall mural. Such intrusive additions suggest that the major temples were still revered but probably used in new ways, following the shift in power from Pagan to the Ava region in the 14th century. Dhamma-yazika Stupa, temple on east face. (DS)

Gotama Buddha culminated a lineage of 28 Buddhas. Eight of the 28 are represented here. Payathonzu. (DS)

closely examined or enjoyed. Pagan's art, therefore, could scarcely have served a didactic function, such as educating the masses or as refresher courses for the monks.

The probable reason is that these sacred images were considered an important part of the efficacious nature of the donation. The paintings and sculpture played therefore an "iconic function" (Brown, 1997). The same is probably true for the celebrated Buddhist murals inside the Ajanta caves in India which require strong, modern artificial light. Although Pagan's works of art are beautiful and were certainly appreciated by the ancients, this was not a culture comfortable with our dictum "art for art's sake." Pagan's monuments were built for the accumulation of merit to listen to the inscriptions. The grander the conception and expense, the greater the merit. Similarly, the same spirit motivated some of the ancient residents to spend large sums for the copying of Pali manuscripts, which were stored in expensive chests in monasteries and probably never read.

For art to perform its iconic function, the subjects had to be represented in acceptable fashion, and this generally meant in a complete form. This way of thinking about art is demonstrated by the fact that it was important to represent the entire set of 547 *jatakas*, either in mural painting or terracotta plaques. It is true that in some temples the sequence of the paintings is slightly out of order or that a few tales are even omitted, but the intent was served because it was considered bascially a full set. In other cases, not all the 547 tales were depicted but only the first *jatakas* from the major divisions of the *jataka* collection. Such examples underline the importance of completeness. The same approach probably governed the selection of sculptural themes, such as the depiction of the 28 Buddhas and perhaps the Eight Great Events.

There were important exceptions to this usual rule, and these reveal a more complex religious environment. The Nagayon is a good example. Here only certain *jatakas* were selected and assigned major portions of the wall surface. Such a selection suggests a deliberate decision, if not by the donor then by the artists or a monk. The Nagayon's interior is among the darker ones at Pagan, and no one could be expected to properly view any of these especially chosen episodes. This example suggests that there is a great deal of nuance that has yet to be understood. Perhaps if we knew more about the rituals at Pagan, many of these questions could be answered.

Why This Buddha and not That Buddha

The subject matter, or iconography, of the painting and sculpture largely reflects the Theravada traditions associated with the Pali canon and influences from the Mahayana art of Pala India. Mahayana and Theravada subject matter co-existed at Pagan, at least in a handful of important temples, despite the overwhelming Theravada religious environment. However, none of the hundreds of stone inscriptions and thousands of ink captions at Pagan can be construed as strictly Mahayana in inspiration, nor are there any temples whose subject matter is solely Mahayana.

One example pertinently highlighting these issues are the murals at the Kubyauk-gyi temple in Myinkaba village. The subjects are virtually all drawn directly from the Pali canon, except two prominent painted fourteen-armed bodhisattvas flanking the entrance to the sanctum. Such bodhisattvas are rightly associated with Mahayana art, and they were almost surely borrowed from Pala art, although no identical comparisons have been found in India. Would it be fair then to conclude from the subject matter of the murals that this temple was mostly Theravada with a touch of Mahayana? Pala sources contributed Mahayana imagery, but it was incorporated into a thoroughly Theravada context. In this process of borrowing, Mahayana subject matter was not necessarily misunderstood or perceived as merely decorative in Burma, but it was thought not to conflict with the pervasive Theravada orientation of the murals and society. For Pagan's residents, the distinctions made by modern scholars between Theravada and Mahayana were probably of little consequence. The terms Theravada and Mahayana themselves are nowhere in the inscriptions. However, why certain Mahayana themes were chosen and others rejected, and the factors determining their placement within temples must be investigated.

Jatakas are rare in the Mahayana art of eastern India but were a major component of Pagan painting and ceramic art, often identified by their titles taken from the Pali canon. The Pali *jatakas* appear in a few temples whose murals are filled with Mahayana subjects. The best example is the Abeyadana where the entrance hall was devoted to *jatakas*, but the inner walls were dominated by Mahayana and even Tantric deities, almost certainly adapted from Pala sources. Like the Kubyauk-gyi (Myinkaba), the Abeyadana reveals how the two disparate types of imagery co-existed within a basically Theravada climate.

One class of miniature stone sculpture found at Pagan and elsewhere also illustrates the combination of a Mahayana theme borrowed from Pala India with subject matter only popular in Theravada countries, like Burma, Sri Lanka and Thailand. The Buddha sits in the centre, in the earth-touching gesture, while tiny figures illustrating the Eight Great Events in the Buddha's life (birth, death and so on) are located on the outer register. This theme is widely found in Pala art and at Pagan. The inner register bears figures representing the Seven Weeeks that the Buddha spent at Bodh Gaya, a theme found in both Pali and Mahayana Sanskrit texts but one which never achieved importance in India.

The Eight Great Events, outer register, and The Seven Weeks, inner register, are shown in this miniature stone sculpture, Pagan Museum. 17 cm high. (DS)

Original stone Buddha in niche inside sanctum of Pahto-thamya. (DS)

Spikes in the Buddha's Ears

One unique stone sculpture exemplifies the full complexity surrounding the sources for Pagan art. This image features a seated, emaciated Buddha flanked by two standing male figures thrusting spikes into his ears. It was found at the Kyauk-ku-umin cave temple, together with other sculptures depicting common scenes from the Buddha's life, and is now in the Pagan museum. The spikes-episode is not in the standard biographies of the Buddha but is found in one story within the vast Pali canon where two cow herders teased and distracted the Buddha by pushing spikes in his ears. The Buddha remained unaffected and harboured no ill-will (*Mahasihananda-Sutta, Majjhima Nikaya*). A slightly different version appears in the Sanskrit *Lalitavistara*, but the spikes are omitted. It is also found in an early Sanskrit text from Gilgit in ancient northwestern India where the cow herders are replaced by naughty boys and girls who pushed spikes in and out of the ear holes. This theme is depicted now and then in palm-leaf illustrations and on the wooden outer boards binding manuscripts in Pala art, and among Nepalese and Tibetan painting on cloth (Wujastyk). It appears only twice at Pagan, among the sculptures from Kyauk-ku-umin and on one miniature stone plaque featuring the life scenes of the Buddha.

What were Pagan's sources for this unique sculpture? Did the artists or patrons turn to a rather obscure section of the Pali canon that is nowhere else represented at Pagan? More likely, the sculptors took their inspiration directly from illustrated Pala examples brought to the city from India and based on Mahayana sources. If that is true, then we must ask if Pagan residents were conversant with the particulars of the story, or was it simply copied from an illustration from Pala India without much understanding. Also, why was this theme never repeated again at Pagan? Was it because it was never that popular in Pala art? The answers to these questions go right to the heart of the subtle interaction between Burma and its neighbours.

Little is known about the selection of subject matter used in individual temples, for both sculpture and painting. Was the donor directly involved in selecting the themes? Was it left to a site foremen or monk, or was it a group decision involving a number of participants? For example, the presence at the Nagayon of only certain *jatakas* implies a degree of reflection and discrimination that went beyond a standard request for all 547 *jatakas*, or the revered last ten stories. But who made these decisions and why? Were there differences between monuments dedicated by members of the royalty and ministers, or even differences between male and female donors? If there were sharply distinguished Buddhist sects at Pagan, did their individual orientations influence the choice of subject? We have no ready answers to these questions, but these are simply a few of the fundamental issues that visitors should keep in mind.

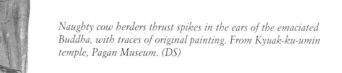

Naughty cow herders thrust spikes in the ears of the emaciated Buddha, with traces of original painting. From Kyuak-ku-umin temple, Pagan Museum. (DS)

Mural Painting

Pagan's interior walls were covered from top to bottom with mural painting. From slightly over 900 temples created between the 11th and 14th centuries, nearly 350 still have some portions of their murals. A number of the temples retain more than fifty-percent of their original painting. Water seepage from leaky ceilings has been the worst threat, but the arid climate of Upper Burma generally served the interests of painting. The Department of Archaeology has sensitively restored a handful of temples, with the help of Unesco, beginning in the 1980s with the Kubyauk-gyi (Myinkaba). Other projects include the Nagayon where work is still ongoing. After removing accumulated dust and grime, an acrylic resin water emulsion mixed with locally sifted earth is injected by syringes into hollow and detached spots and insect tunnels (*Pagan Newsletter, 1985*).

Building up damaged wall surface with specially prepared injections. (DS)

Pagan's painters had an inexhaustible reservoir of subject matter, much of it taken from the Pali canon but also from Mahayana Pala art. As a measure of the diversity, no two temples are identical, or even somewhat similar. In fact, one is struck more by endless variety, even among temples from the same general period. Not only was the subject matter incredibly varied, but the placement of themes within a temple differed dramatically. For example, the 547 *jatakas* contained around the sanctum corridor in the Kubyauk-gyi (Myinkaba) are restricted only to the entrance hall of the Abeyadana.

U Ba Tint restoring murals in Kubyauk-gyi (Myinkaba), 1987. (DS)

One temple, the Alopyi (no. 374) is devoted largely to depictions of the Buddha delivering sermons (*suttas*, Pali), a theme of much less importance at the Kubyauk-gyi (Myinkaba) and other early temples. The Loka-hteikpan focuses on Mt. Meru and other subjects, including the last ten *jatakas*, while the Kubyauk-gyi (Wetkyi-in) concentrates on the Eight Great Events, the Seven Weeks and the 28 Buddhas. Such diversity is no less true of 13th century temples.

Many murals can be identified with some certainty, since ink inscriptions are painted beneath the compositions on a special blank band. The epigraphs identify the scenes and can generally be related directly to specific sections in the Pali canon. No Mahayana or Tantric imagery is identified by an inscription, perhaps because the models from eastern India were

Hundreds of green glazed tiles devoted to all 547 jatakas *are within niches in the roof terraces of the Ananda Temple.* Jataka *no. 524. (DS)*

Religious painting on cloth was probably commonplace at Pagan but few examples are known. This depicts jataka *no. 96, found in debris on the floor of temple no. 315. Pagan museum.*

accompanied by captions in Sanskrit, a language with its own written characters that was unintelligible to most residents. The earliest ink inscriptions are in the Mon language that was gradually eclipsed by Burmese by the second half of the 12th century, at least according to current thinking. Both languages were sprinkled with Pali loan words.

Artists almost certainly used rough drawings or paintings on cloth as models for their vast store of subject matter. For example, not even a team of painters could construe from memory all 547 *jataka* stories, including all of the captions. The original models were probably made by members of society able to read the *jatakas* in Pali, together with an artist who sketched a scene based on this description. For *jatakas*, the models almost certainly did not come from Pala India, since the *jatakas* were rarely represented by Pala artists and the captions at Pagan are in Pali and Mon, languages not in use in Pala India.

Since many scores of temples were under preparation simultan-eously, there was probably a need for numerous groups of painters; a single painting crew would almost certainly have been insufficient. Each group probably used different models for the same subject matter, such as for the *jatakas*, since crews would be working at the same time but at different temples. Perhaps these diverse workshops and their models can be identified in the future, based on their different compositions and captions. The ancient situation can be perhaps likened to the rebuilding of Pagan taking place now, with many work crews exchanging tools and building materials among different temples going up at the same time.

The *jatakas* on the side wall of the Loka-hteikpan arranged in parallel horizontal rows suggest how models were used. The two top registers feature *jatakas* with Mon captions, while those in the remaining rows are identified by Burmese inscriptions. It is improbable that Mon painters worked on the top rows and Burmese on the bottom, or to think that Mon devotees only read the top rows, and the bottom ones were intended only for Burmese. The most likely explanation for this strange juxtaposition is that different painted models were used for the different registers. For the painters and patrons, it mattered little if the captions were in Mon or Burmese, since the *jatakas* did not serve a didactic purpose but were a part of the iconic nature of the temple donation.

Research by Françoise Boudignon on the Samugga *jataka* (no. 436) suggests that artists restricted themselves to the same episode for each *jataka*. However, the same scene could be depicted in very different ways, despite the identical subject matter. For example, the Buddha appears in this *jataka* as an ascetic, and the tale involves an ogre, a damsel and the son of the Wind God. In the example at the Kubyauk-gyi (Myinkaba), the ascetic faces the ogre on the right, with the other protagonists are behind the ogre. A glazed plaque depicting the same *jataka* at the Mingalazedi presents the same characters, but the demon is on the left and the two other figures are placed in the centre.

Another *jataka* (no. 524) from the Kubyauk-gyi (Myinkaba) shows a cluster of five or six men carrying a long snake, moving

from left to right. The same *jataka* among the ceramic tiles at the
Ananda depicts the identical moment, but only four men carry the
snake and they proceed in the opposite direction. This example and
others point to the use of numerous but different illustrated models
by both ceramic and mural artists. Artists were of course free to
interpret these models to some extent, and perhaps many of the
noted differences simply reflect individual preferences, such as the
number of men carrying the snake and the direction in which they
moved.

Another issue to be more fully researched is the degree to which
the *jatakas* and other scenes from the Pali canon adhered to the
stories as we know them today. For example, the Pali *jataka* as we
read it specifies that sixteen men carry the snake, a number never
found at Pagan. In the same vein, there was at least one other *jataka*
series in use at Pagan that extended the series from 547 to 550. To
compare these *jatakas* with the earliest surviving examples in Sri
Lanka and neighbouring Thailand will perhaps reveal interesting
connections.

One painted cloth was found at Pagan in 1984, rolled up and
concealed by debris on the floor in a chamber of a temple (no. 315).
It was restored in Rome and is now in the Pagan museum. It depicts

*Small section once belonging to
cloth painting shown opposite,
Pagan Museum. (Courtesy Alain
Mahuzier)*

Painting restoration at Nagayon, a joint project between Unesco and the Department of Archaeology. (DS)

a number of episodes from *jataka* no. 96 in five surviving horizontal registers arranged in parallel vertical rows. It is over a metre in height but was a great deal longer. The story goes from top to bottom and left to right, each scene identified with Burmese captions below. It has been assigned to the first half of the 12th century (*Pagan Newsletter*, 1988; Pal, 1999). Underdrawing in black pigment was placed over a whitish layer, made either of gypsum or light clay, followed by an application of colour. This lavish painting was surely dedicated to a temple and never used as a model. It proves, however, that painted cotton cloth was available. Palm-leaf manuscripts were probably too small and fragile to be used as direct models. Folded books made from paper may have been in use in early Pagan, but none have survived.

Mural Technique

Burmese artists exclusively utilized the dry-fresco technique, or *fresco secco*, in which paint is applied on a dry wall surface. This differs from true-fresco, or *fresco buono*, where the colours are placed on a wet plaster surface; when the plaster sets, then the composition is united with the wall. Italian Renaissance painters perfected true-fresco, and it was favoured too by artists in 20th-century Mexico, such as Diego Rivera. Dry-fresco wall painting was used in India, but few early examples have survived. The best known are the Buddhist caves at Ajanta. South India has preserved a great deal of wall painting, but these traditions had no bearing on early Burma. In eastern India during the Pala period (c. 750- c. 1200) wall painting was perhaps common, but only traces survive at the Buddhist centre of Nalanda. In early Burma, the Pyu and the Mon may have had painting traditions, but nothing has come down to us.

Wet-fresco artists in the West completed relatively small areas each day, since they were compelled to finish their work before the surface dried. Also, mistakes were difficult to remedy, since a fresh application of plaster proved hard to blend with the surrounding dry surface. No such restraints faced the dry-fresco artists of Burma who never needed to pace themselves against a drying surface. Major errors were likely corrected by re-coating the surface with another application of lime, but this has yet to be detected. At Pagan the brick wall surface was first coated with an evenly spread layer of mud. For the mud to adhere, the brick was chipped with a chisel, a technique beginning in the 12th century, according to Pierre Pichard and Rudolpho Lujan, Unesco's chief painting restorer at Pagan (Pichard, Lujan, 5, 242). After the mud hardened, a thin smooth coat (1-3 mm) of lime combined with minute sand particles was applied and allowed to dry. The underlying coat of mud was replaced by several layers of stucco by the 13th century, providing greater protection against insects and weathering. The actual paint was applied over the dry lime surface. Artists started with light colours, such as yellow ochre and pale yellows, followed by stronger ones, such as red ochre, vermilion, greens and blues (likely from indigo). For the eyes of figures or for flowers, white paint composed of lime was used. The pigments were likely bound by a vegetal gum or a type of glue mixed with water. By the 13th century the paint became

thinner, and new colours were introduced, such as purple and red lacquers, chrysocolla, and a copper-based green. Early painting is found at the Pahto-thamya, Nagayon, Abeyadana, and the Kubyauk-gyi (Myinkaba), while later examples from the 13th century are seen at the Tayok-pyi, Payathonzu and Nandamannya. By the Konbaung period (1752-1885), a white priming layer comprised of chalk or clay was applied over the layer of lime. Also, brighter and more vibrant pigments were introduced at this time. Examples are the Upali Thein and the Ananda Temple Monastery. Painting techniques developed between the 14th and 18th centuries have been little studied.

Grids ensured compositional symmetry. The fresco was never finished, for unknown reasons. Shrine wall of temple no. 1244, c. 13th century. Head restored. (DS)

The Layout of Temple Murals

The forethought required for designing a painted temple interior would have challenged the scientific mind of Leonardo and the beatific vision of Michelangelo. Such complexity can be appreciated by a peek inside the Kubyauk-gyi in Myinkaba where over a thousand compositions are contained within individual frames of various sizes. To ensure symmetry the primed wall surface was first crisscrossed with a vast grid of horizontal and vertical lines throughout the interior. Each line was created from a paint-soaked string snapped against the wall. The resulting boxes became the frames for the compositions, and these were of very different sizes, depending on the need. For the *jatakas* the frames were usually square and quite small, but some narrative panels were over two metres long and a metre high, such as in the Nagayon temple. The grids are concealed now with painting, but a few can still be detected.

Grids were not only used to create boundaries for individual figurative compositions. In one example, horizontal and vertical lines frame parallel rows of roundels within a vaulted ceiling (no. 148). Additional lines can be seen going through the centre of each

Rare unfinished painting at Pagan, in corridor of Payathonzu. Figures outlined in black were never filled in with colour and detail, for unknown reasons. (DS)

roundel. This case illustrates that the grid ensured that each roundel would be identical and the rows symmetrical. Another example shows a grid surrounding a restored brick Buddha set against the rear wall of a temple (no. 1244). The centre of the grid at the top is the apex of the tapering halo of the restored Buddha. This grid, composed of hundreds of tiny boxes, made certain that the painted ornament on either side of the Buddha was symmetrical. Examples can seen throughout Pagan (nos. 246, 1075, 2092). Grids may have been used to enlarge preparatory drawings, as they were in the Renaissance, but there is no evidence for this yet in Burma. Grids can also be seen among Konbaung era painting in the north entrance hall of the Sulamani.

Once the grids were in place over the dry lime coat, then outlines for the figures were drawn within the square or rectangular frames. The next step was for artists to apply the colours. A few preparatory drawings have survived, where the final painting was left undone for unknown reasons. Perhaps the best examples of compositions revealing various levels of completion are tucked away in the inner corridor of the Payathonzu temple. Figures are first faintly outlined in lead, and then in dark black pigment, before the application of colour within the confines of the lines. At some early stage, a red background was provided. The faces and certain other details were saved for last, probably to be done by specialists. It is not known why these paintings were incomplete here. Burmese mural painting followed essentially this tradition for centuries, witnessed among the unfinished sections at the mid-19th century Kyauk-taw-gyi temple bordering the lake at Amarapura. In many cases, however, preparatory drawings were probably not used, since the compositions were not only very small but their execution appears more spontaneous, such as among the *jatakas* inside one of the entrance halls of the Payathonzu, and at Kubyauk-gyi (Wetki-in), the Sein-nyet-ama and many other temples.

Detail of Jataka 357, *wicked elephant vanquished by a bird, Kubyauk-gyi (Myinkaba), 1113.*

Artists based their work on forms that were outlined. For example, an elephant would be conceived first as a basic outline that was later filled in with a solid color. Tonal gradations, used in European painting to create depth and a sense of three-dimensionality were unknown. At Pagan depth was created largely by the overlapping of figures. Proper proportions were of no interest, inasmuch as people could be taller than elephants on one occasion and smaller on another. Similar conventions are found in Pala manuscript painting. Pagan pictorial devices can be best understood by perhaps contrasting Pagan's murals with familiar Western painters, such as Vermeer who relied on subtle tonal variations and a distinct light source.

Early and Late Styles

Two major phases marking Pagan painting can
be identified easily. The earliest is witnessed at
the Pahto-thamya, Nagayon, Abeyadana and other
temples from the late 11th or early 12th centuries.
The only dated murals from this early phase is
the Kubyauk-gyi (Myinkaba), 1113, but this
sophisticated painting suggests a long period
of development beginning in the 11th century.
Perhaps the murals at the Pahto-thamya are earlier
than the Kubyauk-gyi (Myinkaba), but by how
many years or decades cannot yet be shown. The
early painting at Pagan, however, reveals a strong
debt to Pala pictorial conventions found in its
illustrated palm-leaf manuscripts. Future studies
can perhaps determine if there was a time lag
between these two regions, based on dated
manuscripts and datable temples.

The later phase emerged fully by the 13th
century, and can be appreciated at the Payathonzu,
Tayok-pyi, Nandamannya and numerous other
temples. The complex steps linking these two
phases, or styles, are yet to be worked out, but
the traits associated with the later phase probably
began by the middle of the 12th century, with no
fixed year or moment when the older style evolved
into the later one. The reasons behind these
changes are unknown, but perhaps they reflect different influences
from India, combined with indigenous contributions. Closer
inspection will undoubtedly reveal a number of phases and sub-
phases in Pagan's ancient painting.

*Late style painting, suggested by the
painted arch and corner pilasters and
boldly overlapping elements. Interior
of 13th-century Payathonzu. (DS)*

These two phases, or styles, reflect two fundamentally different
approaches to the wall surface. To appreciate this transformation, we
can compare the early Kubyauk-gyi (Myinkaba), dated to 1113, with
the later Payathonzu from the 13th century, at least a century later. In
early mural painting, the wall is conceived as a flat surface existing
merely to display murals and stone sculptures within niches. In the
later phase, however, the painted wall surface is principally conceived
in architectural terms. For example, at the Payathonzu, each sanctum
wall is framed by painted corner pillars, designed to simulate an
interior with real columns. To the degree that artists were attempting
to fashion an interior with three-dimensional qualities, they were
motivated by a strong sense of *trompe l'oeil*. Implicit in this approach
to the wall surface is a conscious desire to create symmetry. For
example, the striking asymmetry of the Loka-hteikpan interior
frescos would find no place in 13th-century painting.

A winged kinnara *dramatically
protrudes over background
ornament. Payathonzu.*

Another major contrast with earlier painting is a conscious
striving to create depth by overlapping major components. For the
Payathonzu, this would include huge painted frames on each wall,
comprised of tall pillars joined by a prominent arch. The frame on
the rear wall highlights the central brick Buddha. Large *kinnara*-
birds perched on the tops of these pillars are painted directly over

86

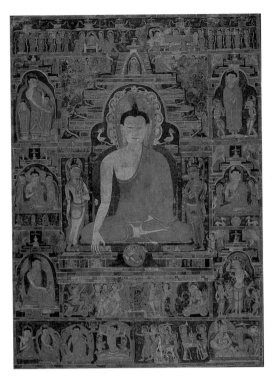

Life scenes of the Buddha, Tibet, c. late 11th or 12th century, cloth painting. (Courtesy Zimmerman Family Collection)

Above right: Late Pagan painting shares compositional features with Nepalese and Tibetan painting. Nandamannya. 13th century. (DS)

Central Buddha, restored in the 1990s, colours clash with surrounding ancient stucco and painting. Abeyadana. (DS)

small seated Buddhas arranged in parallel rows, a device that boldly enhances depth and three-dimensionality. This attitude toward painting is unknown in the early 12th century where overlapping was used but never served to create different dramatic visual layers within the interior as a whole. For example, in the early Kubyauk-gyi (Myinkaba), one or two hands of the multi-armed bodhisattvas extend over their frames, but timidly and with little effect.

Another major later development is the use of large rectangular painted panels, usually featuring a seated Buddha, surrounded by auxiliary scenes contained in small niches and sometimes with a simple narrative scene at the base. At the Payathonzu, Nandamannya, and the Kubyauk-gyi (Wetkyi-in) and other temples these panels were used quite regularly. Their compositions are reminiscent of cloth and silk hanging scrolls, or *thangkas*, associated with the Himalayan kingdoms of Nepal and Tibet. Specific connections have not yet been worked out, but the influence may stem directly from Pala India where similar cloth paintings have not survived.

The later painting style is also marked by whimsy, inventiveness and even playfulness unknown in the earlier temples. For example, again at the Payathonzu, from the mouth of an aquatic creature, or *makara*, comes a long, sinuous snake on which several figures frolic. Such an ensemble is unknown in Pala art or in Nepal and Tibet and is just one of numerous examples highlighting a flourishing indigenous imagination. This entire composition is less than 30 cm long. Such subject matter requires close examination to be fully enjoyed, unlike earlier painting whose large bold patterns are easier to appreciate from a distance. This sensibility is also mirrored in the

Intrusive Buddhas were painted over earlier tan coloured washes, starting at least as early as the 14th century. A horoscope dated to 1376 protrudes over this Buddha at the Htilominlo, proving that it was painted sometime before that date. (DS)

exterior stucco work on later temples which is more intricate and ornamental. Another later development was the covering of major portions of the interior walls with a light coloured tan wash, rather than with figural painting. This trend begins well before the Sulamani temple, dated to 1183. Interior walls are framed with continuous horizontal bands of thin ornament, but the vast bulk of the wall is covered in a light wash. This was true even in modest temples, such as surrounding the sanctum at the Kubyauk-gyi (Wetkyi-in). There were exceptions among some later temples, such as the Tayok-pyi, whose walls are covered completely with figural painting. By contrast, however, early temples are always marked by a *horror vaccui* in which the entire surface is filled with figural painting or ornament. The entrance halls of the Ananda were covered in murals, another mark of its early date.

All of these aforementioned major changes can perhaps be related to evolving pictorial traditions in Pala India, combined with strong indigenous contributions. Monastic centres of Pala art went into decline with the rise of Islamic dynasties in eastern India starting in the 13th century. It is often said that Pala artisans shifted to Burma, but no painting can be yet definitely associated with actual Pala craftsmen. From a religious point of view, Pagan turned increasingly to Theravada Sri Lanka for inspiration, but the 13th-century imagery at Pagan retained Mahayana elements, such as at the Payathonzu. This parodox underscores the notion that Pagan remained essentially a Theravada society, but one which incorporated Mahayana imagery, without a committment to Mahayana ideals and practices.

Virtually all of Pagan's major brick Buddhas were vandalized, beginning when Burma's capital shifted to Ava in the 14th century. Ancient Burmese treasure hunters sought metal relics contained within. Brick Buddha before restoration. (DS)

Later Pagan Painting: 14th–19th Century

The course of painting is less well charted following the 13th century, but there was a sharp diminution of Indian influences. The majority of temples were completely abandoned during this long period, which probably started in the 14th century after the capital shifted to Ava. The major temples, however, continued to function, albeit in a limited way. This is suggested by scores of Buddhas painted intrusively within the corridors of important temples throughout Pagan, placed directly over murals original to the time of construction. These later additions were made for merit, as their ink inscriptions testify. An early example at the Htilominlo features a later Buddha added directly over the original painted wall surface. This Buddha was then later partially covered by an ink horoscope dated to 1376, proving that the Buddha must have been painted some time before that. This Buddha and others in the Htilominlo are accompanied by bold red ink inscriptions by a leading monk named Anandasura. His exact dates are unknown, but he was influential in the fourteenth century, since his inscriptions are found throughout Pagan. Examples are found at the Dhammayan-gyi and his characteristic red 'signature' peeks through one small flanked off section of the Thatbyinnyu's whitewashed walls to prove his presence.

Ceiling ornament at Thatbyinnyu. (DS)

Jataka painting suggests the shift in style by the 15th century,1442 A.D. Temple no. 225. (DS)

Seated Buddha with hole in chest made by ancient robbers (Temple no. 331). (DS)

Extensive refurbishing of monuments occurred over the centuries and indicates how temples were considered 'living monuments' with donations of sculpture and painting viewed as acts of merit. The most striking examples occur at the Sulamani whose corridors are dominated by late 18th-century compositions.

Painting from the fifteenth century can be appreciated at a monastery (no. 225) dated by an inscription to 1442 and located close to the Irrawaddy near the Shwe-zigon. The murals owe much to ancient painting but anticipate developments in the sixteenth and seventeenth centuries.

Mural work from the Konbaung period is well represented at Pagan, with dated examples from the late 18th century, such as the Upali Thein and the Ananda Brick Monastery and scores of other temples. Many 17th-century examples can also be found at Pagan (no. 889). Burmese painting now stands on its own, completely free from Indian sources. A new interest in everyday life scenes emerged, and the compositions are freer and more spontaneous than in the early painting. *Jataka* scenes are cast in contemporary Burmese environments, complete with soldiers carrying rifles and European merchants. Ancient themes continue, such as the 28 Buddhas and the Seven Weeks, but they are treated somewhat differently. By this period too there is no specifically Mahayana subject matter. Some subjects are given special emphasis, such as the Buddha preaching in revered places in India, recounted in the Pali canon. Also, by the early 19th century painted books, or *parabaiks*, appear, but comparisons between these works and wall paintings has only recently begun (Herbert, 1993). By the mid-19th century European pictorial conventions were incorporated into Burmese painting. Examples are at the Kyauk-taw-gyi in Amarapura, near Mandalay, and at the nearby Mahamuni Temple, inside the compound gates. The painted panels placed high among the walls of the corridors facing the Ananda and Shwe-zigon are good examples of 20th-century popular painting, some reflecting single-point perspective absorbed from European art as early as the 19th century.

Sculpture

Sculpture formed an integral part of the temple's design and was coordinated with mural painting to complete the monument. Smaller and less important images were fashioned from sandstone and placed in wall niches, while the principal Buddhas were always much larger and therefore made of brick covered with stucco and painted. The hundreds of brick images within temples were nearly all renovated during the 1990s and are now covered in loud colours clashing with the surrounding ancient stucco and murals.

Virtually all of the stone sculpture at Pagan is now replaced inside the temples by hollow gypsum replicas created from moulds during the last twenty years. These faithful replicas are easily detected by rapping them with our knuckles. Scores of the originals are on view at the museum, with the remainder in storage. One original seated stone Buddha can still be seen inside the sanctum of the Pahto-thamya.

Stone sculpture from ancient Pagan is not on public display outside of Burma, contrasting with Khmer sculpture that can be seen in many museum worldwide. Contrary to popular imagination, the English colonial government in Burma shipped no major works of stone sculpture from ancient Pagan to the British Museum or the Victoria & Albert Museum, London. There have been isolated thefts at Pagan, but the Burmese Department of Archaeology have ably protected Pagan's stone scuplture. A standing stone Buddha stolen from Pagan in the 1980s appeared in a Sotheby's catalogue (New York, Oct. 28, 1991, Lot 104), but it was quickly spotted and saved from the auctioneer's hammer. The two most egregious cases of theft involved two Germans illegally removing mural painting and glazed tiles at the turn of the last century, but these were isolated incidents. Most of this material is in the Museum für Indische Kunst, in Berlin. A far greater threat is the theft of 18th and 19th century marble and wooden Burmese works appearing in shops in Bangkok and worldwide.

Solid core temple, after clearing, outer side wall of sanctum, Buddha with hands in teaching-gesture, no. 1362.

Widespread looting began at Pagan even during the ancient period, beginning probably in the 14th century when the capital shifted to Ava. No value was attached to frescos, stone sculptures, and glazed tiles, so these were passed over at the expense of relics interred within stupas and buried within large seated brick Buddhas covered with stucco. Indeed, there were few brick Buddhas that were not vandalized before colonial rule began in the late 19th century. Visitors to Pagan, even in the 1980s, would have found virtually all of the large brick figures and stupas gutted by fortune hunters centuries earlier. For example, one ink inscription dated to 1735 records the repairs made to three Buddhas damaged by robbers in the temple at the Dhamma-yazika stupa. Another, dated to 1401, mentions repairs to images made necessary by theft (Than Tun, 1996).

Some of the relics inside the brick Buddhas were likely made of metal (bronze, silver and gold) and were probably sold to be melted down. Only a few of such ancient relics have survived. They were often placed in the head, in the centre of the chest, and beneath the seated figure, proved by the crude incisions in these three places made by the ancient robbers. The relics inside the large Buddhas were contained in small stone boxes, surrounded by solid brick.

Fanciful crocodile, or makara, *with rampant lion in its mouth, stucco, Tayok-pyi.*

Brick Sculpture

Pagan's probably most revered Buddhas were located in the sanctums and faced the entrance hall. These were always seated, with their lowered right hand symbolizing the enlightenment at Bodh Gaya and the triumph over Mara. Additional large Buddhas in solid core temples were frequently placed on the side and rear walls. In fewer cases, sculptures depicting the major events in the Buddha's life were placed on the rear and lateral walls, also created in brick and covered with stucco. In one newly cleared temple, one of the Buddhas on the side of the shrine is in the teaching-gesture, while the Buddha on the rear is shown reclining (no. 1362).

Buddha head with metal rod in ear, upper terrace, Pahto-thamya. (DS)

Recently cleared bodhisattva, brick and stucco. Entrance hall. Temple no. 1362.

The fired bricks forming the outer facing of these large images were cut into shapes whose contours conformed to the outline of the figure. In some cases, long and wide cylindrical stones were used to form the legs, and perhaps the arms, that were covered with stucco. Where intricate detail was required, then thin flat metal strips served to hold the stucco in position, as an armature inside a solid core. Such metal devices were sometimes used to form fingers or to fashion ears and can still seen protruding from damaged sculptures. Small unrestored seated Buddhas in the four shrines of the Pahto-thamya illustrate some of these techniques. For example, a portion of the waist is composed of two large bricks cut into a semi-circular shape and which partially extend into the supporting wall. In some cases, the faces alone were made of stone and set into a brick figure; examples can be seen in the museum.

Large standing male figures often placed at the rear of the entrance hall were also made of brick and stucco. The pair were likely the bodhisattvas Lokanath (Pali), and Metteyya (Pali), the Buddha of the Future, who could also be represented as a bodhisattva. These tentative identifications are based on newly read ink inscriptions discovered in a 13th-century temple at Hsale (no. 13). In this temple, the seated Buddha figure appears on the rear wall (west), while Lokanath is painted within a window chamber on the right (north) and Metteyya appears on the left (south) (*Pagan Newsletter*, 1986). Both standing figures can be seen from the entrance, as if flanking the central, seated Buddha. The small figure of a seated Buddha is not found in the headdresses, nor do we find a miniature stupa, attibutes of Avalokiteshvara and Maitreya, respectively.

Most of these figures in brick have been clumsily restored, such as those in the Ananda Temple. One fragmentary example can be examined at the Kubyauk-gyi (Myinkaba), while those at the Nagayon are heavily restored and freshly painted. The finest example only came to light as recently as 2001, following the clearance of a collapsed temple, near the Mingalazedi (no. 1362). Only a small portion of the body is attached to the wall, allowing the figure to turn dramatically toward the shrine entrance. This bold touch and the pristine stucco make this sculpture exceptional.

Techniques for making brick and stucco images must have been forever evolving, but the steps in this development have not been yet studied. By the Konbaung period stucco sculpture included figures in raised shallow relief, such as scenes from the life of the Buddha above the doorways at the Ananda Temple Monastery.

Stone Sculpture

Sculpture was placed inside niches within entrance halls, corridors and the inner walls of sanctums. The average size measures approximately a metre in height. Stone perhaps accorded greater status to the donor, while brick and stucco images were presumably less costly. Stone was certainly more durable than brick, but that was unlikely a factor in its adoption. The figures were painted, but only traces remain, such as the black lines forming eyebrows, white pigment within the eye sockets, and red for the robes.

Stone sculpture was an essential component in the earlier temples from the 11th and early 12th centuries, but its use sharply diminished by the second half of the 12th century and became even less common in the 13th and 14th centuries. In the early temples, such as the Nagayon, sculpture appeared in niches in the entrance chamber, the sanctum and both sides of the corridor surrounding the sanctum. Other temples from the same period, such as the Kubyauk-gyi (Myinkaba), restricted stone sculpture to the side walls of the sanctum and to only one wall of the corridor

Lion, brick and stucco from Sein-nyet-ama.

encircling the sanctum. The Kubyauk-gyi (Myinkaba) is dated to 1113 and was dedicated by a member of the royal family. Nearly twenty years later no stone sculpture was employed in the royal Shwegu-gyi monument, dated to 1131. Stone figures were used in temples following the Shwegu-gyi, but it was no longer as common. The reasons behind this decline are unknown. Stone perhaps became too costly, but there were probably more complex reasons. Perhaps working hand in hand with these changes was the fundamental shift in temple design that occurred by the second half of the 12th century (see Architecture section). By that time windows were replaced by imposing doors on the sides and rear of sanctums, competing in size and importance with the wide entrance halls. Spacious, uninterrupted wall surfaces flanking these doorways became ideally suited to painters. A glance at the ground plans of temples from these two different stages illustrates how the wall surface had dramatically changed, both on the exterior and interior of the temples.

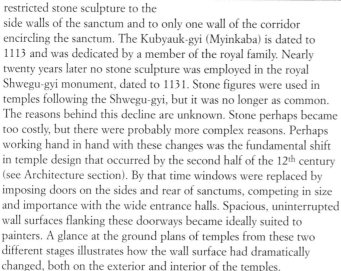

Buddha in the earth-touching gesture. The earth-goddess and the demon Mara crowd the base. Pala style, c. 9th-10th centuries. H. 55.2 cm. (Courtesy Asian Art Museum, San Francisco)

Two phases of sculpture can be readily identified. The earliest is best appreciated at the Ananda and among scores of figures removed from the the Pahto-thamya, Nagayon, Kubyauk-gyi (Myinkaba) and the Kyauk-ku-umin that are now at the Pagan museum and in storage. Like the first phase of Pagan painting, a strong debt to Pala sculpture from eastern India can be noted, but the figures could never be mistaken for Indian works. The earliest dated sculpture is found at the Kubyauk-gyi (Myinkaba), 1113, but stone carving certainly started in the preceding century. Sculpture from this early period is quite homogeneous in style, but future studies should be able to discern differences. The subsequent phase is best illustrated by sculpture from the Kubyauk-gne (no. 1391), dated by a stone inscription to 1198. These figures are fuller, squatter and stiffer. Some of the same features are noted in painted Buddhas. This second phase certainly started well before the dated works in the Kubyauk-gne, but the steps in this development have not yet been established. Another dated sculpture demonstrating these late features is a small seated bronze Buddha in the National Gallery of Victoria, Melboune, dated

Inner corridor, Kubyauk-gyi (Myinkaba), with seated Buddha replicas, 1113. Each Buddha is paired with the particular tree under which he attained enlightenment painted above its niche. (PP)

Buddha with hands in teaching-gesture, temple no. 1029. (DS).

by an inscription to 1293 (Guy, 1995). One large seated Buddha in the entrance hall of the Dhammayan-gyi can perhaps be dated by a nearby ink inscription to 1343. Its crude figural style is probably indicative of the direction in which sculpture had turned by the 14th century. Other large figures in this style are found in one of the temples facing the Shwe-san-daw and inside the eastern temple at the Dhamma-yazika temple.

Buddhist Themes

Stone workers chose from far fewer subjects than painters, but the selection varied widely nonetheless. Unique in its complexity are the scores of sculptures depicting scenes from the life of the Buddha inside the outer corridor of the Ananda. The sculptors drew directly from the Pali text, the *Nidanakatha*, or at least a source closely modeled on it. The episodes, beginning with the Buddha's conception and ending with his enlightenment, conform remarkably to the *Nidanakatha*. The original text is usually dated to the 5th or 6th century and almost certainly came to Burma from Sri Lanka at some early stage. This text is faithfully reproduced in stone at the Ananda, to a degree never seen elsewhere at Pagan or even within the wider Buddhist world. For example, the infant Buddha is shown placing his feet on the head of the ascetic Kaladevala. Also, the Buddha reposes in three pavilions or palaces, built by his father. Described as five, seven and nine storied in the *Nidanakatha*, these very three pavilions are depicted in stone at the Ananda, with the correct number of stories. Another scene features the Buddha collapsed on the ground, fainting from his fast at the end of six years practicing asceticism. These aforementioned scenes are rarely, if ever, depicted in Buddhist art. It has been recently suggested that there was a Sanskrit Buddhist component in the series, a possibility that needs more investigation (Galloway). Numerous sculptures in the four entrance halls of the Ananda range over other incidents in the Buddha's life, also taken from the Pali canon, such as the Descent from the Heaven of the 33 Gods, and the Defeat of the Nalagiri Elephant.

One popular theme among sculptors was the 28 Buddhas, drawn from the *Nidanakatha* and another Pali source, the *Buddhavamsa*. These Buddhas are typically found in the niches encircling the sanctum, such as at the Kubyauk-gyi (Myinkaba). Painted above each niche is the special tree associated with each Buddha's enlightenment, carefully delineated from one another. Seventy niches inside the corridor and sanctum at the Abeyadana were intended for sculpture, but only a handful survived into the 20th century. In style, they resemble those in the Nagayon, Kubyauk-gyi (Myinkaba) and the Ananda. They have been removed to the Pagan museum.

Buddha fainting after his fast. This rarely depicted subject in Buddhist art is drawn from the Nidanakatha, *a Pali text influential at Pagan. (DS)*

Stone Buddha possibly associated with an ink inscription on the wall above it, dated to 1343, Dhammayan-gyi. East entrance hall. (DS)

Sculptures similar in subject matter to those in the entrance halls at the Ananda also appear in the entrance hall at the Nagayon. Inside the corridor encircling the sanctum are the 28 Buddhas, placed on both sides of the corridor, unlike at the Kubyauk-gyi where sculpture was restricted to only the inside wall of the corridor. The series at the Nagayon begins on the front wall of the sanctum and goes clockwise. It then jumps to the outer corridor wall and continues in clockwise fashion. Each of the 28 Buddhas is shown twice, immediately next to each other. Individual Buddhas are first shown in the meditation-gesture, with figures relating to each biography in shallow relief on the base. Beside it is a depiction of the same Buddha, showing his enlightenment, with his lowered hand. Niches for stone sculpture were probably planned for the corridor of the Pahto-thamya, but a change in design occurred during the temple's construction, and the niches on the rear wall of the sanctum were bricked up. These few examples suggest the diversity marking these stone sculpture series, both in their depictions and in their placement among these early temples. The few sculptures that were planned for temples from the second half of the 12th century and the 13th century appear to focus on the life of the Buddha, such as those in the Kubyauk-gne (no. 1391).

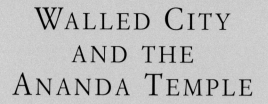

WALLED CITY AND THE ANANDA TEMPLE

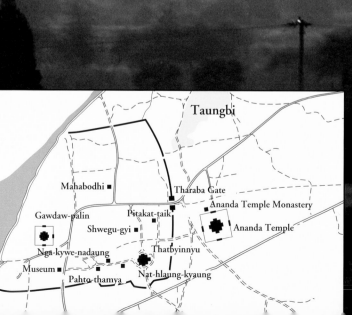

ANANDA

Previous pages: View from Mingalazedi Stupa toward Walled City at dawn. Thatbyinnyu Temple in centre. (PP)

The Ananda is based on a cruciform ground plan, with symmetrical entrance halls. Glazed plaques line the foundation and jataka tiles are placed in niches within the roof terraces. The tower has been restored numerous times, following earthquakes, but the temple's appearance is largely original. (DS)

Date: c. 11th-12th centuries

The Ananda temple ranks as one of Burma's most revered shrines, together with the Shwe-zigon also at Pagan, the Mahamuni in Amarapura, and the Shwedagon in Yangon. Worship never ceased at the temple, even following the city's eclipse starting in the 14th century. Endless refurbishing has included the whitewashing of its frescos and numerous re-applications of stucco and paint on the exterior. Four huge, wooden, gilded Buddhas in the centre of the temple are the focus of devotion, but these were added long after the temple's founding. The crowning tower sustained heavy damage in the 1975 quake, but the appearance of the temple is essentially the same as the day it was completed.

Scores of stone sculptures in the outer corridor are unequalled for portraying the life of the Buddha in such rich detail, at Pagan or elsewhere in Burma. Also, over fifteen hundred glazed plaques on the exterior combine Buddhist subjects in a unique configuration. Three modern corridors blending European and Burmese architectural traditions are also attractions.

The Ananda is a masterpiece of perfect proportions, appearing neither too squat or too lofty. A brilliant vision guided the architects, not unlike the inspiration behind the Parthenon or the Taj Mahal.

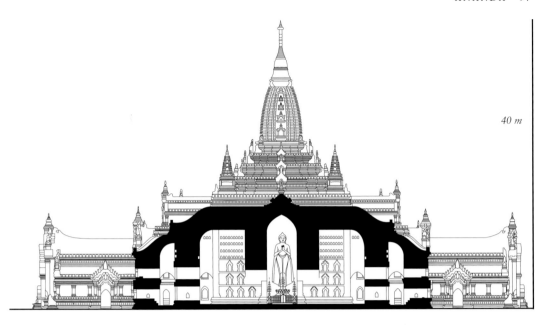

40 m

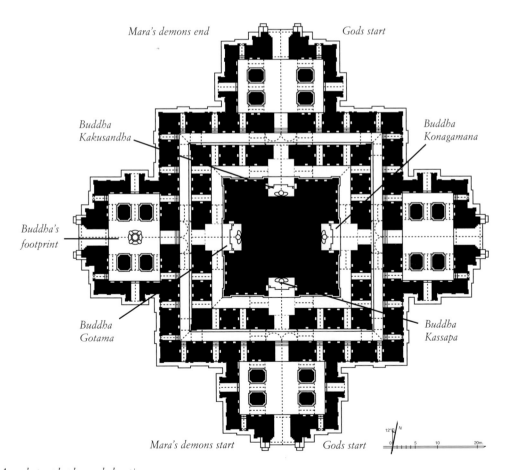

Mara's demons end

Gods start

Buddha
Kakusandha

Buddha
Konagamana

Buddha's
footprint

Buddha
Gotama

Buddha
Kassapa

Mara's demons start

Gods start

12°

N

0   5   10   20m.

Ananda temple plan and elevation.

Miniature stupas on compound wall.

History and Legend

Burmese chronicles attribute the founding of the temple to King Kyanzittha, but firm evidence about who constructed the temple or when it was built is missing. That no donor inscription is associated with Pagan's most important temple highlights the difficulty in reconstructing the history of the city. The temple came to be known in the 18th century or slightly earlier as the Nanda, based on a legend claiming that Kyanzittha emulated the legendary Nanda-mula Cave in the Himalayas when he designed the temple. In the 19th century or earlier, the temple also came to be called Ananda, after the name of one of the Buddha's celebrated disciples.

The temple's real patron and its original name are unknown, however. The monument is usually dated to around 1100, based on the style of its stone sculpture, the use of Mon language captions incised on the glazed tiles, and its legendary connection with Kyanzittha.

The Ananda is likely the first of Pagan's enormous temples, but extensive building activity certainly took place long before its creation. The earliest dated structure at Pagan is the Kubyauk-gyi (Myinkaba), built by Kyanzittha's son in 1113. A number of temples are thought to be late 11th century, such as the Pahto-thamya, Nagayon and the Abeyadana, but it is safer to think of them as late 11th or early 12th century, like the Ananda.

Visit

The vast temple emerges into view after leaving the Walled City from the Tharaba Gate. The expansive area in front of the west gateway is reserved for traders and merchants during the annual festival culminating on a full moon day in December-January. Footware is deposited just inside the north and west gateways, the two main public entrances today. A morning visit is recommended, since the compound flagstones grow toasty as the sun rises.

Pilgrims visiting the Ananda purchase vases brimming with flowers and place them around the central gilded Buddhas. Devotional activities also include lighting candles at the base of the Buddhas and quietly intoning prayers while kneeling in the narrow passage ways. Senior monks are now and then commissioned to chant from Pali texts, the sacred syllables drifting throughout the temple and outside, boosted with electronic amplification.

The Gateways

Imposing gateways resembling miniature temples are set into each of the four walls of the square compound. Inside each

Ananda gateway, south.

are two heavily restored
seated figures, with one leg
pendant, probably representing
bodhisattvas. Similar figures,
though unrestored, are in the
gateways of the Nagayon
temple. The gates at the
Ananda are largely original,
but their exterior has been
repeatedly resurfaced with
stucco and whitewash. A
continuous row of miniature
stupas adorns the exterior face
of the compound wall,
probably added to the original
wall during the 19th century in
the Konbaung period (1752-
1885). Each wall is roughly
three metres thick at the base.

The two public entrances
today are on the north and west sides, but the principal one during
the 19th century was on the north. A 19th-century British mission
recorded a "wooden colonnade, covered with the usual carved gables
and tapering slender spires." (Yule, 37). This old colonnade adjoins
the north gateway, now packed tightly with shops. To one side is
Pagan's first museum, with its original blue and white enamel sign
bearing the date 1904. On the other side is the multi-storied Ananda
Temple Monastery, with its 18th-century wall painting.

Modern corridor, south. (PP)

The Modern Outer Corridors

Three long corridors were established within the compound wall
during the early 20th century. Each is designed somewhat differently,
but all combine European and traditional Burmese elements. The
two on the north and west are lined with shops and form the main
avenues leading to the temple today.

The west corridor was completed on April 14, 1925, recorded
in an inscription on raised stucco at the entrance. It took one year to
finish, having been begun the previous year on a certain day at 9:00 in
the morning. In two niches placed at the end of the corridor, facing
the temple, are sculptures of the donors, a husband and wife from
Hsale. Above the souvenir shops are modern painted panels recording
the deeds of Anawrahta and Kyanzittha. Dozens of small oval-shaped
terracotta votive tablets salvaged from the ancient period are placed
high on the exterior walls.

*Ancient votive tablets such as this
one are found in the west corridor,
exterior wall.*

The south corridor was finished in 1929, the gift of a husband
and wife and their family, recorded in an inscription. Panels lining the
walls depicting at least one of the Buddha's previous births, or *jatakas*,
were probably hung soon after the hall was finished. The signature of
the artist, Maung Saw Maung, can be made out on the panels, and he
describes himself as a famous painter from Mandalay. Some figures
are dressed in court costumes of a by-gone age. Artists were exposed
to European painting as early as the 18th century, and indigenous

West entrance hall, right, and corridor, left, leading to the Ananda, donated by a family in 1925.

painting came to be greatly influenced by Western pictorial conventions, such as perspective and modeling.

The north corridor has no panel painting, only in the entrance hall preceding the main temple where eleven examples are devoted to at least one *jataka*. The corridor itself was finished in 1932 by a woman and her family from Twinya village, south of New Pagan. The ceilings of the corridors are enlivened by repeated designs formed by metal strips inserted between the rafters in parallel rows.

The Temple Plan

The Ananda is unique at Pagan for many reasons, beginning with its symmetrical ground plan. A huge central block is fronted on all sides with wide, long entrance halls of equal dimensions, forming a cruciform shape. Since the four entrance halls are equal in size and so long and low in relation to the central block, the temple appears two-sided rather than four, from every point of view. Other large temples at Pagan may appear symmetrical like the Ananda, such as the Sulamani, or the Thatbyinnyu, but one entrance hall is always slightly longer than the others, and one major Buddha dominates the conception.

This ground plan highlights equally the four enshrined standing Buddhas. Also, the glazed plaques surrounding the base appear to be in a continuous row, although divisions are created by the entrance halls. The genius of the Ananda plan can be only appreciated today from the east gate, since no modern corridor was built on that side.

The principal ancient entrance at the Ananda is unknown, since the symmetrical plan itself offers few clues. However, it may have been the west side since sculpture featuring the biography of the Buddha begins there. Also, the *jataka* tiles in the tower begin on the west face. The west face also is oriented toward the Walled City, perhaps another consideration.

Two concentric corridors encircle the enormous central block whose four deep niches contain the gilded wooden Buddhas. The outer walls are pierced by numerous windows, one set above the other, admitting light into the first corridor which passes directly into cross-passages leading to the inner corridor. This design ensures that the interior sculptures are well lighted.

Mara's demons in procession, glazed tiles, west side. All the demons face north. (DS)

The Glazed Tiles

The Ananda showcases over fifteen hundred green glazed tiles set into exterior niches, all identified with Mon characters incised on their base. The basement tiles are devoted to the army of Mara and numerous deities, while the upper terraces feature tiles dedicated to the *jatakas*. The roof tiles were never designed to be closely viewed, since no ready access was ever planned to the terraces. The majority of the plaques are in their original niches, with only minor modern fiddling.

Tile production began by placing the clay in a square mould, probably of wood. The figures, such as men, women, animals, carts, boats and trees, were formed separately and carefully attached. A Mon inscription was incised on the bottom of each plaque, and small circular ornaments were applied around the rim. The tiles are very thick, roughly 6 cm. The green plaques are in a variety of hues dependent on the composition of the glaze and firing conditions.

Other glazed complete *jataka* series are found at Pagan encircling the terraces of *stupas*, such as the Mingalazedi and and Dhamma-yazika, but the Ananda is the only temple designed with glazed *jatakas* in the roof terraces.

Roof terraces. Glazed jataka *tiles in niches. The series begins on the west face. Public access to the roof was never intended by the ancient architects. (DS)*

Mara's demons – west face

Encircling the west face of the temple are hundreds of tiles portraying the army of Mara, the demon-king symbolizing the worldly attachments that the Buddha eschewed.

The demons are depicted in pairs, with few exceptions, and are shown marching to the left, toward the north. Many stand on their own two feet while others go to battle on animal mounts (Guillon). A common category includes men with unpleasant faces, made more disagreeable by snakes emerging from their mouths, ears, eyes, or even noses. A typical Mon caption reads, "Mara's army with snakes coming from their eyes." At least one illustrated palm-leaf manuscript from Nepal

Top: 'Gods holding elephant-goads', Mon caption, east face. All of the gods move in the direction of the east doorway.

Above: 'Mara's army with snakes issuing from their noses', Mon caption. All of Mara's demons proceed in the same direction, toward the north entrance.

also depicts snakes coming from the mouths of Mara's demons, so eastern India is probably the origin for this unusual rendering (Pal, 1985, 192). It is also found in Pala sculpture, though rarely, and at least once at Ajanta. Snakes emerging from the mouths of Mara's soldiers also feature in the *Lalitavistara*, a Mahayana text.

Other no-gooders appear deceptively harmless, such as little waddling ducks, but these cute, innocent creatures were probably included in the phalanx to illustrate Mara's all-encompassing and beguiling powers, a theme in Pali literature. Mara, for example, could even hide within the stomach of a disciple of the Buddha, assume the form of a ploughman or a bullock, or could create an earthquake or a landslide. The message is clear: "keep a clean mind, since even a duck in your nearby pond can cause mischief and spoil your day, if not your life."

Mara's demons appear only rarely in ceramics at Pagan but commonly in frescos. However, no fresco series repeats many of these demons, such as the characters with the snakes. One or two small stone sculptures of Mara's demons, from a ruined stupa (no. 1339), are displayed at the museum. Ferocious figures in trios line the south side of the Mingalazedi stupa basement but are not Mara's demons, judging from their Burmese captions.

The Gods – east face

Hundreds of deities on the east face represent the major players in the Pali Buddhist universe, such as the Regents of the Four Quarters, their 28 Generals, the Four Kings of Death, and many other divine beings, including special mythical birds, snakes, gods, goddesses and others (Shorto). Among the ink inscriptions at Pagan many of the same deities are listed within a group attending a sermon of the Buddha. One inscription from a Pali text at the Nagayon lists attendees at one of the Buddha's sermons as including "gods (*devas*), *yakkha* (spirits), Gandharvas, snakes, Suparnas and Kumbhandas of the ten thousand world systems." (*Digha Nikaya*, 20). Some of these protagonists appear in later painted Burmese manuscripts, surrounding Mount Meru, but the Ananda should not be associated with Mount Meru (Herbert, 2002).

Unlike the demons facing in a single direction, the gods are divided into two moieties, each moving toward the east door. Both groups largely mirror each other, with some exceptions. The procession to the right side of the entrance is led by the chief gods, Brahma and Sakka, standing together on a single plaque next to the doorway. The three-headed Brahma holds an umbrella, while Sakka grasps a conch, their usual attributes at Pagan. All of the figures are identified by Mon glosses. Gods and goddesses are usually in trios, holding different auspicious objects identified in the glosses, such as lamps, banners and vessels.

The *Jatakas*

The tiles on the roof terraces comprise the most complete surviving ceramic *jataka* series at Pagan. They begin on the southwest corner of the lowest terrace and wind around the temple in a clockwise direction, ascending to the sixth topmost terrace. Each of the first 537 *jatakas* is accorded a single tile and is identified with its Pali name and number. The order conforms to the standard collection of Pali *jatakas* known today. The last group of ten tales, known as the Mahanipata, were considered most sacred and their complete telling consumes a total of 389 tiles. The plaques on the last two terraces are smaller than the others, since the terraces themselves become smaller. The last ten stretch over much of the top four terraces, the first (no. 538), beginning in the middle of the north side, immediately abutting *jataka* no. 537, with no special break marking the division. The number of the last ten *jatakas* begins with 538 and runs serially. The Mon captions briefly describe the action represented. The order of the last ten *jatakas* differs somewhat from the sequence in the standard Pali collection.

'Mahosadah decides the case of the bull – 671', Mon caption. Each of the last ten jatakas *extends over numerous tiles. They numbered serially, and this example is 671 in the sequence and belongs to* jataka 546. *The last tile is numbered 920, from the Vessantara* jataka.

Prince Vessantara, his wife, and children. This jataka *completes the series of 547. (DS)*

Death of the Buddha. Sculpture presenting major events in the Buddha's life are within 16 niches in each entrance hall. East entrance hall.

Maya's Dream, south entrance hall.

Exposed stone and brick voussoirs, inner corridor. (DS)

Opposite: Standing Buddha in central niche, gilded wood. South side. (PP)

Below: Recently uncovered ancient murals, north entrance hall. The subjects cannot yet be identified. (DS)

Right: Seated Buddhas, until recently concealed by whitewash. East entrance hall. (DS)

The Entrance Halls

The entrance halls are showcases for sculptures illustrating the main events in the Buddha's life. Each hall contains sixteen images. The majority have been heavily painted and gilded but are otherwise as fresh as the day they left the workshop. The subjects and their positions on the walls are nearly identical in all four halls, with some probable shifting over the centuries. At the rear of each hall on the side walls are Maya's Dream and the Death of the Buddha. Other familiar subjects include the Buddha's Descent from the Heaven of the 33 Gods, the Birth of the Buddha, and the First Sermon at the Deer Park.

In the north hall stucco has flaked off to reveal a triple arch made up of alternating brick and stone voussoirs. Similar arches can be detected high within the outer corridor where they distribute the weight down into the walls. The stone voussoirs extend deeper into the wall than the bricks, designed to secure the face of the wall to the inner fabric.

New Painting Discoveries

The entrance halls were once completely covered with frescos but were whitewashed sometime in the late 18th or early 19th century. Recent cleaning has uncovered small portions of the original painting, in the north and east entrance halls. Parallel rows of unidentified narrative scenes appear on the piers, while rows of seated Buddhas filled the vaults above. The ceiling was painted with roundels. Thin orange-coloured lines used within some of the figures resemble those in the frescos of another early temple, the Pahto-thamya.

An ink inscription in late 18th- or early 19th-century characters in the east hall records a donation by a military leader from Yangon, made for the sake of obtaining 'nebban', or *nibbana* (Pali). His act of merit should be associated with a row of painted Buddhas immediately below.

The inner corridors may also have been covered with original mural painting, but we cannot be sure. The walls of many later large and small temples had no figurative painting but were covered with a tan coloured wash, accented by painted borders, such as the Sulamani and the Thatbyinnyu.

Detail of standing Buddha, south side. (PP)

Footprint of Buddha, west entrance hall. (DS)

The Buddha's Footprints - West Entrance Hall

A huge circular stone slab dominating the west entrance hall is incised with impressions of the Buddha's footprints. Worshippers often make offerings here before proceeding to the inner sanctum. This may be the original location of the footprints but it is uncertain, since no similar stone footprints remain inside temples today. Carved inside the footprints in very shallow relief are small auspicious symbols contained in square frames; they are said to total 108, a number specified in certain Pali texts. Surviving ancient stone footprints at Pagan number no more than a handful, but one can be seen at the museum, recovered from the Lokananda stupa (no. 1023).

Worship of the Buddha's footprints began very early in India but cannot be documented in Burma until the Pagan period. The prints are often found painted on the ceilings of entrance halls, such as the Loka-hteikpan. The veneration of the footprints increased following the Pagan period, and even entire temples became dedicated to them, such as the 19th-century Settawya temple at Mingun, near Mandalay. One 18th-century reference records that stone footprints were placed in carts and wheeled about to obtain offerings (Cox, 111). The sanctity of the Buddha's footprints is recognized throughout Buddhist Asia, but especially so in Theravada countries, like Sri Lanka and Thailand.

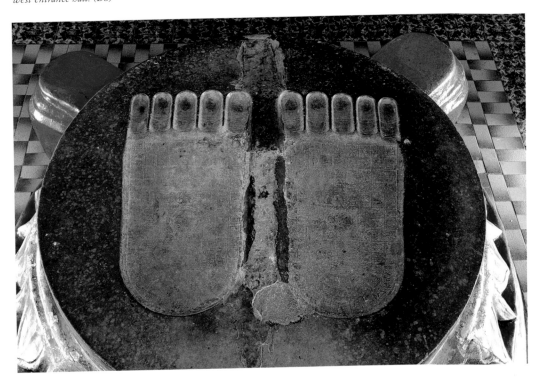

The Four Gilded Buddhas

At the heart of the temple are four majestic gilded wooden Buddha images standing in deep tall niches within the central block. These Buddhas are believed to represent the historical Buddha, Gotama, and the three Buddhas preceding him in the present era. Gotama is considered the 28th Buddha in a sequence extending into mythical time. The 25th, Kakusandha, is believed today to be in the north niche, while the 26th, Konagamana is in the east, Kassapa, the 27th, is in the south, and Gotama, the 28th, is in the west. Kakusandha and Kassapa are shown with their hands raised together at their chest in the teaching-gesture. Konagamana's lowered outstretched hands resemble Buddha figures associated with Mandalay in the 19th century and earlier. Gotama's right hand is raised in the gesture-of-reassurance.

The Buddhas on the east and west sides are believed to be 18th century, while the other pair is thought to date from the ancient Pagan period. However, it is more likely that all four images belong to the Konbaung period, from the 18th or early 19th centuries. We must remember that no Buddhas that are the chief focus of devotion in ancient Pagan are made of wood. Moreover, the central image within a sanctum is never shown standing, always seated. If there were originally standing images in these shrines, they would more likely have been made of brick and covered with stucco. It is more probable, therefore that there were originally seated Buddhas in these four niches.

Even the identity of these four Buddhas is speculative, apart from believing that they represent the last four Buddhas in the influential sequence of 28. For example, none of the Buddhas are associated with the cardinal directions in canonical Pali literature. Also, the hand-gestures by themselves provide no clue. It is also probably not without significance that the identifications made in the 20th century by Luce and others, differ completely from those recorded in the 19th (Yule, 39).

Outer corridor and 18th-century wooden doorway. Stone Buddhas in niches.

Early 20th-century floor tiles, east side

Disciple of Buddha, south side.

First sculpture in the Buddha's life series. The Buddha-to-be in Tushita Heaven, lower tier, west.

Below: No. 7. Dream of Maya, lower tier, north.

Skylights piercing the lowest roof terraces admit a shaft of light at certain times of day, striking the Buddhas with dramatic effect. Artificial lighting installed over the last decade has unfortunately spoiled the "very powerful and strange effect", as one early observer noted. (Yule, 38). Also, lining the side walls of the deep chambers are additional sculptures placed in niches, barely visible due to their height. Their subject matter can be identified, but their narrative connection to the overall conception of the monument has not yet been worked out.

The original bases of the wooden images cover the entire floor of the chamber and are heavily repainted and regilded. To the sides in special niches are kneeling stone figures, thought to represent the chief disciples of each of the Buddhas. On the west side are two figures said to be the patron, King Kyanzittha, and his Mon religious advisor, Shin Arahan, but there is no firm evidence for this. That nearly identical kneeling figures are found within a small 18th-century shrine in the northern part of the Ananda compound is one more reason for thinking that all of these kneeling figures inside the Ananda are much later (see temple 2168). The example on the south side is my favourite, poised as if to spring out of its niche.

A Biography in Stone – the outer corridor

Eighty stone sculptures inside the Ananda narrate the compelling story of the Buddha, starting from before his birth on earth and ending with the enlightenment beneath the Bodhi tree at Bodh Gaya. The series encircles the wide outer corridor located only steps beyond the rear of the entrance halls. To appreciate the story from start to finish in the correct order requires two circumambulations of the corridor, the first round focusing only on the bottom row of niches and the second round only on the top tier where the story concludes.

The sculptures were based either on a 5th- or 6th-century Pali text known as the *Nidanakatha*, or more probably from later works based directly on this source. A remarkably close correspondence exists between this text and the sculptures, suggesting that the stone carvers, who were likely illiterate, modelled their work on drawings based upon the text.

Too many details in the sculptures conform to the text to believe that the craftsmen fashioned these from common lore. There are a number of scenes that appear to be unprecedented in ancient Buddhist art, such as the Buddha fainting. A handful of stray Buddha figures outside the narrative were likely inserted into niches for unknown reasons, replacing original images. Apart from these later additions, these sculptures have not been removed from their original niches for roughly a millennium, a long time to be sitting still, gazing down at pilgrims, and, more recently, foreign tourists.

Outer Corridor – Lower Tier: (West Wall)

The story begins after leaving the western entrance hall and upon entering the outer corridor, a short distance from the Buddha's footprints. It starts immediately to the left of the entrance, on the outer wall. The sculptures are arranged in two parallel rows, each image sheltered within a quatrefoil niche. The series begins with the bottom register and winds completely around the temple in a clockwise direction. The very last sculpture depicts the Buddha seated beneath the Bodhi Tree, located in a niche next to the western entrance in the upper tier. These sculptures were probably painted originally but have been repainted in new colours many times in subsequent centuries. In the mid-19th century they were covered with a type of gum resin and vermilion, whereas many are now of gold colour, with red backgrounds.

The series begins immediately to the left of the doorway as we enter the first corridor, facing north. The first sculpture shows the seated Buddha-to-be, or bodhisattva, in the company of two kneeling gods in Tushita Heaven, prior to his birth on earth (no. 1). He wears princely garb, with his right hand lowered. The second panel depicts the Buddha's mother, Queen Maya, sleeping with two attendants below. In the next panel the Four Guardians of the World have transported the sleeping Maya to the Himalayan mountains and placed her beneath a huge *sala* tree. The next two feature the four consorts of the Guardians and Maya, first her anointment in the Anotatta Lake, suggested by water lotuses, followed by her dressing in special garments. In ancient Buddhist art worldwide, this section of the narrative is rare, if not unprecedented.

No. 12. Birth of Buddha, lower tier, north. The infant emerged from her right side.

Lower Tier: North Wall

The images on the north wall begin with the Conception where Maya is shown on a heavenly couch. In the next panel the Buddha-to-be assumes the form of a white elephant, with a white lotus flower in his trunk (no. 7). In the form of a white elephant, he circled around Maya's bed three times and, "appeared as though to have entered the womb making an opening on the right side" (*Nidanakatha*, 67). Maya is shown sleeping and the tiny elephant is shown by the side of the couch. In the next panel she reveals the dream to her husband, King Suddhana. And then Maya shown is guarded by four gods with swords, conforming exactly to the *Nidanakatha* text. Next, Maya asks permission from the king to visit her parents for the childbirth and her departure. She is then shown carried aloft on a palanquin, in a niche immediately after the central doorway. The next panel features the birth in Lumbini Park where Maya grasps the flowering *sala* tree, and the infant Buddha emerges from her side (no. 12). (The Buddha's mother will die seven days later and the child-rearing will fall to her sister, Prajapati, but her death is not represented). The text says nothing about being born

No. 20. Infant Buddha and ascetic, lower tier, east.

No. 26. Buddha in seven-tiered pavilion, lower tier, south.

No. 29. The Buddha's manly regime, holding a sword and a bow, lower tier, south.

from her side but claims that the Buddha "left his mother's womb . . . like a man descending from a stairway . . . unsmeared with any impurity arising from the mother's womb, . . . like a precious gem placed on a silken cloth" (*Nidanakatha*, 70). The next scene depicts the Buddha supported by four standing figures representing the Hindu god Brahma who held the Buddha in a golden net. The narrative continues with the four Guardians of the World receiving the Buddha on a carpet of antelope skins. In the next panel two mortals receive the infant on a fine cloth, as the text specifies.

Lower Tier: East Wall

The first panel likely represents the Buddha holding special medicinal sandalwood in his hand, a gift from Sakka in one of his previous lives. This medicine was put into a pot, and it is likely Sakka holding this pot. [Luce identified the scene as the Buddha flanked by Brahma and Sakka]. The next two panels depict the Buddha taking his first seven steps, but in the narrative this episode belongs immediately before his appearance holding the medicinal sandalwood. The *Nidanakatha* specifies that Brahma held a white umbrella and that Sakka carried a fan, conforming exactly to these reliefs. The next panel shows the seated Buddha surrounded by flying gods, rejoicing at the birth of the Buddha. This is followed by the infant Buddha and his father seated before the ascetic Kaladevala who was asked to forecast if the child was to be a spiritual world leader (no. 20). The father instructed the infant Buddha to pay homage to the ascetic but suddenly the Buddha unexpectedly thrust his feet on top of the ascetics head! This was a reversal of normal roles, since a child was expected to place his own head at the feet of the ascetic. Indeed, under normal worldly circumstances the Buddha's behaviour would be unacceptable. However, the ascetic immediately recognized the child's greatness and told the king that it was destined for his son to become a religious leader. Tension between the Buddha and Hindu ascetics is a leitmotif in Buddhist literature.

The next relief, after the doorway, probably represents the moment when eight brahmins examine the Buddha for auspicious markings. Seven held up two fingers to indicate that these marks would mean that the child would supercede his father and become a Universal Monarch. But the brahmin named Kondanya raised a single finger to prophesize that the infant will become the future Buddha. Here on the base are four seated men, although the Pali text specifies eight. The next panel possibly represents the seated Buddha, attended by royal ". . . nurses of great beauty who were free from all faults", following the episode with Kondanya (*Nidanakatha*, 76).

Then come two panels devoted to the moment when the shadow of a tree protecting the Buddha refused to budge during the course of the day. His shocked maid-servants reported this miracle and in the accompanying panel his mother and father kneel beside him beneath the tree, after witnessing further proof of their unusual son. The surprise, amazement, and awe surrounding such miracles, together with the Buddha's trifling prank played on the ascetic Kaladevala, is reminiscent of Krishna's infancy and childhood. One did not influence the other but rather such themes in both biographies stemmed from the same cultural sensibilities in early India. The last panel on the east wall jumps to the Buddha's late adolescence, after his marriage, when his father tried desperately to shield the Buddha from suffering. He constructed three pleasure pavilions, for each of the three seasons, with nine, seven and five stories. Taking no chances, his father equipped these pavilions with forty-thousand dancing girls, "like a deity surrounded by bands of heavenly nymphs" (*Nidanakatha*, 77-78). Each pavilion is represented in a separate panel, with the required number of stories, again conforming precisely to the *Nidanakatha*.

Lower Tier: South Wall

The first two panels continue the depiction of the pleasure pavilions (no. 26). The third sculpture on this wall is difficult to assign to the narrative but perhaps represents the young seated prince assuming a formal position within the court. The Buddha's poor father was soon chided by his kinsmen for spoiling his son, arguing that the prince would be unable defend the realm in time of war. The Buddha's father, therefore, started his son on a manly regime, beginning with archery. The young man is shown in a stiff pose, holding a sword in one hand a bow in another (no. 29).

No. 30. *The Four Sights: an old man, lower tier, south.*

The gods agreed that it was time to set the youth's spiritual quest in motion, and therefore staged the Four Sights, exposing him to suffering. From his chariot he witnessed an old man, a sick man and a corpse and a hermit (no. 30). Each scene is depicted in a separate relief, the second beginning to the right of the door.

Two of the next three panels are difficult to identify and perhaps are out of order. In the text, after the sight of the hermit, the divine craftsmen named Vissakamma ties an elaborate turban on the Buddha's head. This can be seen by skipping one panel where the cloth turban is being wound. The preceding sculpture perhaps shows attendants holding the cloth for the turban, but this is uncertain.

Lower Tier: West Face

The first panel depicts the Buddha on a chartiot, facing a kneeling figure. This may represent the noblewoman Kisa Gotami to whom the Buddha gives his string of pearls. Luce identified this scene as a messenger giving the news to the Buddha about the birth of his son, Rahula, but this comes a bit further in the narrative. (That Kisa Gotami appears among the paintings at the Pahto-thamya reinforces this suggested identification). After giving his necklace to Kisa Gotami, the Buddha then returns to the palace where he is surrounded by maidens, two of whom seem to stroke his arms or are in the act of dressing him. This panel comes after the vision of the hermit, but it may have originally been placed after the panel showing the kneeling woman before the chariot.

The remaining scenes on the west wall depict the dramatic departure from the palace. He is first shown, recumbent, entertained by musicians. In the centre of the next relief the Buddha is seated, contemplating the sleeping courtesans, "some of them with saliva pouring out of their mouths, . . . some grinding their teeth" (*Nidanakatha*, 82) (no. 38). The next shows the Buddha with his

No. 38. *Buddha observing sleeping courtesans, lower tier, west.*

trusted horse, Kanthaka, and his groom, Channa, who was instructed to saddle up the mount. The last panel before the door shows the Buddha gazing at his sleeping wife whom he is now to abandon, perhaps the most poignant moment in his new life of renunciation.

Top Tier: West Face
The narrative now continues on the other side of the doorway on the top tier. The first scene shows the Buddha preparing to mount his steed for his secret departure in the night. To muffle the clitter-clatter of the hooves, four gods carry the horse aloft in the adjoining panel (no. 42). The next illustrates the moment on the journey when Mara, disguised, tempts the Buddha with a precious bejewelled-wheel. The demon appears on the upper right, as if on a cloud. The adjacent panel shows the progress toward the Anoma River, the horse purposely shown with his head lowered, suggesting its exhaustion. The next panel shows the trio again, before the horse leaps across the river, the groom holding the tail.

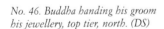

No. 42. Buddha departing from the palace, top tier, west.

Top Tier: North Face
The first panel on the north wall show the group on the opposite bank, the Buddha presenting his jewellery to the groom. The next scene shows the Buddha removing his jewelled turban and cutting his hair, inaugurating his life as a recluse. In the next panel Sakka catches the Buddha's hair and his turban which he entrusts to a jeweled casket; Sakka is shown in the upper right, holding aloft the casket that was enshrined in a special stupa in the Heaven of the 33 Gods. Then comes a depiction of a Brahma named Ghatikara presenting the robes of a recluse to the Buddha. The following features the Buddha with the kneeling Ghatikara and the groom with the now unsaddled mount. The horse dies of a broken heart, realizing that he will never see his master again but is reborn as a god in the heavens.

No. 46. Buddha handing his groom his jewellery, top tier, north. (DS)

The next sculpture, the Buddha in the earth-touching gesture, does not seem to belong to the sequence, evinced also by its very different throne-back. Next is the scene of a 'walking' Buddha, denoting his journey to the town of Rajagaha. He is then shown standing with his alms bowl, followed by a panel in which he is shown eating from the bowl. The last panel on this face shows the crowned king of Rajagaha offering his kingdom to the Buddha.

Top Tier: East Face
The first two panels on this side show the Buddha conversing with two ascetics, Alara Kalama and Uddaka, rejecting a form of trance that he learned from them, each represented in a separate relief. After leaving them, he journeys further and meets five hermits and for six years practices austerities in their company, represented by

the Buddha seated in a pavilion. Near the end of those six years he undertook a fast, his emaciated chest revealing his rib cage beneath his taut skin (no. 59). Alarmed, the gods attempted to infuse "divine energy through the pores of his skin", indicated by two gods rubbing this elixir into his arms (*Nidanakatha*, 89). The Buddha was nonetheless overcome and fainted, his five associates shown at the base, a god kneeling over him beside a tree. The first panel after the doorway on the east wall is likely an intrusive addition. The Buddha then approached Bodh Gaya, a village now in northeastern India. A landowner's daughter named Sujata had made offerings to a tree-spirit inhabiting a banyan (*nigrodha*) tree belonging to a goatherder, wishing for marriage and the birth of a son. She instructed her maid to make the daily offering, seen in the next panel. The maid spots the Buddha, mistaking him for the god of the tree who has finally manifested himself in physical form. She rushes back and brings Sujata who offers the seated figure beneath the *nigrodha* tree a golden bowl filled with milk-rice, enriched by the gods. She kneels on the left, below, holding the vessel. The next image is likely a later addition, since the Buddha is shown in the meditation-gesture which does not fit into the narrative. The last sculpture on this face shows the Buddha eating from Sujata's bowl.

No. 59. *Buddha fasting, top tier, east.*

Top Tier: South Face

The first panel depicts the seated Buddha with a small bowl placed on his two folded hands. The next sculpture is likely intrusive, since the Buddha is shown in the earth-touching gesture and the backdrop of the sculpture does not match those in the series. This is followed by the Buddha with two banner-wielding gods in procession to the Bodhi tree. Before appearing before the Bodhi tree, a grass-cutter offers the Buddha eight bundles of grass on which to sit. The next five panels present the Buddha standing, the first one with the grass cutter and others in which the Buddha holds the grass, but with his free hand in different positions. Why this incident should run over so many panels is curious. Then comes the seated Buddha in the earth-touching gesture, with a small kneeling female holding aloft a pot. She is possibly Sujata, offering the milk-rice, but this would not fit into the narrative at this point, and it is therefore possibly not in its original location. [This composition is strongly reminiscent of Pala sculpture where the kneeling figure with a pot represents the

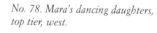
No. 78. *Mara's dancing daughters, top tier, west.*

Earth Goddess at the time of the Enlightenment]. The next panel depicts the Buddha, with Sakka, with his conch, and Brahma with an umbrella, both deities present in the text.

Top Tier: South Face

The next panel is likely a later addition, since it does not fit the narrative and its backdrop is similar to other such panels. Then comes the Buddha beneath the Bodhi tree, with the demon Mara standing beside him. The neighbouring panel shows Mara's three daughters, dancing seductively on the base but to no avail (no. 78). This incident occurs on the fifth week after the Buddha's enlightenment, according to the *Nidanakatha*, in the vicinity of the goat-herder's tree. The sculptors carefully made this tree different from the Bodhi tree in the adjacent panel. The other weeks the Buddha spent at Bodh Gaya are not-represented, so the series skipped to this popular episode. The second to last sculpture shows the Buddha again, with six *devas* at the base. This panel does not illustrate a specific episode in the narrative but may refer to the gods who initially doubted his claim to enlightenment. The final relief shows the Buddha with his hand lowered, signifying the enlightenment.

The Remaining Corridor Sculptures

The inner wall of the outer corridor and both sides of the inner corridor are lined with Buddha images in niches, predominantly in the earth-touching and teaching-gestures. A handful of figures show the Buddha without his cranial bump and his left hand touching the lotus base, a highly unusual feature. Another small group reveal the Buddha, also without the cranial bump, with his right arm resting across his chest, another unexplained pose. Whether these depictions and the many other images conform to a narrative has not yet been determined. The large cross-passages have rich stucco pediments, with seated male figures in the centre, perhaps bodhisattvas. The simple, flat surrounds for the niches were probably originally elaborately crafted with stucco ornament, but all of this was removed and the surfaces are now painted a gold colour. It cannot yet be determined if the walls of the corridor were painted with figurative painting, as the entrance halls were.

Enigmatic Sculpture in Cross-Passages

Cross-passages leading from the exterior to the outer corridor admit light deep into the interior; a second set of cross-passages links the outer corridor to the inner. There are a total of forty passageways, each with two small niches on its sides. Some sculptures placed in these niches are of modern date while the majority belong to the ancient period, a handful on display at the museum. These are much smaller than the narrative reliefs in the outer corridors. About fifteen appear to be *jataka* scenes but arranged in no particular order and only tentatively identified by Luce. Others are episodes from the Buddha's biography, such as his death. Were these ancient images intended for these niches? Were they originally part of a distinct narrative sequeuce and did it relate to the other sculpture in the temple? These questions need more investigation.

Some of the sculptures within the cross-passages may represent jatakas *but many cannot be identified, such as this example, north side. (DS)*

Wooden Doorways.

Enormous double teak wood doorways from the late 18th century separate the entrance hall from the inner corridor. An English envoy to Burma in 1797 recorded that the Ananda had been "repaired and beautified by the present prince of Pagaan (sic)" and also added, "that the avenues to the inner cloister had great folding grated gates" (Cox, 415, 417). These "noble frames of timber" are supported by an iron ring at the top and a stone cup at the base (Yule, 38). The principal ornament is at the top, with two types of birds (north, east) and sets of horned deer (south, west). Similar doorways were probably added to the Shwegu-gyi at roughly the same time. The central section is latticed, with small gilded metal rosettes. Seated or squatting guardians are placed on the bottom, at the right.

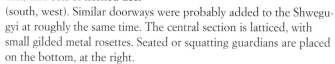

Eighteenth-century doorway, east. Detail.

Highlights in the Compound

Within the vast compound are several smaller shrines of interest. In the northwest corner is a open-air shrine known as the To-thwe-gyi (no. 2163) and inside is an exquisite, seated crowned Buddha from the ancient period, heavily gilded. Another small shrine in the compound, dating from the 18th century, contains a seated Buddha, flanked by two kneeling disciples resembling those inside the Ananda (no. 2168).

The largest is located on the south side, a temple known as the Tha-gya-kyi-hpaya (no. 2170), perhaps from the 14th century.

The Legacy of the Ananda

The Ananda has been under continuous worship since its founding nearly a thousand years ago. The temple is spoken of in the same breath as the celebrated King Kyanzittha, but definitive evidence linking the two is unlikely to be forthcoming. The enduring religious and cultural prestige of the Ananda is measured today by the numerous temples built throughout Burma that are loosely based on its groundplan and elevation.

The Ananda was also evoked in the mid-19th century royal Kyauk-taw-gyi temple on the south shore of the lake near Amarapura. This was not a true replica, since there are many fundamental differences. However, the four entrance halls are symmetrical, reproducing a cruciform plan, and the tower is reminiscent of the Ananda. The famous Mingun Pagoda, near Mandalay, also turned for inspiration to the Ananda, since its original conception included tiles whose subjects were based directly upon those of the Ananda.

Mara's demons with snakes issuing from their mouths. Tile made for the late 18th-century Mingun Pagoda modelled after ancient Pagan examples. Department of Archaeology, Mandalay. (DS)

ANANDA TEMPLE MONASTERY

Date: 1775-1786

Highlights

★ 18ᵗʰ century frescos
★ dated monastery, 1775-1786

This brick monastery belongs to a fresh wave of construction and refurbishing at Pagan in the late 18ᵗʰ century. The mural painting represents new trends in Burmese painting, such as a focus on scenes drawn from everyday life.

Visit

This monastery can be combined with the grand Ananda temple, since it is located only steps outside its compound wall, to one side of the north entrance. Its proximity to Pagan's most sacred shrine is probably no coincidence, and stupas and temples of the same period are clustered nearby. Its original name is unknown, but it is often called Ananda Ok Kyaung, or literally the Ananda Brick Monastery. There were wooden monasteries at Pagan from the same period but few examples survive. This brick monastery follows wooden examples to the degree that the ground floor is elevated and the entrance and rear are faced with wide staircases. A somewhat later brick monastery from the first half of the 19ᵗʰ century can be seen at Ava, known as the Maha Aungmye Bonzan Monastery, with an entirely different design.

Main entrance

No. 22

No. 3

No. 4

N

1 2 3 4 5   10m.

Ground plan of the Ananda Monastery.

A Half Million Bricks .... or Almost

Four long formal inscriptions record the dedication of the monastery. Two are on the front wall of the sanctum, one in Pali on the left and the other in Burmese, both prominently outlined. On the rear wall is the other pair, also in Pali and Burmese. The Pali text is mixed prose and verse, while the Burmese versions are solely in prose. The texts are similar and dated in the Burmese and Buddhist eras.

The phases of construction can be pieced together from these four inscriptions, together with one record inside the inner sanctum and one caption describing the donors. The monastery took ten years or slightly longer to complete. Ground breaking began on the full moon day of *Phussa* (December-January), 1775, the same day marking the culmination of the annual Ananda Temple festival. The actual building of the monastery was largely completed on the fourth day of the dark half of the month of *Phagguna* (August-September), 1779, and dedicated the next month. However, it was not until six years later, in 1785, that the monastery was completely finished, on the full moon day of June-July (*Asalha*), according to the latest date included in the formal inscriptions. The caption beneath the donor, on the front wall of the inner shrine, states that the brick work and plastering were finished in 1778, and

The Ananda Temple Monastery, rear, from roof terrace of the Ananda Temple.

The inscription enumerates the major expenses which totaled 3,950 ticals of silver.	
450,000 bricks	1,800 ticals
Carriers of red ochre and water	600
Master brick masons	600
1,500 viss of lime	150
1,500 viss of molasses	150
100 sheets of buffalo leather	50
Ten labourers	500
Master cement masons	600

that the *jatakas* and other wall painting were completed in 1786, a year later than the completion-date mentioned in the formal donative epigraphs. The painting therefore was done sometime between 1778 and 1786. It probably took months, rather than years, most likely between 1785-6, the last thing to be finished.

The donor was the Royal Archivist at Pagan who shared the merits with his parents, teachers, relatives, the "King who is Lord of the Earth and Water", the guardian gods of the Buddhist Community lasting 5,000 years, beings inhabiting the 31 planes of existence, and the god of Death ("Yama"). By his donation he hoped to attain nirvana (*nibbana*, Pali), to be reborn in the presence of the Buddha of the Future, Metteyya, and to become an enlightened being. These are among the same religious goals expressed in numerous ancient inscriptions from Pagan. He also hoped to have a complexion of gold and to have the sweet voice of a *karavika* bird (Tin Lwin).

The donor presented the monastery to the Venerable Mahathera Sudhammalankara, a 66 year old monk who was ordained for 40 years and who headed the Parupana sect at Pagan. The lower storey was for his use, and the upper was reserved for the benefit of the Buddhist community, or *sangha*. A twelve-line inscription inside the sanctum on the rear wall mentions the name of his teacher, the Mahathera Shin Gunasiri. The Parupana faction advocated that novices should cover both shoulders with the monastic robe when representing themselves before the laity, while a competing group maintained that it was proper to conceal only one shoulder. The issue was hotly contested for nearly a century until it was finally decided by King Bodawpaya (1782-1819) who ruled in favour of the two-shoulder faction. The Parupana evolved into the most influential Buddhist division in Burma, known today as the Thudhamma.

The Buddha severing his hair after leaving the palace. Stucco ornament above doorway.

The inscription on the rear wall inside the sanctum lists the names of three master masons, all brothers, another indication that craft occupations were hereditary. The single date in this epigraph mentions only the year in which the monastery was begun, 1775.

The monastery is described in the formal inscriptions as three-tiered, with four surrounding enclosures, three staircases, 18 doors and 37 cubit high. None of the epigraphs mention the reigning King Bodawpaya, whose capital was Amarapura, near Mandalay.

Exterior

On the wide terrace encircling the ground floor are small scenes in raised stucco above the doorways, many with inscriptions. These reliefs depict the Buddha's life in the palace and his departure from luxury and family, poignant themes for monks. Above the central door is the Buddha's groom shown carrying the trappings belonging to the dejected horse taking up the rear, all identified in the incised cartouche. To the right of the doorway is the Buddha leaving the palace on his horse, and on the left is the Buddha cutting his hair, after his departure from the palace. Each entrance is associated with a specific completion date, recorded in an incised inscription on each doorway. The central one was finished on the auspicious full moon, while the flanking pair were completed on the waxing and waning of the same month, in 1782. These stucco figures were probably among the last things finished on the exterior of the building, but the interior murals were not completed until four more years.

On the other side wall the spaces above the doors contain animals, birds and figures, probably representing *jatakas* which await identification. The rear wall is devoted to the first three of the Four Sights prompting the Buddha's departure from the palace (an old man, a sick man and a corpse). The other side wall has the following: the sage (last of the Four Sights), the Buddha's horse, and the Buddha leaving his wife and son.

Ancient motifs continue into the 18th century, such as kirtimukha *faces. Outer wall of shrine.*

The Buddha's dejected horse and groom return to the palace. The groom carries the horse's trappings. Dated by an adjacent, incised inscription to 1782. (DS)

The Frescos

The frescos differ greatly from the earlier, ancient Pagan painting, both in style and content. The palette is richer and the style far bolder and more spontaneous. Compositions are generally larger and are also not restricted to separate frames but rather flow into one another. The painting was probably the last work to be completed, finished in 1786, according to the caption on the front of the sanctum wall. Scores, if not hundreds, of 18th and 19th century shrines with painting survive at Pagan and in upper Burma, but this work ranks among the finest, together with the painting in Pagan's Upali Thein ordination hall.

Mount Meru in the inner sanctum. (PP)

In the 18th century, artists and patrons felt under no obligation to depict the entire series of 547 *jatakas*, as was true in the ancient period. The *jatakas* at this monastery begin with the first in the series and perhaps conclude with no. 27. At least half are now missing due to their condition. A few of the tales are well-known today in Burma, and from one evolved the popular maxim, "You can get rich from selling a mouse."

Couple embracing, inner sanctum. (DS)

The Central Sanctum

Inside the sanctum in the centre of the rear wall is a depiction of Mount Meru surrounded by seven mountain ranges or continents, each represented by pillar-like forms. Two roundels contain a hare and a peacock, symbols of the moon and sun, respectively. In this cosmology the world we inhabit is the southern-island or Jambudipa (Pali). Depictions of Mount Meru are as old as the ancient Pagan period, and the best known example is at the Loka-hteikpan temple. Large mythical animals cover much of the interior surface, two large Garuda birds, or *galons* (Burmese), a *kinnara* and *kinnari* (birds with human heads, male and female, respectively), and two dragons. These creatures may be directly associated with Mount Meru, since manuscript painting from this time also includes their depictions, apart from the dragons (Herbert,

Garuda inside the sanctum. (PP)

2002). The artists could not resist a racy whimsical touch, even within the central sanctum. A couple embrace, one with a hand on the other's breast. A caption below on the right leaves no doubt about the subject, "Oh snatching breasts, disgraceful." This engaging scene is visible on the left wall, in one corner, as we enter.

A single-line inscription near the base of this wall contains an enigmatic riddle whose answer contains the date of the temple: "Young people in the eastern part of the household come to carry water, like a beauty contest, but everyone looks the same. That is the date." Above this inscription is a domestic scene, with several young nude girls. Perhaps the designers felt that the elderly monk would do well to contemplate such an enigma, together with these titillating illustrations.

Outer Wall of Sanctum

Outside the sanctum door on the far left is a depiction of the monastery itself and the donors, visible behind the modern metal grate. The inscription below summarizes the salient details of the longer donative texts but adds that the donors

Ceiling ornament. Interlocking circles and floral motifs are reminiscent of ancient designs.

and family (mother, father, son and daughter) arrive at the monastery. At the top of the monastery stairs stands a monk, ready to receive them. The family is placed within a mountainous setting, facing the monastery. The daughter brings up the rear, bearing a lacquer object on her head. Such a depiction of contemporary events, even if they did not occur in reality, was unthinkable in ancient Pagan and represents new thinking about the place of art in society.

Much of this front wall is taken up with battle scenes, and a newly read inscription suggests that they belong to the Bojajaniya Jataka (no. 23) in which the Buddha-to-be appears as a horse to defend the ruler of Varanasi against seven attacking kingdoms.

The outer sanctum wall on the left (east) is devoted to the ascetic Sumedha who is told by the Buddha Dipankara that he will be reborn as Gotama Buddha. The climax of the story is in the middle of the wall, between the two small windows, where Sumedha prostrates himself before Dipankara, spread over a puddle to keep Dipankara's progress dry. It concludes with Sumedha's meditation beneath a tree, next to his monastery, on the far left.

The rear wall features the last and most revered *jataka* (no. 547), the tale of Prince Vessantara who gives up his kingdom and family. Much is damaged but we can make out a number of protagonists, such as the royal white elephant, and the wicked brahmin sleeping in a tree with deities below protecting the children.

The other side wall features two *jatakas* where the bodhisattva takes the form of a deer. In the southwest corner is the Tipallattahta-miga Jataka (no. 16), and in the northwest the Kharadiya Jataka (no.15).

Jataka 3, the Serivanija.

Detail from Jataka 3 showing the Buddha-to-be with gold pot.

Detail from Jataka 3.

The Corridor (Outer wall)

The corridor is devoted entirely to *jatakas* in two horizontal registers, interrupted only by the small windows and the median doorways. The murals begin with the first *jataka* and probably conclude with no. 27. The top register containing eleven *jatakas* is in good condition but the bottom panels are badly weathered. Rather full descriptions of the action are given in the ink glosses written in Burmese in the thin registers beneath the murals.

The *jatakas* are ordered in their basic sequence in two parallel registers on each wall, begining at the bottom, and proceed in a clockwise direction around the main shrine. They begin not at the entrance but on the side wall, on the left. On the first wall (east), the two *jatakas* on the bottom were almost certainly nos. 1 and 2 (no longer visible). The top register contains first no. 3 (Serivanija) and no. 4 (Cullakasetthi). The top register of the rear wall is devoted to no. 7 (Katthahari) and ends with no. 8 (Gamani). The bottom register of the rear wall likely contained at least nos. 5 and 6.

The bottom register on the last side wall (west) probably contained a number of *jatakas*, perhaps beginning with no. 9. The painters were perhaps short of space on this wall, since they choose to jump over to the exterior of the shrine wall to place *jatakas* 15 and 16. Back on the corridor wall (west) begins no. 19 (Ayacitabhatta) and proceeds with nos. 20 (Nalapanna), 21 (Kurunga) and 22 (Kukkura). The front wall (north) begins with no. 25 (Tittha), followed by no. 26 (Mahila-Mukha) and possible no. 27 (Abhinha), to conclude the series. All of the depictions are confined to a single wall, apart from the Cullakasetthi *jataka* that starts on a side wall and partly wraps around onto the rear wall. The ceiling of each corridor is ornamented differently.

Three *jatakas* in particular are easy to discern on the side walls.

Left Wall (east)

The Serivanija (no. 3)

Unfolding on the left wall as we enter the interior is the *jataka* about the Buddha-to-be and his wicked cousin, Devadatta, who were competing travelling merchants. Devadatta first meets an old woman who is keen to trade an old bowl for a trinket for her grand-daughter. Devadatta realizes that the bowl is made of gold but tells her that it is worthless, planning to return later to get it for a song. The Buddha-to-be also recognizes the bowl's real worth and gives the old lady his entire stock of trinkets. He is shown at the bow of the boat, holding aloft the bowl, while Devadatta expires by the edge of the river, angry and disconsolate about the loss of the bowl. This *jataka* is popular among theatregoers. The role of Devadatta was immortalized in the 1970s by the actor Shwe Man Tin Maung.

Cullakasethi (no. 4)

This tale begins immediately to the right of the previous one and takes up the entire right half of the wall, and even extends partly on to the rear wall. The Buddha-to-be saw a dead mouse on the road, prompting him to say aloud, "Any smart fellow could pick this mouse up and make a fortune." He was overheard by a young man who sold the dead mouse to a tavern-owner to feed his cat. One

investment led to another, including selling fuel to a potter whose kiln workers are depicted. He also negotiated with a sea trader, whose ship we see on the right. Now a tycoon, he visits the Buddha-to-be who presents his daughter to him in marriage.

Above and below: Details of foreign ship and potters from Jataka 4.

Right Wall (west)

Kukkura (no. 22)

One *jataka* on the opposite side wall (west) tells the story of a king of Varanasi who goes on a dog-killing spree after the leather fittings on his horse carriage were eaten by a dog. The Buddha-to-be is a dog who convinces the king that it was his own dog that destroyed the leather. To prove his point he asks the king to feed his dog grass, whereupon the royal dog vomits to reveal the leather trappings. The king recognizes his error in punishing all dogs for the mistakes of one. In a pavilion on the far right are three dogs, the one at the end is likely the Buddha-to-be.

King's men slaughtering dogs suspected of eating the leather fittings of the horse carriage. From Jataka 22. *(PP)*

THARABA GATE AND WALL

Highlights

★ only surviving gateway to
ancient city

★ brother-sister nat shrines

Date: 11th-12th centuries

Visit

The Tharaba Gate is the only formal entrance to the Walled City today, but there were likely others. The upper parts of the gate are missing completely, but traces of the barrel vault once covering the wide passage can still be seen.

Stucco survives on the outer side of the gate, in patches above the box-like shrine on the right. Familiar patterns used on temple walls are found, such as the *kirtimukha* frieze and the inverted V-shaped motif. The work lacks the robustness found at the Kubyauk-gyi temple, dated to 1113, but it is hard to date this stucco with much precision.

Two brick shrines were added to the front of the gate, probably in the 18th or early 19th centuries, designed to house two *nat* figures. On the right is the *nat* named Hnama daw (sister) and on the left is Maung daw (brother).

These two shrines are the focus for novitiate ceremonies when young boys at Pagan enter the monastery for a short period. They are brought to the gate by their parents early in the morning with the rising sun. Later on the same day a full-fledged monk shaves the head of the boy. For girls, an ear-piercing ritual occurs.

Exterior of Tharaba Gate, nat shrines from the late 18th or early 19th century on either side.

Other openings to the brick city walls can be seen, but no parts of the gates can be detected, nor can we even be sure if these breaches were original entrances. Three can be seen on the east and south sides, and one on the north. The wall bordering the river was washed away completely. The walls probably date between the 11th and mid-13th centuries, based on radiocarbon dates and the stucco ornament still adhering to the Tharaba gate (Grave, Barbetti).

A low moat roughly 60 metres wide still encircles the walls. Water, pumped from the river, fills part of the moat near the gate. The only paved road within the Walled City passes between the Tharaba gate and a crude gap in the wall near the museum. This road was probably a major artery leading from north to south, for centuries.

Above right: Sister nat.

Middle: Local children on the morning of their tonsure and ear-boring ceremonies.

Lower: Ancient stucco ornament adhering to outer side of gateway.

Above: Brother nat.

PITAKAT-TAIK

Highlights

★ early Pagan temple renovated in the 18th century

★ early stone windows

Date: ancient Pagan period, renovated 1784

The Pitakat-taik is a building from the early Pagan era whose appearance was completely altered in the late 18th century. The king most active in the city's later rebuilding was Bodawpaya (1782-1819) whose capital was Amarapura, near modern Mandalay. A document associates the refurbishment of this monument to 1784.

Visit

This Pitakat-taik is located within the Walled City, beside a motorable dirt path leading from the main paved road near the Tharaba Gate.

The function of the Pitakat-taik in the Konbaung period (1752-1885) is uncertain, but it is usually identified as a library, or repository for palm-leaf manuscripts. Some have even speculated that it preserved the Pali canon captured from the Mon in Lower Burma in the 11th century, but this is impossible to confirm.

The original, underlying structure belonged to the ancient Pagan period, but its exterior was transformed completely in the refurbishing. Its ancient plan is based on a square, hollow sanctum covered by a cloister vault and encircled by a vaulted corridor. It

The Pitaka-taik is an ancient temple completely renovated in the late 18th century. The original entrance hall replaced by narrow verandah.

likely had a separate entrance hall, now replaced by a long verandah reached by three wide staircases.

Over 80% of the temple's stucco ornamentation survives in good condition, especially on the façade and within the sloping roofs. The stylized peacock in the centre of each terrace, with its abbreviated chest and head, is a hallmark of later Burmese architecture and is never found in the ancient Pagan period.

Left: 18th-century stucco ornament still survives on stairways.

Abstract peacock design on the roof terrace.

Refurbishment and the Windows

The way in which the later builders changed the exterior walls is difficult to assess, but nine perforated stone windows date to the ancient period. Some were probably salvaged from ruinous temples nearby, while one or more may have belonged to the original structure. The re-use of these centuries-old stone pieces underscores the fact that most of the temples at Pagan were in ruins, which was also true until the early 1990s. The smaller windows likely belonged to ancient monasteries.

Stone window, probably from an ancient monastery, reused in the 18th century.

An English envoy to Burma in 1795, Michael Symes, records visiting a libary at Pagan, and some scholars have identified the Pitakat-taik with his description (Symes, 383). He mentions, however, that the entire building was surrounded by a verandah and that he spotted 50 large manuscript chests through the window, an amount that would fit only uncomfortably in the interior.

Building from the Konbaung period and the reign of Bodawpaya is well represented at Pagan, such as the Upali Thein and the Ananda Temple Monastery. Bodawpaya made a pilgrimage to Pagan at least once, dedicating a gold finial at the Shwe-zigon and taking possession of a white elephant that had been captured in Lower Burma. One of his queens also made a donation at the Thatbyinnyu, recorded in a long painted inscription in the temple's corridor.

SHWEGU-GYI

Highlights

★ commanding views of temples
   within the Walled City

★ 18th–19th-century wooden doors

★ dated temple, 1131

Date: 1131

The Shwegu-gyi affords excellent views of the major monuments within the city walls. The time it took to build was a mere seven and half months, important evidence for estimating construction times at Pagan. The dramatic interior illumination heralds experiments developed in the second half of the 12th century. It also is the first dated temple at Pagan to be designed without stone sculpture, an important trend. It was extensively refurbished sometime during the late 18th or 19th century when its original frescos were whitewashed. Its interior stucco work ranks among the best at Pagan.

Visit

The temple is located in the heart of the Walled City, to the south of the paved road leading from the Tharaba Gate. This and the Pahto-thamya are now the only temples inside the city walls with access to the upper terraces.

History and Inscription

The temple was built by King Alaungsithu who, in 1131 succeeded his grandfather the great Kyanzittha, said to be responsible for the Ananda. His donation is recorded on two slabs set into the wall of the sanctum, facing the central image, but this may not be their original location. The temple was begun on April 19, 1131, and

Gods on temple plinth, rear. Brick and plaster.

This temple was completed in only seven and half months, according to an inscription. Entrance hall on the right.

finished on December 16, 1131. This information proves that this medium sized temple required only seven and a half months to finish.

The inscription is a poem of a hundred Pali verses and records the king's command: "Make a pleasing lovely room, a fragrant chamber [*gandhakuti*, Pali] for the mighty Seer, Gotama Buddha." It is the only inscription at Pagan dated to the Shaka era, a system of reckoning years started in early India. It was rarely used in north India by the time of the Pagan period but was more common in south India.

A lengthy painted inscription to the right of the central Buddha is undated but probably belongs to the late 18th or early 19th century. It is entirely in Pali and mentions that the temple was built by Alaungsithu and includes the name "Pugaramapura", or the City of Pagan. Another ink inscription inside is dated to January 23, 1771, and records that the entire temple was refurbished (Than Tun, 1996). This work likely included the wooden doors, the crude chapels on the sides of the sanctum, and the first whitewashing of the interior walls.

This royal temple points north, another indication that directional orientation was never a hard and fast rule at Pagan, at least in the early period. Modern excavations of brick mounds in front of the temple are conjecturally associated with Kyanzittha's palace.

Exterior

At the rear of the temple was once a glorious row of gods beaming down from the top of the tall foundation wall. Only an handful of these seated, crowned figures survive today, their hands clasped together in homage, but more than fifty were intact as recently as the 1950s. These impressive figures once encircled the building, accented by rounded crenellations, some still filled with green glazed tiles, with a register of bold lotus leaves.

The stucco work on the exterior has been renovated, but original bits and pieces can be seen. At the base of many of the doorways are matching niches intended for seated male figures, built of brick and covered with stucco, a feature at the Ananda Temple and other later temples, such as the Sulamani and Dhammayan-gyi.

Each of the entrances has enormous teak double-doorways possibly dating from refurbishment of 1771. The pair facing the shrine has fanciful lions at the top while the others have birds holding stalks in their beaks (see page 132). These door are likely from the same period as the even larger examples in the Ananda.

Entrance hall

The façade of the entrance hall is framed by restored double-arch pediments. The doorway inside leading to the central sanctum was entirely renewed. In one corner is a short dated stone inscription of King Bayinnaung (1551-1581) from when he was in Pagan raising a *hti* at the Shwe-zigon stupa. The inscription was brought from somewhere else and relates to land taxes.

Interior

The sanctum interior is dominated by a Buddha seated on a high base within a huge niche formed from the central core. The plan departs from the norm, since the architects made the space facing the Buddha much wider than the side and rear corridors. Also, the enormous vault in front of the principal image springs low, rising steeply near the floor. These devices create the feeling of a separate, spacious area rather than a narrow corridor surrounding the sanctum. In addition, the Buddha figure protrudes into the hall, allowing the worshipper closer access to the seated image than if it were deeper inside the niche. This unusual interior space may be appreciated by standing in any corner of the shrine.

The interior is well lit, with nine doors and windows. Two small square openings placed high on the wall of the shrine near the Buddha's head shed additional light. This bright, open interior contrasts to the dark inner sanctums of many temples at Pagan, such as the Kubyauk-gyi in Myinkaba, built in 1113, only 18 years earlier. The addition of side and rear doorways marks the direction in which Pagan builders were moving.

Opposite: Restored seated Buddha in niche. The interior is flooded with light issuing from doorways and windows, unlike many dimly lit early Pagan temples.

Outstanding stucco work with traces of original paint frames the niche on the rear wall.

A fanciful crocodile, or makara, *enlivens the cusped arch. This stucco can be dated to 1131.*

Wooden doors were probably part of the refurbishment of the Shwegu-gyi in 1771 and resemble those inside the Ananda Temple.

The Shwegu-gyi is the earliest dated temple to show this important feature. Each wall is also pierced by multiple windows, a feature that virtually disappears among later temples, such as the Nandamannya.

There was also no stone sculpture planned for the interior, another major departure from earlier practices in such temples as the Ananda, Nagayon and many others. This begins a trend at Pagan, and by later in the 12th century few temples were designed with stone images.

The inside was extensively refurbished in the late 18th century. Traces of the original 12th-century fresco can be picked out with difficulty beneath the later whitewash, such as parallel rows of seated Buddhas.

The rear of the sanctum wall still preserves its original niche, however, a tour de force of ancient stucco work, with faint traces of original painting. Note the unusual frieze of *kirtimukhas* and suspended garlands encircling the base of the outer sanctum wall.

The Roof Terraces

A staircase in the entrance hall leads to the upper terrraces. The tower has been restored recently, but the two lower terraces retain rows of original square green glazed tiles alternating with stucco lotus medallions. This is the first dated use of glazed ceramics at Pagan. Much re-plastering in modern times has occurred, but some original ornament survives on the small corner shrines.

Exterior niches with seated figures are also found at the Ananda and were also used in later temples, such as the Sulamani, 1183. Brick, covered with plaster. Restored.

The earliest dated glazed ceramics in Burma, 1131. The square green insets alternate with stucco lotus medallions. (DS)

PAHTO-THAMYA

Date: 11th-12th centuries

This temple within the city walls is among the earliest at Pagan, dating to the the late 11th or early 12th centuries. It features some of the finest of the city's early painting.

Visit
The Pahto-thamya can be approached from either a dirt road leading from the museum or on the same road leading from the Thatbyinnyu. The watchman living at the side has the key to the temple which is opened more than it is locked. Sadly it has fallen into neglect but is of tremendous importance for early Pagan.

No inscriptions tell us when the temple was created, but it may have been built sometime before the city's first dated temple, the Kubyauk-gyi in Myinkaba, 1113. The ink inscriptions are all in Mon, an indication of an early date. Its modern name means "The Temple with Many Children". The same name appears in the *Glass Palace Chronicle* where it is attributed to a king whose reign is too early for its likely date.

The huge central brick Buddha inside the sanctum, from opening in corridor. Its base and much surrounding stucco are largely original.

The dramatic outline of the temple is best appreciated at a distance, from one of the sides. The bulbous dome is divided into twelve vertical sections by raised foliated ribs. These segments continue uninterrupted into the umbrella-spire that was faithfully restored following the last earthquake. Each umbrella ring is clearly articulated, unlike other more common examples where the rings merge closely together and lose their individuality. These rings and the bands relate directly to similar motifs found on small stone stupas from eastern India. A hemispherical dome with twelve ribs is found in one 13th-century stupa (no. 394), but this is rare.

The rigorously plain wall surface is unusual, compared to other early temples, such as the Nagayon and the flamboyant Kubyauk-gyi (Myinkaba). For example, the brick windows are framed by simple unadorned surrounds, with no elaborate pediments. The simplicity of the walls, however, contrasts with the crennelated lower terrace and a continuous row of miniature vases set within a baluster. There are also no rows of header bricks or stones visible in the walls, perhaps another indication of its early date, but this has not yet been fully researched.

Entrance Hall

The large pediment above the east-facing entrance has been replaced, but immediately above the arched doorway are two wooden beams once concealed in the brick fabric. (Wooden lintels set into the deep window openings are seen inside).

The poorly preserved frescos in the entrance hall depict seven rows of individual seated Buddhas with various hand-gestures and attended by disciples. None of these have ink glosses. The ceiling reveals traces of painted roundels.

A 22-line ink inscription on the rear wall is placed over one of two original standing figures that once flanked the entrance. The long text is in Pali and Burmese and perhaps records a repair to the main image. Beneath this is an inscription in red dated to 1668.

Inner Sanctum

The square inner shrine is illuminated by light from the entrance hall, two windows on the sides and from three skylights set into the roof terraces. The large central Buddha was restored a number of times, but the base is untouched. The two seated flanking Buddhas have recently been completely renovated. The main image was framed by a massive throne, portions of which come to life with the aid of a torch. This arrangement of three Buddhas within a sanctum is rare at Pagan (see temples nos. 320, 1081, 1148).

The single stone Buddha within a niche on the east wall is now one of the few original sculptures that can be appreciated in its intended setting. This sculpture conveys the best of Pagan's

The spire toppled in the 1975 quake but was faithfully restored, in 1976 and 1984. Twelve-sided dome with vertical bands is unusual. Side view, from south. (DS)

Original stone Buddha in the earth-touching gesture, inside the sanctum.

sculptural style at the end of the eleventh and the beginning of the 12th centuries and resembles the dated sculpture from the Kubyauk-gyi (Myinkaba), 1113. (The image on the opposite wall was recently removed to the museum for safekeeping.) The long niches on the north and south sides of the walls were perhaps reserved for recumbent images depicting the Dream of Maya and the Death of the Buddha. Other niches indicate the outlines of standing figures.

The massive arch framing the entrance to the sanctum is a tour de force in conception and execution. Comparable arches and pediments are found on the other three sides of the sanctum, each ornamented with a tower topped with a stupa ending in a small bulbous finial.

The wide passage leading to the sanctum was once covered with murals. Intrusive painting with Burmese captions can be made out with difficulty. On the right is a seated Buddha, identified as "Gotamahpaya", (or Lord Buddha). To the side is a kneeling figure holding a floral ornament, beneath which is a short inscription mentioning a royal or noble donation ("Min . . . . kaungmhu"). On the left side is a five-line inscription refering to another donation. It refers to *nats* (spirits) and a tree-spirit ("*yokka*"), or *yakkha* (Pali). The same kneeling figure holding a floral offering occurs also. He wears a long tapered hat often associated with hermits, or *yathe* (Burmese), and the term hermit appears in the inscription. These additions probably date to between the 14th-16th centuries and closely resemble intrusive compositions at the Abeyadana, also in the corridor leading to the shrine.

The Frescos

Both sides of the inner corridor and inside the sanctum are filled with murals whose subjects are drawn from a wide range of Pali sources. There are no Mahayana elements, as at some other early temples, such as the Abeyadana.

Roughly sixty percent of the painting has survived but most in poor condition. Luce and his colleague Col. Ba Shin painstakingly deciphered hundreds of Mon ink inscriptions and identified most of the compositions. Only a few panels, along the south wall have been completely cleaned, but they suggest the once brilliant colours. Other segments have been recently cleaned, revealing new compositions unavailable to Luce and Ba Shin. The large panels focus on the life of the Buddha, beginning from his birth and ending with his death.

The frescos start on the outer wall of the corridor, immediately to the left of the shrine entrance, and proceed clockwise. These start with the Buddha's conception and end with the Buddha seated beneath the Bodhi tree. The narrative then jumps from the outer wall of the corridor to the inner wall, beginning immediately to the left of the shrine doorway and proceeding clockwise entirely around the sanctum. The story appears to continue inside the shrine.

The original plan of the temple probably included stone images on the outer wall of the sanctum, suggested by six niches that were bricked up on the rear wall. It is unknown why the design was changed, but it created a nearly continous surface for mural painting.

Stucco vase belonging to the Buddha's throne.

Outer wall of Corridor

The narrative painting begins immediately to the left of the entrance, on the east face. There are a total of twenty-four panels, each over a metre in height, but only four or five can be made out readily. Where niches and windows do not interrupt the wall, the panels are over two metres long. The first three panels were too fragmentary for Luce to read but probably were devoted to scenes prior to the Buddha's actual birth.

The only restored panels are limited to the adjacent side wall, in the south corridor. Here the first scene is the Birth of the Buddha, followed by the prediction of the sage Kaladevala who visits the infant. The Mon inscription translates: "This is when the hermit Kaladevala worships the lord Bodhisattva and prophesies that he will become a Buddha." It makes an interesting contrast with the same scene at the Ananda, where the infant Buddha places his feet on the head of the ascetic, conforming exactly to the passage in the *Nidanakatha*.

The neighbouring scene depicts the inspection of the Buddha by brahmins, assigned to detect any auspicious signs. The caption at the bottom reads: "This is when the hundred and eight brahmins look at the auspicious marks of the lord Bodhisattva." The small child wears a crown and is marked with a halo. The brahmins are positioned in front of him, while behind him are four court ladies. The multi-storied pavilion in which the action takes place likely reflects the wooden architecture of the day at Pagan.

Other easily readable scenes are on the opposite side of the sanctum, on the north wall. At the beginning, on the left, we find the Buddha mounted upon his horse. The caption states: "This is when the Reverend One mounts his horse . . . . all the *devas* [gods] show

Top: The Buddha departing on his horse, outer wall, corridor, north. (DS)

Above: The Buddha severing his hair, outer wall, corridor, north. (DS)

The infant Buddha, held by his father, inspected by brahmins for auspicious signs. Outer wall of corridor.

their approval." Next is the Buddha severing his headdress before his renunciation of the world. The last three of the twenty-four episodes ends on the east wall. No glosses survive, but Luce felt that the last three scenes were likely the following: the offering of milk-rice by Sujata, the casting of the bowl into the river, and an event connected to the Bodhi tree.

Above this wide narrative band are four parallel rows of seated Buddhas, with hands in the teaching and earth-touching gestures. A partially cleaned segment is found in the southwestern corner.

The Death of the Buddha, right of shrine door, inner wall of corridor. (DS)

Plain treatment of walls contrast to the flamboyant stucco ornament of roof terraces. Patho-thamya. South side. (DS)

Inner Wall of Corridor

The narrative skips across the outer corridor and begins immediately to the left of the shrine doorway. Each side wall has eight panels, while the rear has six, each divided by a painted pillar. The sequence starts with the theme of the Seven Weeks at Bodh Gaya. It was probably drawn from the Pali *Nidanakatha*, or sources closely modelled on it.

It begins with the Enlightenment beneath the Bodhi tree, representing the first week. In the same week to prove himself to the doubting gods he rose into the air and replicated himself. This is represented by the seated Buddha, with his hands in the teaching-gesture, surrounded by four other figures. The second week concerns the Buddha standing, gazing at the Bodhi tree without blinking, a sign of his supra-normal powers. For the third week the Buddha walks to and from on a Jewelled Walkway; the standing Buddha is shielded by an umbrella held by the god Brahma, an uncommon addition and one not mentioned in the *Nidanakatha*. The remaining four weeks are depicted on the south side of the sanctum, beginning with the Buddha preaching the *Abhidamma* inside a Jewelled House. The next shows the Buddha tempted by the Daughters of Mara. The demon himself is dressed regally and is shown with a number of young women. The next panel features the the snake-king Muchalinda shielding the Buddha with his hoods from a storm. The last week is heavily abraded but should be the gift of the four-bowls by the "world-guardians" (see two figures to the right of the Buddha, with bowls) and likley includes the two merchants who receive strands of the Buddha's hair (see the figure on the lower right).

The theme of the Seven Weeks was important in ancient Pagan and common too in the Konbaung period. This example at the Pahto-thamya is unusual, since it includes the episode of the Buddha's replication after the Enlightenment. It is included in the *Nidanakatha* in the sequence we find at the Pahto-thamya, but is rarely represented as part of the Seven Weeks elsewhere. The Seven Weeks was known in Mahayana literature but was always more important in Theravada societies, such as in Thailand and Sri Lanka.

The other panels surrounding the wall cannot be identified, but there are 18 seated Buddhas encircling the shrine, some in the teaching-gesture and others in the earth-touching. Some are inside pavilions, while others sit below cusped arches, surrounded by different trees. One is holding a bowl. Two standing Buddhas appear at the beginning and end of the north wall. The last panel, to the right of the sanctum door, features the Death of the Buddha, recumbent with disciples. A similar scene, in brick and stucco, occupied this

Buddha in roof terrace shrine.

identical position in the Abeyadana. Luce did not suggest a meaning for these Buddhas, but perhaps they can be linked to important episodes following his departure from Bodh Gaya.

Above these tall narrative panels are four parallel rows of seated Buddhas, shown in either the teaching or earth-touching gesture. Four more rows appear on the outer wall of the corridor, and are also similar to those found in the entrance hall.

The story of the Buddha's life continues inside the sanctum, on the right wall, next to the seated Buddha on the right. Luce was able to make out at least ten episodes concerning the Buddha's early travelling ministrations, beginning with the First Sermon at the Deer Park and ending with his return to Kapilavastu. This register proceeds around the sanctum in a clockwise direction, but it is difficult to make out now. More life-scenes in sequential order are presented above this register, but beginning above the Buddha on the right side and continuing on the north wall. Dozens of other scenes identified by Mon captions are located high on the walls, all drawn from the Pali canon. Also, high within the shrine was a horizontal register depicting all 28 Buddhas, the surviving single caption devoted to the Buddha Padumuttara, found above the entrance. Beneath that register were dozens of panels illustrating the "sayings" of the Buddha, or *suttas*, from the Pali canon, also set out in a clockwise fashion beginning in the northeast corner, according to Luce.

Buddha in teaching-gesture, outer wall of sanctum. (DS)

Upper Terraces

A stairway in the entrance hall leads to the upper terraces. One or two of the single Buddhas in the four roof shrines have been partially restored, but some are untouched, permitting a close examination of how each figure is built up entirely of cut brick and covered with stucco. The waist for example is made up of two projecting curved bricks that are at the same time secured into the fabric of the wall. Inside the fingers, wrists and ears were often long, thin flat metal strips around which, the stucco was formed, like an armature.

NGA-KYWE-NADAUNG

Highlights

★ rare glazed stupa

Detail showing remains of the green glazed bricks which once covered the entire stupa.

The stupa's top was missing for centuries but was restored conjecturally in the 1990s (see opposite). Metal bands around the stupa were installed following the 1975 quake. (DS)

Date: c. 11th-12th centuries

This unusual glazed stupa lies in the heart of the Walled City, just beside the dirt road linking the Nat-hlaung-kyaung Hindu temple and the Pahto-thamya temple. Stupas covered completely in glazed bricks are rare at Pagan, with only one other surviving example, the Sintzedi (no. 377). The Sintzedi stupa is somewhat larger and has two high square concentric basement terraces once covered in stucco. The original base of the Nga-kywe-nadaung is missing but may have been circular or square.

The entire crowning section had disappeared by the early 20th century, and its replacement is totally conjectural. An unevenly shaped cavity exceeding a metre was discovered at the top that was likely caused by early treasure hunters. The earthquake in 1975 produced severe cracking and the steel rings encircling the stupa today were added in 1981.

This familiar green glaze is found throughout Pagan's ceramic ware. Each of the exterior bricks is made from a curved mould and then fired with a glaze. Since the shape of the dome is uneven the curvature of the brick moulds for the different layers required precise calculation. The earliest dated green glazed ceramics occurs at the Shwegu-gyi temple, dedicated in 1131, but its use certainly started earlier.

Bulbous stupas like this are not uncommon at Pagan, but the genesis of its shape cannot easily be traced. Some scholars argued that the stupa was connected to a 10th-century king mentioned in the *Glass Palace Chronicle,* but Luce rightly debunked this.

NAT-HLAUNG-KYAUNG

Date: c. 11th-12th centuries

This temple is the only surviving shrine dedicated to Hindu worship at Pagan. If it was constructed for an Indian community or whether it was patronized by Pagan's Buddhists is debated, but Hinduism undoubtedly played an influential role in court life. It governed secular rites, such as coronations and palace consecrations, while Buddhism advocated the renunciation of worldly ties. Hinduism was, and remains important in neighbouring Theravada countries, such as in modern Thailand where the state symbol is the mythical Garuda bird associated with Vishnu.

Vishnu was especially important at Pagan, at least for king Kyanzittha. Brahmin priests invoked this god as they consecrated wooden posts at the dedication of his palace. This Pagan ruler also traced his spiritual descent from Vishnu and the deity Rama who is considered one of Vishnu's manifestations.

Hindu temple in foreground, glazed Nga-Kywe-Nadaung to right, Patho-thamya in rear. From roof terrace of the Thatbyinnyu. Irrawaddy in distance. (John Listopad)

Visit

This temple lies between the towering Thatbyinnyu and the Pahto-thamya, in the heart of the Walled City. It was originally much grander, losing long ago its entire outer wall that once encompassed

the sanctum we see exposed today. Its plan was unusual, since it was designed with two concentric inner corridors, similar to the Ananda. Where the missing outer corridor vaults once sprung from the wall can be seen in the surviving rows of brick placed at an oblique angle high on the temple wall outside. A wide entrance hall would have extended beyond the modern brick platform.

Above left: Central sanctum after restoration.

Above right: Vishnu upon Garuda. Once in Berlin, captured by Russian troops in 1945 and now missing. H. 120 cm. (Courtesy Museum für Indische Kunst)

Stone sculpture – The Avataras of Vishnu

Small stone sculptures set into niches on the exterior depict the manifestations, or *avataras* (Sanskrit), of Vishnu. All of the niches are filled, save for three on the façade. The most well known figures are Krishna and Rama, hero of the *Ramayana*. The *avataras* often number ten in Hindu texts, a figure that even included the Buddha. There is a total of six *avataras* in this Pagan temple, but only five can be safely identified; the three empty niches on the front of the temple perhaps held additional ones.

On the north wall in the first niche on the left is the deity Balarama, the brother of Krishna, identified by his plough resting on his left shoulder. The last sculpture on this same wall is Rama, with his bow. The first figure of the rear wall is too damaged to identify but the second sculpture is Vamana, the drawf-*avatara*, with a staff and a tiny jar suspended from his right arm. The south wall begins

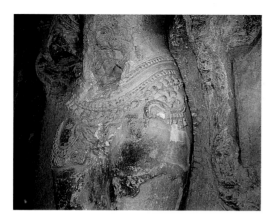

Vishnu, waist ornament before destruction on the sanctum wall. (DS)

with Narasimha, the man-lion *avatara*, shown disembowelling a demon strung across his waist. The last *avatara* is the two-legged boar Varaha, shown with the tiny earth goddess grasping his tusk as he rescues her from a cosmic flood. On the facade the single surviving sculpture is probably the Hindu sun deity Surya, recognized by two upheld lotuses.

Sanctum

A heavy stone threshold and matching jambs form the entrance way; the stone lintel was replaced long ago. Inside is a large, solid, square brick core dominated by a wide vertical niche featuring Vishnu sleeping upon the serpent. The original brick and stucco composition has now been entirely replaced by one in concrete. The original entwined tails of the serpents are still visible, on the right side within the niche.

In Hindu mythology Vishnu lies dormant upon his serpent in the cosmic ocean, awaiting the god Brahma to arouse him from within. Brahma disturbs Vishnu's slumber and then emerges from the god's navel and the universe comes into existence. The single figure of Brahma is usually shown seated upon a lotus whose stem connects to Vishnu's navel. This myth and its representation was popular among the Khmer in Cambodia and in India. In this example at Pagan, however, not one but three major Hindu deities appear on separate lotuses, Brahma, Vishnu and Shiva, from left to right, respectively. This peculiar rendition is found at Pagan only one other time, on a stone image, now in the museum, found loose in a minor temple (no. 1612). The same theme is seen on a handful of other small sculptures from lower Burma, in Mon country. If this odd depiction of Vishnu began at Pagan and spread to Lower Burma or whether it came to Pagan from the Mon remains unclear. There are also examples at Shri Kshetra, but they are likely of Pagan period date.

Shiva, displayed in old Pagan Museum. (Courtesy John Listopad)

Above this large composition in opposite niches are new replicas of original sculptures made of brick and covered with stucco. The pair show the four-armed seated Vishnu riding upon his vehicle, the Garuda bird.

In the centre of each of the other walls of the sanctum were once four-armed, standing images of Vishnu, made of brick and stucco. The three were sheared off the wall in the 1990s, and we are now left with concrete examples, holding fanciful objects unknown to the originals. For example, the Vishnu on the rear wall has acquired two extra arms to make six.

A life-size four-armed stone Shiva previously inside the temple is now in the museum. It was found with a stone Vishnu riding upon Garuda that was removed to a Berlin museum but taken by Russian troops during the occupation in 1945. A plaster cast was made of the object before it was looted, but the whereabouts of the original in Russia remains unknown. We cannot say where in the temple these two figures might have been, but they may have been placed in the now missing entrance hall. The two empty shallow niches on the front of the sanctum wall do not match the sizes of either of these two stone sculptures.

The interior frescoes are in miserable condition, but we can make out rows of seated figures on the inner wall of the sanctum surrounding the restored standing Vishnus. The outer wall facing the sanctum was designed with at least two large horizontal registers of painting but little can be made out.

It has been suggested that the temple was used by the city's Indian merchants, but it more likely featured in royal religious ceremonies. Its exact role at Buddhist Pagan, however, leaves unanswered issues at the heart of this Asian civilization.

Vishnu reclining on serpent, three gods emerging from his navel. Pagan Museum. Found in temple no. 1612. H. 81 cm. (DS)

Central niche before restoration. (DS)

Vishnu before destruction, brick and stucco. North wall. (DS)

THATBYINNYU

Date: 12th century

While some Pagan temples are celebrated for their girth, the Thatbyinnyu is known for its height. It is the tallest temple at Pagan, competing with a modern twenty-one floor office building. It also departs from all the other major temples, since no Buddha image was planned for its principal entrance. Instead, the main Buddha sat within the upper storey shrine, facing east. The interior has been whitewashed, but the rear hall retains a good deal of original painting.

Visit

Little is known about the history of the temple, since its founding is unrecorded in stone inscriptions. The chronicles attribute it to Alaungsithu, grandson of the legendary builder of the Ananda. It may date to the second half of the 12th century, more or less contemporary with the other mammoth temples at Pagan, such as the Sulamani, Gawdaw-palin, Htilominlo and Dhammayan-gyi.

The tallest temple at Pagan, the Thatbyinnyu dominates the skyline within the Walled City. The principal Buddha sits within the central shrine on the first storey, unlike other major temples in which the chief image is enshrined on the ground floor.

Its modern name, Thatbyinnyu, derives from Sabannu (Pali), or Omniscient One, an epithet of the Buddha.

The temple's size, central location and sanctity ensured that worship never ceased here, like the nearby Ananda. Later, intrusive Buddhas were likely painted on the walls, but all are now covered by whitewash. The earliest probably belonged to the 14th-century monk Anandasura whose red ink inscription appears in the rear corridor, beneath a flaked off section of whitewash. This monk commissioned painted Buddha figures within all of the major temples, following the capital's move to Ava when the temples experienced limited use.

A queen of Bodawpaya (1782-1819) left a 17-line inscription in red ink in one of side halls. The king is styled Hsinbyumashin, or Lord of White Elephants, a title he assumed in January, 1785. It records her visit to Pagan ('Pagam') and mentions the capital, Amarapura. It also states that the first donor of the temple was Alungsithu and gives the temple's name as Thatbyinnyu. She donated rest-houses ('tazaung') and also repaired some damaged stucco, or 'ingaday' (Burmese), but we cannot be sure if this refers to repairs at the Thatbyinnyu. She hopes that her donation will last 5,000 years, a reference to the anticipation of the Buddha of the Future, Metteyya. The year of the inscription appears in a flaked off portion. A Burmese document states that King Bodawpaya ordered the whitewashing of the walls of the temple and the restoration of all of the images, and that the work was completed on October 18, 1790 (Than Tun, 1996).

Stairways lead through the centre of the temple to the Buddha enshrined above which faces east. Two encircling vaulted passages inside the structure help reduce the total volume; such entresols were used in many of Pagan's largest temples. (DS)

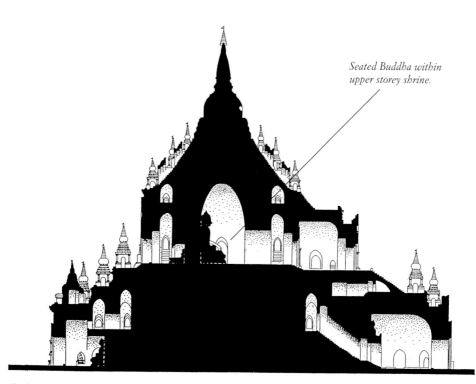

Seated Buddha within upper storey shrine.

Thatbyinnyu elevation.

Rear entrance hall with original ceiling painting. Restored Buddha. (DS)

The Exterior

The row of windows high on the ground floor is similar to those at the Dhammayan-gyi, but here they open on to a separate floor, a lower entresol, a device used in many large temples to reduce the mass of the brickwork.

Three wide, square terraces encircle the second floor, and there are a further three terraces and a second entresol above the second storey supporting the *shikhara*. At the corners are small stupas, now all restored. Hundreds of empty small niches line the terraces, and it has been suggested that these were intended for *jataka* tiles, which is unlikely for many reasons.

Interior

All of the major large temples were designed with a single Buddha figure dominating the ground floor, facing the entrance hall. The rear of the hall in the Thatbyinnu, however, is pierced by a staircase leading to the top storey. Surrounding the entrance to the stairway are two standing figures and a large pediment ending in a stupa finial. It all has been refreshed many times, but probably reflects its basic original appearance.

It is difficult to gauge the age of the restored central Buddha in the upper shrine. It faces east and is in the earth-touching gesture. The upper storey has been closed to the public for a number of years.

The only remaining painting belonging to the period of construction is found in the rear hall. The best work survives in the ceiling above the restored Buddha. The side walls were painted originally in a light coloured tan wash, defined by vertical registers,

One of the original vaulted gateways. North side.

creating large panel-like
sections. On the right and
left sides were large intrusive
paintings, perhaps belonging to
the 14th-15th century, but these
are difficult to see now.

Compound Wall and Bell

The compound wall was rather
small for a temple of these
dimensions, perhaps suggesting
that space within the city walls
was in short supply. Only small
portions of the wall survive,
covered in thick vegetation,
but one gateway on the north
still stands.

Two enormous square
stone piers once supported a
bell, outside the entrance to
the temple, now concealed by a
modern monastery. Inscriptions tell us that bells were donated to
temples but this is the only tangible evidence relating directly to bells.
The bell has been missing for centuries. The square pillars were badly
damaged in the 1975 quake and then rebuilt. The many separate
stone blocks are sculpted with floral designs in low relief, recalling
the technique at the Nanpaya.

*Square stone supports once supported
a huge bell. (John Listopad)*

Queen's inscription in corridor. (DS)

*U Nyein Lwin, Department of
Archaeology, reading ink inscription
recording donations made by one of
Bodawpaya's Queens, late 18th-early
19th centuries. South corridor. (DS)*

MAHABODHI

Highlights

★ Replica of the Mahabodhi Temple in India

The Mahabodhi Temple at Bodh Gaya, India, commemorates the spot where the Buddha obtained his enlightenment. (DS)

A corridor linking the temple to a small shrine in the rear is an unusual feature.

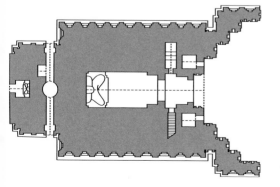

Date: c. 12ᵗʰ–13ᵗʰ century, with recent refurbishing

This monument commemorates the Mahabodhi temple in Bodh Gaya, India. Full-scale replicas of the original temple were created from time to time throughout the Buddhist world, and this example at Pagan is the earliest surviving example. It is traditionally attributed to King Zeyatheinhka (1211-1235), but its actual foundation date is uncertain.

Visit

The Burmese were familiar with the Bodh Gaya temple in India, since King Kyanzittha (1084-1112) dispatched a mission there, recorded in a stone inscription found at Pyay, or former Prome. His repairs were unspecified, but it is suspected that he added a typical Burmese pediment above the entrance, composed of a cusped arch topped with multiple vertical elements. This pediment replaced a large tableau featuring a recumbent Buddha. This alteration and others in the ancient period are reflected in some twenty miniature stone models of the Bodh Gaya temple found throughout the Buddhist world (Guy, 1991). Two late 13ᵗʰ-century Burmese inscriptions at Bodh Gaya refer to other Burmese donations, but what they relate to cannot be fixed.

The Pagan Mahabodhi temple shares basic affinities with the original. The chief characteristic is the pyramidal tower that departs from the ubiquitous, curvilinear *shikhara*, as seen at the Ananda. Other similarities include small shrines placed on the terrace corners, a row of Buddha figures at the base of the wall, surmounted by a frieze of *kirtimukhas* and two parallel rows of niches containing small Buddhas. This special type of tower was not limited to the Mahabodhi temple and appears elsewhere at Pagan in other temples, such as the Kubyauk-gyi (Wetkyi-in).

The Mahabodhi temple in India was also known to Pagan's residents via small, imported clay votive tablets depicting the temple. Painted representations of the temple, on palm-leaf or cloth, most likely also came from India, their influence reflected in a general fashion in numerous Pagan wall paintings.

The original Mahabodhi shrine inspired Southeast Asians long after the ancient period (Brown, 1988). The next major replica in Burma was built in Bago, or former Pegu, near Yangon, dating to the 1470s. Here, smaller monuments commemorating each of the Seven Weeks that the Buddha spent at Bodh Gaya were constructed in the vicinity (Stadtner, 1990). A similar replica was made earlier in the same century in Thailand, at Wat Chet Yot, in Chiang Mai, which also had shrines representing the Seven Weeks. Somewhat later in Thailand, another model was built in Chiang

The Mahabodhi Temple at Pagan, side view from south.

Above left: Refurbished stucco ornament, side wall.

Above right: Seated Buddha in niches, side wall.

Enigmatic shaft within the rear corridor. (DS)

Rai. Some claim that the smaller monuments surrounding the Mahabodhi at Pagan commemorate some of the Seven Weeks, but there is no strong evidence. However, compared to the other replicas, the example at Pagan is the most faithful representation of the Indian original.

Bodh Gaya continued to be important in Burmese Buddhism, with various missions sent to inspect the site in the 19th century. King Bodawpaya (1782-1819) even contemplated an invasion to liberate the temple from British rule, but the idea was fortunately shelved. During his reign one large model of the Mahabodhi was built in the hills above Mingun, near Mandalay, complete with shrines denoting the Seven Weeks. The temple also appears in a late-19th century fresco at the Mahamuni temple, near Mandalay. This depiction is perhaps based on photographs, since it so realistically conforms to photographs of the temple taken at this time.

A square chamber within the tower contains a seated Buddha, facing east. An inscription on the chamber wall dated to 1442 records the donation of a bazaar tax for the maintenance of the temple (Than Tun, 1996). The exterior for has been redecorated with crude stucco figures that are "execrably rough and inaccurate", as a 19th-century visitor already observed (Yule, 42).

Joined to the rear of the temple is a separate chamber containing a Buddha facing west, reflecting a similar feature found on some of the ancient stone models. A short, narrow corridor separates the chamber from the main body of the temple and in the centre is a peculiar shaft open to the sky. This circular hole was perhaps intended for an artificial Bodhi tree, since the original tree at the Mahabodhi temple in India was located immediately behind the temple, as it is today. The two seated Buddhas in three parallel rows on each of the outer side of the temple porch are also seen in at least three of the ancient stone models of the Bodh Gaya temple.

To one side of the Mahabodhi is a recently excavated temple, whose base is located a good deal below the present ground level. It was likely built before the Mahabodhi, but its exact date is unknown.

Miniature stone replica reflects the ancient appearance of Bodh Gaya and resembles the temple at Pagan. c. 11th century. 11.3 cm. (Courtesy Ashmolean Museum, Oxford)

Mahabodhi in India depicted in late 19th-century mural, Mahamuni temple, Amarapura. (DS)

Below: Wat Chet Yot, 15th century, Chiang Mai, Thailand. (DS)

GAWDAW-PALIN

Date: 12th century

The Gawdaw-palin is counted among the largest temples at Pagan, and only the Thatbyinnyu offers any competition in bricks and mortar, within the city walls. Burmese chronicles attribute the start of the temple to Narapatisithu and its completion to Zeyatheinhka, but we cannot be sure of its date since no original inscriptions have survived. Extensive refurbishing in the Konbaung period (1752-1885) or earlier has left only hints of its original painting. The entire tower toppled in the 1975 quake but was restored between 1976 and 1982 and further strengthened in the early 1990s.

Visit

The Gawdaw-palin sits in the southwestern corner of the Walled City and can be combined with a visit to the nearby museum. A low wall and four Konbaung period gates surround the temple today. The monument is of the solid core class with encircling corridors on both stories, similar to other two-storied temples at Pagan, such as the Sulamani, Htilominlo and the Thatbyinnyu. Large, seated east-facing Buddhas are enshrined on the top and bottom. The temple was likely constructed in the second half of the 12th century, judging

The entire tower was lost in the 1975 quake but is now restored.

from its resemblance to the Sulamani temple dated to 1183. The Gawdaw-palin has no inner storey, or entresol, separating the ground floor from the second storey.

The exterior has been resurfaced and whitewashed many times, so only traces of the original work survive. The inner corridor is flooded with light through numerous doors leading from the compound. Few of the original green ceramic insets survive on the basement, but they are more numerous within the roof terraces. The top storey is surmounted by terraces, crowned with a massive, restored *shikhara*. The shape of the tall segmented shaft rising above the tower is completely conjectural.

Faint traces of original ceiling painting surivive throughout the temple, made up of roundels containing five small circles, a design also found at the Htilominlo and other temples. There was probably no original figurative painting, but the wall surface was covered with a light tan wash and framed by painted registers at the top and bottom. In this way, it resembled the Sulamani, Thatbyinnyu and other large temples which also had no figurative mural painting.

The interior tells the story of successive restorations. One certainly took place in the Konbaung period when the main image was restored, and the wall behind painted with designs, dominated by a Bodhi tree. Small Buddha images with painted surrounds were placed against the inner side of the corridor. Such additions were common in that period and in the 20th century, witnessed in the Sulamani, Shwegu-gyi and other temples.

Above the principal Buddha at the rear is a delightful owl whose wide black eyes echo those of the Buddha below. The old metal finial that tumbled down during the earthquake in 1975 is preserved inside one of the side halls, a melancholy tribute to a universe forever in flux.

A 19th-century stupa, containing four marble Buddhas, sits in one corner, near the modern entrance. An octagonal stupa is found in the adjoining corner from the same period, designed for worshippers to honour the day on which they were born. This stupa can be seen in the watercolour by Colesworthy Grant, painted from the roof terrace of the Gadaw-palin temple in 1855.

An owl, perched high above the restored Buddha at the rear of the temple, c. 18th century. (DS)

Late 18th- or early 19th-century gateway.

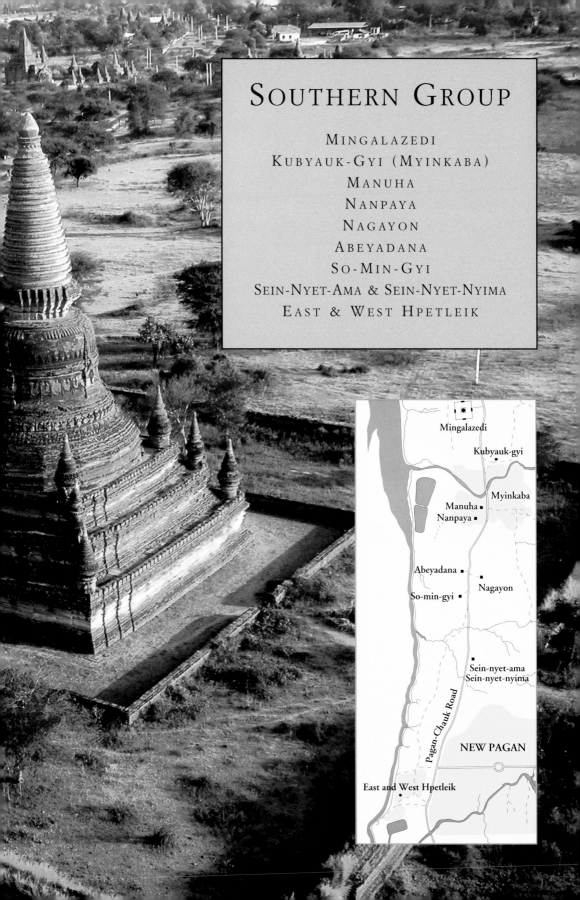

SOUTHERN GROUP

MINGALAZEDI
KUBYAUK-GYI (MYINKABA)
MANUHA
NANPAYA
NAGAYON
ABEYADANA
SO-MIN-GYI
SEIN-NYET-AMA & SEIN-NYET-NYIMA
EAST & WEST HPETLEIK

Mingalazedi
Kubyauk-gyi
Myinkaba
Manuha
Nanpaya
Abeyadana
Nagayon
So-min-gyi
Sein-nyet-ama
Sein-nyet-nyima
Pagan-Chauk Road
NEW PAGAN
East and West Hpetleik

MINGALAZEDI STUPA

Highlights

★ panoramic views of Pagan
  and river

★ unique glazed tile series

Date: 12-13th centuries

The Mingalazedi stupa affords breathtaking views of Pagan's major monuments and the surrounding countryside, especially in the early morning or late afternoon. Its terraces boast nearly a complete set of *jataka* plaques, together with unique Buddhist tiles on the basement plinth. The Mingalazedi probably dates to the 12th or perhaps the early 13th century.

Visit

The Mingalazedi lies off the main paved road leading from the Walled City, just south of the junction with Anawrahta Road. The stupa must have been the hub of much activity, since two smaller stupas and a number of monastic buildings were built between its inner and outer compound walls. An inscription found in a monastery within the precinct is dated 1285 and records donations of land, cattle and bonded servants. It says nothing, however, about the construction of the stupa.

The patron, King Narapatisithu, was warned in a prophecy that if the monument were completed it would signal the end of his life and the kingdom, according to the *Glass Palace Chronicle*. Nevertheless, his Buddhist mentor insisted that he should finish it, arguing that mortals cannot impede the inexorable law of impermance and thwart death, even if they are kings. Whether the prophecy came true, or when the stupa was built cannot be determined. That the captions of the *jatakas* are in Burmese, not Mon, suggests that it did not belong to Pagan's earliest phase. The Dhamma-yazika, dated to 1197-1198, was perhaps the city's last mammoth building project, maybe together with the Mingalazedi. There was a construction boom in the 13th century, but ambitious projects of the 11th and 12th centuries, such as the Ananda and Dhammayan-gyi, had come to an end.

Previous pages: Southern Group. Paired temple (Sein-nyet-ama) and stupa (Sein-nyet-nyima) within a double compound wall. From southeast. Road on left leads north to the Walled City. Irrawaddy in the distance. (PP)

Kirtimukhas spewing oval motifs, detail, corner stupa on top terrace. (PP)

After removing our footware at the gate, our feet tread on numerous ancient bricks placed randomly within a modern walkway. Short inscriptions stamped into a few identify the names of former villages around Pagan and donors that supplied brick to the capital.

The Stupa

The stucco on the dome is new, together with the spire that was damaged during the 1975 quake. Roughly thirty percent of the stucco remains on the terraces, mostly on the rows of lotuses.

Each terrace is divided into recessed vertical sections, thereby relieving the tedium of a single, flat surface. Large brick lions were once placed at the corners of the first terrace, but only one survives today, in ruins on the southwestern corner. It is similar to the sole remaining example at the Shwe-san-daw. Stone lions may also have guarded the base of the stairs, if one example on the north side is considered to be *in situ*.

Each terrace is topped by rounded crenellations and double lotuses. Rows of now exposed header bricks bind the exterior facing to the inner brick core, along with small, square sandstone blocks that penetrate deeply inside the walls at regular intervals. Restored urns are at the corners of the lower terraces.

Unique glazed ornamentation

Stupa-shaped obelisks at the corners of the top terrace are adorned with remarkable decorative tiles. Here, each tiny *kirtimukha* disgorges an oval shaped motif. The bricks are moulded in a sloping

The stucco ornament covering the dome and the stupa's finial are conjectural. Small stupas on the corners of the terrace echo the shape of the central one. Hundreds of glazed jataka *tiles appear within niches. (DS)*

Glazed tiles remaining on corner stupas on top terrace. (DS)

Jatakas *were planned for all of the terraces. Each is incised on its base with its name and its ordinal number. The best preserved plaques are found on the south side, third terrace.*

Left: No. 446.
Right: No. 449.

fashion conforming to the contours of the underlying brickwork. Pagan artists often used coloured tiles both in exterior ornament, but these at the Mingalazedi are unique for their design and function. Their original colour was green, but they have faded badly, according to Dr. Aung Bo, a ceramic specialist.

The Jataka Plaques

The entire set of 547 *jatakas* begins on the lowest terrace and proceeds clockwise, ascending the stupa sequentially. The first is located immediately to the left of the median stairway. This terrace has 216 niches, but about half are empty and many tiles are heavily damaged, including the first one. Plaques in better condition are found on the upper terraces, especially on the south side. Each is incised on its base with the name of the *jataka* and its ordinal number following the standard Pali sequence. In some cases, there is a brief description of the scene. They are green, with a wide range of hues, like all of the glazed *jatakas* at Pagan. These single *jataka* tiles take up the greater part of the three lower terraces.

The last ten *jatakas* (538-547), or the venerated Mahanipata, begin on the third terrace and finish on the octagonal terrace above. They are numbered in a single continuous sequence. The first of the last ten, the Temi *jataka*, begins on the north side of the top square terrace with number one and ends in the centre of the east face with no. 31. The second then starts on the east side of the octagonal terrace with no. 32, to the left of the stairway, in the centre. The remaining eight *jatakas* proceed clockwise to culminate in the centre of the east face, abutting the first tile of the second *jataka*. The last *jataka*, the Vessantara, begins on the west side and ends in the middle of the eastern face. This important concluding *jataka* was accorded more tiles than any of the others, at least 65. This last terrace has 147 niches but only 116 tiles have survived. Many are damaged and some were never assigned a number. A good many have been inserted out of order in modern times, but the basic sequence of the last ten is correct and matches those at the Hpetleik Stupas, the Ananda and the Kubyauk-gyi (Myinkaba). Plaques on the octagonal terrace are somewhat smaller than the ones on the lower terraces, a practice found also at the Ananda.

Garuda birds in procession, basement tiles, north side.

For some of the missing tiles one must go to the Museum für Indische Kunst, Berlin, whence scores were removed by Fritz von Noetling, in the late 19th century. They are the only significant glazed *jatakas* from Pagan in a public collection outside of Burma.

Unique tile series

The tall walls forming the base of the stupa were designed with a series of tiles found nowhere else at Pagan. Captions in Burmese incised at the bottom of each identify four separate classes of celestials represented on each of the faces: the gods and their chief, Sakka (east), demons (south), snakes (west) and the mythical bird Garuda (north).

Gods in procession with banners, basement tiles, east side.

Each plaque has three identical figures shown moving in procession toward the four median staircases. All bear auspicious offerings, such as flowers, lamps or banners, also identified in the inscriptions. The total was originally 296, but no more than a dozen or two remain today; the *Inventory of Pagan Monuments* listed 53 in the 1980s. The gods are labelled '*devatas*' and 'Sakka'. The demons, called '*philu*', (*bilu*, modern Burmese), are not the demons of Mara's army but rather demons within the Pali universe. The snakes are labelled both '*nagas*'(Pali, Sanskrit) and '*naga* kings'; one of these plaques was mistakenly inserted recently into the lowest terrace at the Dhamma-yazika. The bird-faced deities with wings are called '*galon*', after Garuda (Sanskrit); one can be seen in the museum.

These deities arose originally within a Hindu context in India but were absorbed into Buddhism at a very early date. They appear much later in Burma via Pali literature. This specific combination of deities is unique to Burmese ceramics, but these same gods are linked together in at least one undated Pagan-period inscription, in which the donor records his wish that the fruits of his donation be enjoyed by Sakka, all of the gods and demons, together with the king of the *galons* and *nagas* (Luce, I, 114). These important tiles are often concealed by vegetation and therefore can be overlooked. A fuller and more complex cosmology unravels in the tile series on the east face of the Ananda Temple.

The four small stupas on the top terrace were once covered with ornamented glazed ceramics. (DS)

KUBYAUK-GYI (MYINKABA)

Date: 1113

The Kubyauk-gyi is important for understanding Pagan's development, since it is the earliest dated temple in the city. It was founded in 1113 AD by a prince whose donation is recorded on two stone slabs discovered nearby. The epigraph is unique for Pagan, because its text is repeated in four languages: Pyu, Pali, Mon, and Burmese. The frescos showcase a dazzling variety of Pali texts.

Visit

The temple lies just off the paved road leading south of the Walled City, amidst a stand of toddy palms. The gem-like Kubyauk-gyi comes as a pleasant relief after many of Pagan's overwhelming monuments. It can be followed with a visit to the nearby Manuha and Nanpaya temples, also in Myinkaba village.

The Exterior

A wide entrance hall facing east adjoins a square sanctum encircled by a corridor. The tower is supported by a square terrace and two sloping roofs. The shape of the present spire is conjectural, since the original collapsed centuries ago. Above the entrance hall is a miniature temple, together with small shrines on the corners, reflecting a similar arrangement at the Pahto-thamya, in the Walled

The earliest dated temple at Pagan, 1113, the Kubyauk-gyi in Myinkaba village affords valuable evidence for tracing Pagan's painting, sculpture and architecture. South view, near entrance.

City. Access to the terrace is
by a narrow staircase within
the entrance hall.

The stucco work ranks
among the best at Pagan,
being confident in design and
execution. The encircling frieze
of *kirtimukhas*, for example,
finds little competition at Pagan
in its boldness and its stark
contrast against the smooth wall
surface. Note also the intricate
pediments above the windows,
made of brick covered stucco.

The windows themselves are perforated stones carved in geometric
shapes. Much of the façade crumbled long ago, but a pair of pilasters
brims with frothy vegetation contrasting with delicate looped
patterns. Above the doorway on the left perches an engaging little
kinnara, a mythical union of bird and man, the sole remains of what
was surely a spectacular tableau. *Kinnaras* in this same position were
used at Pagan, even as late as the 13th-century (no. 664). Roughly
60% of the remaining stucco was selected by Unesco for cleaning
and preservation in the 1980s [*Pagan Newsletter*, 1985].

*A kirtimukha frieze and a window
pediment (see also detail below).
The stucco was restored jointly by
the Department of Archaeology and
Unesco in the 1980s. (DS)*

The Murals

The murals are counted among the most important at Pagan,
recognized for their quality, subject matter and the fact that they
are earliest dated pictorial art in Burma. The walls retain roughly
50% of their painting, while only about 5% survives on the ceilings.
The frescos were sensitively restored jointly by Unesco and the
Department of Archaeology between 1983 and 1993. Luce and his
colleagues deciphered decades ago hundreds of tiny ink inscriptions
in the Mon language placed as identifying labels beneath the painted
compositions (Luce, Ba Shin).

The meticulous forethought, planning and execution these murals
represent is staggering, since they required the painting of thousands
of figures within hundreds of small compartments and large panels.
Before work began, the entire wall surface was crisscrossed with
scores of vertical and horizontal lines forming frames to contain
the compositions.

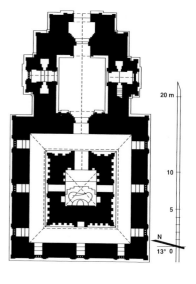

*Hollow core sanctum encircled by
vaulted corridor, faced by wide
entrance hall on east.*

The Entrance Hall

The outer porch has two towering ten-armed bodhisattvas, with
seated, three-headed Brahma figures above. Two-armed bodhisattvas
are in the adjacent vestibule, holding long sinuous lotus stems. The
wide entrance hall itself retains only patches of once spectacular
frescos. Against the rear wall is a fragmentary standing figure whose
brick core was originally covered with moulded stucco; the matching
figure on the left is completely gone, save for traces of its painted
surround. Such two-armed male figures in this position are common
at Pagan, and many suffer from over restoration. They have been
identified as guardians, but they likely represent the future Buddha,

Metteyya, shown as a bodhisattva, and Lokanatha, on the left and right, respectively.

Painting inside the two deeply recessed hall windows is in fair condition, with subjects taken from the "Stories of the Mansions" (*Vimana-vatthu*) in the *Khuddaka Nikaya* in the Pali canon. These tales describe good deeds undertaken by the laity, such as a man who gave a needle to a monk stitching his robe. Luce deciphered about fifteen captions from the roughly eighty-five scenes. They appear to be in serial order, starting in the window chamber on the right (north) and then proceeding to the opposite window (south). The series concludes by awkwardly jumping to the corridor forming the entrance to the shrine, on the bottom of the left wall (south). The tales in this corridor belong to the last section of the *Vimana-vatthu*, suggesting that the series ended here. That the illustrations from this text skipped from the entrance hall to the shrine area signifies that it was important to complete the series, even if it required dividing the painting between the entrance hall and the sanctum area. Before entering the inner corridor are two tall, painted bodhisattvas.

Bodhisattva, passage to inner corridor.

Detail of raised hand.

The Shrine

A newly refurbished Buddha sits within the sanctum, its base retaining much original stucco ornament. Surrounding the Buddha was perhaps the Eight Great Events in the Buddha's life, similar to the rear wall at the Loka-hteikpan. Deep niches in the sanctum and in the corridor walls contained stone sculptures, all of which were removed to the Pagan museum in 1990. Many were replaced by gypsum replicas, for security reasons. Rows of painted seated Buddhas high on the walls and monks below are the major subjects in the sanctum. Luce was unable to read any of the captions.

Corridor to Inner Sanctum

Immediately to the left and right of the entrance are two life-size bodhisattvas, each with fourteen arms, holding various attributes. One or two small dark square sections were left un-cleaned by restorers, so that we can appreciate the layers of accumulated grime.

The painting on the side walls leading to the inner sanctum is arranged in six tiers, with those on the top in good condition. Many of the subjects were drawn from the Sri Lankan chronicle, the *Mahavamsa*, such as the Buddha's legendary visit to the island and events in the life of King Ashoka of India. The scenes are identified by ink inscriptions, and the narrative begins on the left wall (south) and goes from left to right, from top to bottom. On the right wall (north) at the top are two panels on the right representing two Indian cities associated with Ashoka and relics. This pair superficially resembles the '*mandalas*' of Nepalese and Tibetan art (geometric compositions of circles and squares containing deities), but should not be confused with this tradition. The caption beneath the third frame from the left reads: "This is when King Dhammasok takes the relics." The first panel within this top tier depicts the seated King Ashoka, within a pavilion; the caption reads: "This is King Dhammasok."

A king named 'Vijaya' appearing in two of the damaged panels on the left wall (south), prompted Luce to suggest that it may represent the Sri Lankan King Vijaya Bahu I (fl. 1055-1114), a contemporary with King Anawrahta and Kyanzittha. This tantalizing suggestion with many historical implications is unlikely, since this Vijaya should be identified with an earlier legendary Sri Lankan king of the same name mentioned in the *Mahavamsa*. Moreover, traditional painting holds no place for contemporary events.

Decorative bands, above seated Buddhas. Shrine wall, front. (DS)

"If only my wife's body . . . "

Other illustrations within the corridor leading to the sanctum are drawn from different Pali texts, such as the sorry tale of a married man named Soreyya. Once upon a time Soreyya came across a monk bathing and dared to ponder, "If only my wife's body could have such beauty!" (Luce's translation of the now-lost ink gloss). After pronouncing these words, he turned miraculously into a woman, and then abandoned his wife and two sons to settle in a new town, Taxila (an ancient city in northwestern India), where he re-married and gave birth to two more sons. He would have lived happily ever after but he confessed his identity to an old friend, and then, out of shame, Soreyya reverted to being a man and joined a monastery. Just as he thought his mid-life crises was behind him, his fellow monks badgered him night and day with queries about his extraordinary personal history. In desperation, he abandoned the monastery for the forest where he achieved sainthood, ultimately rewarded for his gender-switch. This instructive story is regrettably too weathered to be visible today. The tale is found in a commentary on the *Dhammapada*, known as the *Dhammapada-atthakatha*.

Outer Corridor Wall

Paintings here are devoted largely to the creation of the universe, the story of Gotama Buddha leading to his enlightenment, and his 547 previous birth-stories. Each wall is divided into eleven vertical rows of niches, creating a total of 132 frames for individual compositions. Those in the two highest registers are larger than the ones below but are in poor condition and difficult to read. The bottom row is devoted to miscellaneous subjects from Pali sources.

The narrative order of the birth-stories and all of the other subjects moves clockwise around the sanctum, beginning on the east wall and going from top to bottom. This clockwise direction conforms to conventional Buddhist circumambulation in which the worshipper's right side faces the chief object of devotion, that is, the Buddha within the shrine. This same narrative direction is seen too at the Ananda temple where the life history of the Buddha is told in 80 sculptures progressing in sequence around the inner sanctum.

```
inner corridor – east wall

Scenes from the Life of the Buddha

Conversion of Brahmins            The Four Great Kings, etc.

                                  Dipankara Buddha

Jatakas                           Jatakas

Miscellaneous Sections            Miscellaneous Sections
from Pali sources                 from Pali sources
```

Outer Corridor Wall – Top Row

Standing with our back toward the central shrine, we face the outer corridor wall (east). Look to the top where two parallel rows of large frames encircle the entire temple. These panels are in fragmentary condition and difficult to read. The top register features scenes from the Buddha's life, beginning with the Buddha's mother and ending with the gift of the Jetavana Monastery to the Buddha by the legendary King Anathapindika in India. Luce estimated that there was originally a total of 64 frames but only 43 survive with captions. The series goes in a clockwise direction, or from left to right, starting in the corner (northeast). It begins with Queen Maya's conveyance to the Himalayas by the Four World Guardians. Most of these scenes have flaked away entirely since Luce's recording. The panels that can be best appreciated appear on the rear wall (west) where we make out the Buddha's horse, followed by the Buddha cutting his hair prior to his wanderings (two compositions which also appear at the Pahtothamya on the outer wall of the corridor).

The Pali text responsible for these illustration appears to be the same that guided the sculptors at the Ananda, the *Nidanakatha*. The narrative begins a trifle later here than at the Ananda, with Maya's dream in which the Four World Guardians are transporting her to

The gluttonous King Pasanadi and his court. Animals destined for his table appear to the side. Window in southeastern corner.

the Himalayas. The artists omitted many of the episodes represented in the Ananda sculptures but took the narrative further by picturing certain events after the enlightenment. The murals end with the presentation to the Buddha of the Jetavana monastery, from the concluding episode in the *Nidanakatha*, a scene not shown at the Ananda.

Outer Corridor Wall – Second Row from Top

The second row had a total of 39 panels, also running from left to right. It does not begin in the northeastern corner (unlike Queen Maya), but immediately to the right of the entrance arch. Unlike the top row which was based on one text and followed a continuous narrative, the subjects in this tier are taken from several sources and cover different themes. The first nine panels focus on cosmological subjects, such as the Four Great Kings, and The Regents of the Cardinal Directions, from the *Agganna Sutta* of the *Digha Nikaya*. (Many of these same deities are represented among the glazed tiles on the east basement of the Ananda temple). Other subjects include the mythical king ruling over the island of Jambudipa, Sakka's rule in the Heaven of the 33 Gods, and special signs that foreshadow the appearance of a Buddha. The last four panels on the east wall seem unconnected thematically to the previous scenes, depicting the Buddha's conversion of two brahmins after his enlightenment (from the *Khuddaka Nikaya*). All of these panels are fragmentary.

Boddhisattva, to right of shrine entrance.

Jatakas on the Corridor Wall

The 547 *jataka* scenes dominating the interior are among the freshest and most engaging at Pagan. Each is within a single square frame and identified by a short ink gloss placed in the yellow border below. The Pali title of the tale is given, followed by a brief description in Mon, usually beginning: "the bodhisat was a . . . " [before the Buddha was reborn as Gotama he was known as a bodhisattva]. The tales adhere to the sequence in the standard Pali collection of *jatakas* that has come down to us today, except that the order of the last ten is somewhat different. Only 496 *jatakas* survive from the original 547, and many are in poor condition.

The series begins to the right of the arched entrance high up on the wall, below the two top horizontal registers. It starts with a single frame devoted to the Buddha Dipankara, one of the

Left: Detail from above.

Below: U Ba Tint, painting conservator, 1987. (DS)

Ascetic, detail from jataka.

Four jatakas, *south wall, top, nos. 355, 356, left to right; bottom, nos. 437, 438, left to right.*

previous 28 Buddhas, who prophesized the future birth of Gotama Buddha. This reference sets the thematic link to the actual *jataka* series following immediately to the right. The episode of Dipankara also connects the *jatakas* to the biography of the Buddha, since Dipankara foretold the birth of the Buddha Gotama and he plays an important role in the *Nidanakatha*, the text guiding the top row of panels. (Dipankara also starts off the *jataka* series in the entrance hall of the Abeyadana). The tales then proceed from wall to wall in horizontal rows completely encircling the outer wall. They begin at the top and end near the bottom of the floor. The last *jataka*, no. 547, appears on the north wall, in the sixth frame from the northwestern corner. The remaining, extra frames on the wall tell the story of one or two hermits.

Each *jataka* painting focuses on a single significant action in the complete narrative. The Buddha appears either in human form or often as an animal, each tale illustrating a moral precept centring on selfless benevolence and other virtues. The narrow vertical bands separating the frames are ornamented with small alternating lozenges and circles, an influence from east Indian palm-leaf painting which also appears in Nepalese and Tibetan painting.

Two Lowermost Tiers: Miscellaneous Scenes

These frames are difficult to make out, and many have lost the captions available to Luce. Some scenes are taken from the *Mahavamsa* from Sri Lanka and others from different Pali sources, with little connection to each other, and no clear starting point. However, the frames do move in a clockwise direction when they are part of the same narrative. The *Mahavamsa* sections (on the south wall) record the prowess of an elephant that was offered to a king to drive the Tamils from the island. On the east wall is a story of a woman who tamed a raging elephant with a simple snap of her fingers. On the same wall is the tale of a nude Jain ascetic who converts to Buddhism. Other scenes involve a pregnant general's wife wishing to bathe in a sacred tank. It is tempting to think that these scenes were of more interest to local artists than the standard *jatakas*.

The Window Recesses

The walls lining each of the nine deep window chambers feature large painted panels, with subjects derived from many Pali sources. The first window to the left of the entrance (southeast) features the legendary Indian King Pasenadi surrounded by his court (see page 166). This Buddhist king and the Buddha were great confidants, and he figures in many places in the Pali canon. The paintings on both sides of the window involve the king struggling to trim his waistline, to practice the Buddhist ideal of moderation. On the left wall the king is

seated with his many wives. The caption below reads: "This is the daily quantity of food of King Pasenadi: one buffalo, eight pigs, sixteen fowls, thirty quails, five hundred shrimp and seven measures of husked rice." The domestic animals painted in frames on the left are intended for his table. He can be likened to a Buddhist Paul Bunyon. The Buddha requested the king's nephew to preach the virtue of moderation each time his uncle sat down to one of his prodigious meals. This simple expedient worked, since the panel on the other side of the window shows the same monarch, with the following caption: "These are the sixteen royal concubines, King Pasenadi proceeds to reduce his diet. He becomes handsome again." The king seemingly achieved two goals, pleasing his courtesans and at the same time practicing moderation.

Other window chambers depict certain *jatakas* (no. 380, 546, 257) and scenes from various Pali sources, including one panel from the *Mahavamsa*. Some of the episodes on the north wall lack captions, such as a depiction of the Buddha inside a pavilion placed on a boat.

At the bottom of each chamber are lively white elephants, clasping sprigs of vegetation in their trunks. The Buddha assumed the form of a white elephant before his birth, and white elephants were considered an emblem of royalty at Pagan and throughout Burmese history. The most inventive compositions are found in matching roundels on the three tall steps leading to the windows. Dancers and animals are treated with originality and vigour, revealing the Pagan's artists unbounded creativity when freed from the restraints of strictly religious imagery. One depicts an embracing male and female snake-couple, recognized by their snake hoods.

Inner Walls of Corridor

The four walls are devoted to the 28 Buddhas and important incidents in the life of the Buddha. Stone sculptures of the 28

Compositions on two lowermost tiers of outer corridor walls are drawn from a variety of Pali sources.

Snake-hooded deities, steps in window chamber, north corridor.

King Vedeharaja, jataka no. 546, window in southwestern corner, with detail below. (PP)

Buddhas were once in niches around the sanctum, and above each was painted the individual tree associated with each Buddha. The original images were removed more than ten years ago and those now in the temple are replicas. The series probably begins at the front of the sanctum and proceeds in a clockwise direction, similar to the order found at the Nagayon.

Top Row

Large panels below the ceiling encircle the sanctum in a clockwise direction and feature the Buddha preaching in north India at seven different locations, such as Vesali and Kosambi. They begin on the east, to the right of the shrine entrance, and are identified by Mon glosses. Each sermon is shown in two adjacent panels, one with the Buddha preaching to monks and the other with the king and his court.

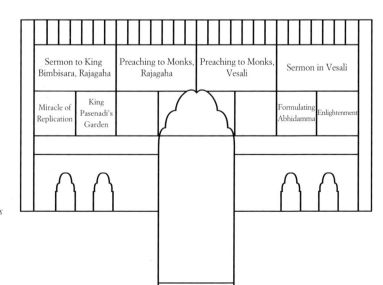

Outer wall of shrine (east.) The lower panels are devoted to scenes from the Buddha's life. The top ones show the Buddha teaching at different sites within India.

Lower Row

The 20 panels on the lower row are more diverse than the top tier. They celebrate the promulgation of Buddhist philosophical teachings known as the *Abhidamma*, incidents from the Buddha's life, and the Three Buddhist Councils held in north India to codify doctrine after the Buddha's death. This row also begins on the east face, to the right of the shrine door, in the northeastern corner.

Shrine Entrance (East)

The series opens with the Buddha's enlightenment, followed by a panel in which the Buddha formulated the *Abhidamma* at Bodh Gaya in a jewelled house. The next two panels, to the left of the shrine doorway, describe the miracle of a giant mango tree grown in a garden belonging to King Pasenadi and the replication of the Buddha in the garden.

Side Wall of Shrine (South)

The first two panels on the side wall (south) show the Buddha ascending to the Heaven of the 33 Gods, followed by a panel of naked ascetics opposed to the Buddha who unsuccessfully try to perform a miracle. In the upper left, four men are shown in a square pool of water, explained by the caption below: "The heretics, ashamed, go and drown themselves in a tank." The next panel shows the Buddha at Anotatta Lake, while the last panel on this side wall depicts the Buddha preaching the *Abhidamma* to his disciple Sariputta.

Rear Wall of Shrine (West)

On the rear wall the first panel on the right shows the disciple Sariputta explicating the *Abhidamma* to 500 monks. However, they already knew these teachings, having previously been bats who lived in a cave visited by two monks who regularly repeated the teachings out loud. These two robed men are shown standing in a trefoil-shaped cave, with small bats clinging to the roof of the rocky interior. The next panel shows the Buddha descending diagonally

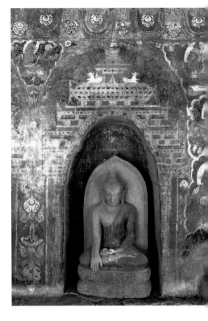

Gypsum replica replacing original stone sculpture now in museum. Outer shrine wall, front. (DS)

Rear wall of shrine. The central panels portray the defeat of Mara.

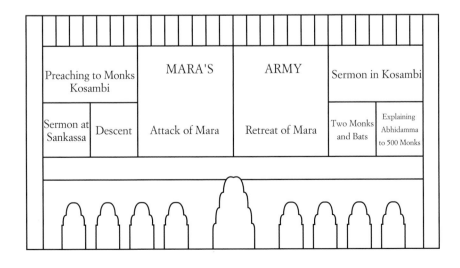

White elephant, window chamber. (PP)

from the Heaven of the 33 Gods, with the three-headed Brahma supporting a tall umbrella. The last scene shows the Buddha preaching a sermon, within a pavilion, before entering the city of Sankassa.

Side Wall of Shrine (North)

The side wall (north) devotes six panels to the story of the three Buddhist councils held in north India following the Buddha's death. The four central panels depict events of the Second Council, presided over by King Ashoka. In the second frame, Ashoka is seen crowned, standing in water, greeting Moggaliputta Tissa. The last panel, on the far left, shows the Third Council, with the venerable Moggaliputta Tissa within a pavilion. This material on the councils is drawn from the the *Mahavamsa*.

Attack of Mara – Rear wall of sanctum

The centre of the rear wall is dominated by a huge composition featuring the defeat of the demon Mara. The attack starts on the left side where Mara is seated upon an elephant and accompanied by dozens of his soldiers and wild animals. The defeated army scampers off, on the right half of the wall. Similar compositions are found on the rear of the shrine walls at the Abeyadana and Nagayon. To either side are stately standing figures, probably representing bodhisattvas.

The Myazedi Inscription: Pyu, Mon, Pali and Myanmar

Two stone inscriptions were discovered in the late 19th century in the vicinity of the Kubyauk-gyi. The better preserved one is now in the Pagan museum and was found near the Myazedi stupa, adjacent to the Kubyauk-gyi. The other was pieced together from four fragments recovered nearby and is now displayed in the compound of the Myazedi stupa. The text is repeated on both slabs in four languages: Pyu, Pali, Mon and Burmese. It is the first dated inscription using

Below right: Enlightenment of the Buddha, shrine wall, front, bottom row, far right.

Below: Formulating Abhidamma in jewelled house, shrine wall, front, bottom row, to the right of door.

Burmese and has enhanced our understanding of the enigmatic Pyu language. Since the inscriptions were not found in their original locations, it must be recognized that there is no certainty that they can be associated with the Kubyauk-gyi.

A prince donated the temple on behalf of his ailing father, Kyanzittha (1084-1112), legendary founder of the Ananda. The inscription refers to the year of the king's accession in 1084, which occurred 1,628 years after the death of the Buddha (reckoned to be 544 B.C.). It then relates that he had been ruling 28 years when his son made the dedication, or in 1112. Luce opined that the monument was likely finished soon after, in 1113. For the welfare of his father, the son dedicated a 'golden Buddha' and a temple (*gu*, Pali; *ku*, Burmese), surmounted by a finial (*athwat*, Burmese), or golden spire shaped like a stupa (*kanchana-thupika*, Pali). This metal Buddha has vanished, but it probably resembled the bronze Buddhas preserved in the museums at Pagan and in Yangon. This image may even remain buried somewhere deep within the brick tower, since a number of metal sculptures have been recovered within the walls of temple towers, ceremoniously interred and never meant to be seen. A spectacular bronze in the Pagan museum measuring over a meter in height was discovered, for example, in the tower of a temple (no. 40), as recently as 1999. This practice was unlikely to have been a precaution against treasure-hunters, but was rather intended to enhance the efficacy of the donation. The king's son also donated for the temple's upkeep three villages bequeathed by his deceased mother, together with their bonded workers. Those obstructing the donation are warned that they will be forbidden from beholding the Buddha of the Future, Metteyya, in future re-births.

The inscription can be seen in a small cage-like structure in the compound of the Myazedi stupa. Also nearby is a modern pavilion with a large tableau of doll-like figures representing all of the chief protagonists from the 12th century, identified by plaques, such as Kyanzittha, his wife, his son, Buddhist dignitaries, and courtiers.

Above left: Bodhisattva, shrine wall, rear, right side.

Above right: Demon in defeat, shirne wall, rear, right side.

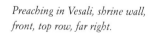

Preaching in Vesali, shrine wall, front, top row, far right.

MANUHA

Floor tiles from the early 20th century were popular throughout Burma.

The Manuha is associated in lore with the Mon king captured by Anawrahta. In the compound is an important nat *shrine.*

The Manuha is a 'must-see' destination for pilgrims, after the Ananda and the Shwe-zigon. It suffered greatly in the 1975 quake but was rebuilt in reinforced concrete between 1975-1980. Burmese lore associates the temple with the Mon king from Lower Burma who was captured in the 11th century and confined to Pagan.

Visit

The temple is located at the southern edge of Myinkaba village and can be joined with a visit to the nearby Nanpaya stone temple.

The long façade faces toward the main road, or east. The three chambers are dominated by enormous seated brick Buddhas, covered with stucco and painted gold. A long extension added at the rear contains a reclining Buddha, facing north. The *Glass Palace Chronicle* claims that the Mon king captured by Anawrahta (1044-1077) donated the largest image in the centre and the recumbent Buddha in the hope that he would never be conquered and taken captive in future re-births. The temple bears the Mon king's name, Manuha, and is yet another example of how Pagan's temples were later incorporated into the national mythology.

There is no solid proof that the temple actually belongs to the ancient Pagan period, and it may be much more recent, either from early in the Konbaung period (1752-1885) or probably from some time before. The ground plan, for example, is not characteristic of the Pagan period. The building at the rear is unlikely to be part of the original design, placed asymmetrically against the back of the

temple. Neither are large recumbent Buddhas a feature of the ancient period but are of more recent origin, such as the example in the compound at the Shwe-san-daw.

A row of whitewashed stucco *kirtimukha* faces can be made out with difficulty just below the roof of the upper storey on the front of the building. These likely mimic ancient designs, but the assessment of the building's age will have to change if it can be proved that this stucco is ancient. Friezes of 19th-century *kirtimukha* imitating ancient designs can be seen at the Myazedi stupa, adjacent to the Kubyauk-gyi (Myinkaba), or in mural paintings at the Ananda Temple Monastery. At the rear of the Manuha is another row of *kirtimukha* below the roof cornice, but these are in typical Konbaung style, with each grinning face shown with two outstretched arms.

The modern corridor leading to the entrance features a huge stone bowl where worshippers, standing on a ladder, deposit money-offerings. A tall column outside in the compound is dedicated to the eight days of the week, with small figures in niches at the base representing each day.

The Nat Shrine

A modern *nat* shrine opposite the column is in one corner of the compound, close to the road. The woman riding the goose is the *nat* known as Thuraberi, after Sarasvati, the Hindu god and consort of Brahma. She symbolizes wisdom and learning, and that is why she holds a stack of books. The grouping on the right represents Popa Medaw, in the centre, flanked by her two sons, the Taungbyon brothers.

The tall column within the compound is dedicated to the eight days of the week.

This large reclining Buddha is in a separate hall attached to the rear of the temple.

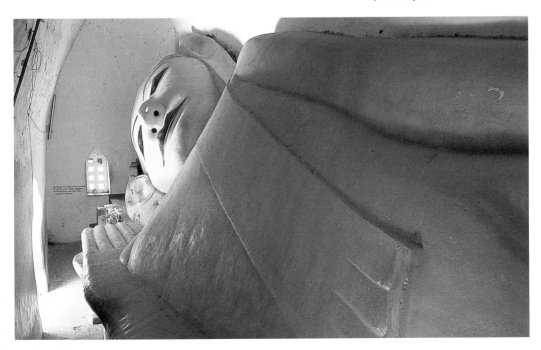

NANPAYA

Highlights

★ rare stone temple at Pagan

★ sculpted figures of Brahma

★ dramatic interior light

Date: 11th-12th centuries

The Nanpaya is celebrated for its masterful stone carving, notably eight large figures of Brahma sculpted on four square piers. Stone used as facing for a brick temple is rare at Pagan.

Visit

The Nanpaya is located in Myinkaba village, a short distance south of the Manuha on the west side of the main paved road. We can walk to the Nanpaya from the Manuha compound or enter on a separate dirt road. The intimate nature of the Nanpaya is a pleasant contrast to the massive Manuha whose white walls are blinding on a clear day.

The Nanpaya's square sanctum is preceded by an entrance hall facing east. Its exterior design is similar to numerous temples at Pagan, but its interior is unusual since it is dominated by four piers. Covering the corridor are half-barrel vaults. Traces of stone masonry flanking the door reveal a missing, narrow outer porch.

Stone facing conceals the temple's brick fabric. The tower and much of the entrance hall have been reconstructed. (DS)

Why Stone?

Stone for exterior facing is noted at only one other temple at Pagan, the Kyauk-ku-umin. The brick-sized stones were first carved

in a nearby workshop and then set into the brick fabric, or carved while *in situ*.

No inscriptions record the histories of these two stone temples, but the fact that this medium was presumably more costly than brick would probably explain its restricted use.

Exterior

The rich relief sculpture surrounding the windows makes a dramatic juxtaposition with the chaste walls and foundation mouldings. The windows are topped by intricate cusped arches, each sheltering a vase from whose pinched rim emanates foliage. This motif is drawn from Indian art where it is known as the 'overflowing vase' (*purna-ghata*, Sanskrit), a symbol associated with fecundity and abundance. Spectacular aquatic creatures, or *makara* (Sanskrit), with frothy, foliate tails make up the ends of the arches. Rising above are ten flame-like projections; in the centre sits a figure with a lotus stalk in each lowered hand.

Above the windows and encircling the walls is a heavily weathered band featuring *kirtimukha*. The best preserved are on the north, to the right of the entrance. At the bottom of the wall is a register of rich foliage inhabited by tiny geese facing the entrance. A goose, or *hamsa* (Pali, Sanskrit) is the vehicle for the god Brahma, but it was a widely used motif at Pagan and should not be connected directly to the depictions of Brahma inside. The finest sculpture is perhaps on the pilasters at the corners, with *kirtimukhas* dominating the top of long V-shaped motifs. The *shikhara* has been largely restored, but there are some original sections on the east and north sides.

Makara, or fanciful crocodile, window pediment.

Top: Two windows and 'overflowing vases' within the cusped arches.

Detail of three-headed Brahma.

The temple is best known for its eight life-sized images of Brahma adorning the four interior piers.

The Sanctum

The inner chamber is preceded by an entrance hall whose fresco work has deteriorated completely. The sanctum is unusual at Pagan, since it is formed by four gigantic square piers joined by arches, a similar arrangement found in the entrance halls of large temples, such as the Ananda and the Dhammayan-gyi. In the centre of the piers is a raised brick platform. If this platform is original is unknown, but it may have supported sculpture. For example, a similar platform in the upstairs shrine at the Kyazin temple (no. 1219) supported four brick Buddhas, placed back to back.

The walls above the piers are conceived like a regular square sanctum, with pilasters on the corners and massive ornamental arches connecting one pier to the other.

The Brahmas

The eight life-sized images of Brahma adorning the four piers rank among the highpoints of Pagan sculpture, proving that the sculptors were no less gifted than the city's painters. Using small blocks to form large wall sculptures is uncommon at Pagan. This technique is also uncommon in Indian art but is noted in some centres, such as at Lalitgiri and Bhubaneshvar in Orissa, and now and then in Madhya Pradesh, such as at Sirpur. It is also a well-known feature of Khmer art.

The Hindu god Brahma was incorporated into Buddhism from
the very beginning where he served the Buddha as a loyal attendant.
Brahma is depicted with three heads, but a fourth is understood to
be in the back. He is shown surrounded by lush vegetation in these
stone reliefs and holds flowering plants. Usually represented in
Hindu art with four-arms, at Pagan the god is normally shown with
only two, and he often holds an umbrella sheltering the Buddha.
Some of the Brahmas are marred by gaping holes in their chests,
probably a result of treasure-hunting in the ancient period.

Above the Brahmas are rows of tightly spaced *kirtimukhas*,
and a lotus band retaining much of its original black, white and red
painting, especially on the southeastern pier. Long V-shaped motifs
capped with intricate *kirtimukha* decorate the corners. How deeply
the stone is embedded into the brick walls can be seen in the
damaged portions.

Lighting Effects
Shafts of light enter the sanctum like laser beams from four skylights
set into the roof terraces, spotlighting the sculpture on the piers at
only certain times of day. No mystical or astronomical links have
ever been suggested, but the temple's ancient architects would
undoubledly have been pleased, if not amused, to realize that their
skylights created memorable snapshots in photo albums worldwide.

Above left: Kirtimukha *frieze
with original paint, interior pier.*

Left: Goose amidst foliage, plinth.

Above: Kirtimukha *on
corner pilaster, exterior wall.*

NAGAYON

Date: 11th-12th century

The temple's murals and sculpture are important examples in Pagan's early history. The sanctum was refurbished completely during the Konbaung period (1752-1885) or earlier. Its spire was repaired after the 1975 earthquake, and its frescos are now under restoration by the Department of Archaeology and Unesco.

Visit

The temple lies just south of Myinkaba village on the paved road between the Walled City and New Pagan. It makes a convenient visit with the nearby Abeyadana and the So-min-gyi.

The Nagayon marks the location where Prince Kyanzittha slept, and a snake, or *naga* (Pali, Sanskrit), watched over him, according to the *Glass Palace Chronicle*. He honoured the spot by constructing a temple after ascending the throne. Its Mon ink inscriptions, sculpture, painting and ground plan ensure its place in Pagan's early period. It has therefore been dated by Luce to about 1090, but it should be thought of as late 11th or early 12th century, until the city's chronology is better understood.

The myth in the Chronicle probably arose because of a large snake-hooded Buddha in the sanctum. This gilded brick image is flanked by two standing Buddhas that were all all part of a refurbishing of the temple executed long after its original

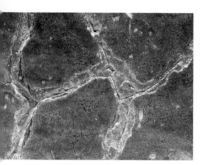

Glazed brick, temple floor.

Nagayon's compound wall and gates.

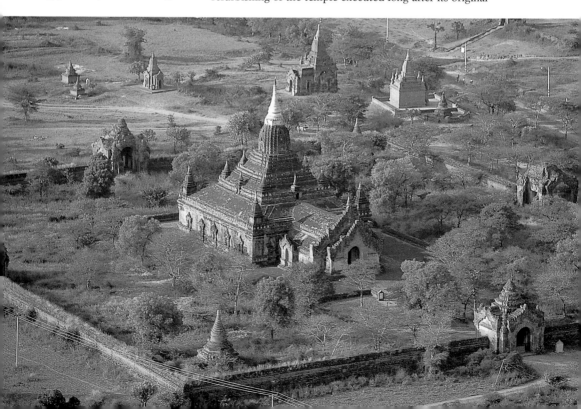

construction. The temple at some stage was named Nagayon, meaning 'protected by a snake.' Later, a myth involving Kyanzittha was likely grafted on to the history of the temple. The temple's original name is unknown.

Its ground plan and exterior appearance broadly resemble the Kubyauk-gyi (Myinkaba), dated to 1113.

Compound Wall and Gateways

The Nagayon is in the centre of a large walled compound and faces north, with four minimally restored gateways. Each resembles a miniature temple, with receding roof terraces and cusped arches. The gate is capped by a small stupa-like dome resting on a large ribbed member, modelled on a similar feature in Indian architecture known as an *amalaka* (Sanskrit). Inside the gate are seated figures with one leg pendant, made of brick with patches of surviving stucco. Similar figures are found in the gates at the Ananda and most likely represent bodhisattvas, though these are larger and completely restored. Traces of original painting can be made out on the ceilings. Inside the compound are four restored stupas symmetrically placed in the corners, probably 12th century additions (nos. 1188-1191).

Exterior

The crowning spire was completely destroyed by the 1975 earthquake but has been repaired. The tower has three terraces, with restored miniature temples and stupas placed on the corners.

The five windows on each wall accentuate the length of the building, but their pediments are restrained compared to the those at the Kubyauk-gyi (Myinkaba). The majority of early temples have three windows on each side of the sanctum. Only a small portion of the original stucco work survives, but it compares favourably with the finest of the early work at Pagan.

Entrance Hall

The wide, barrel-vaulted hall is dominated at the rear by the two heavily restored standing figures made of brick and covered with recently painted stucco. The two are probably the bodhisattvas, Lokanatha and Metteyya, on the right and left respectively, based on identifying ink inscriptions found at Hsale (*Pagan Newsletter*, 1986).

The stucco above the arches in the hall has flaked off, revealing brick and stone voussoirs. Three arches are superimposed for extra strength, a device used at the Ananda and among the later larger temples. The stone voussoirs and rows of header bricks protruding deeply in the wall were designed to affix the outer surface to the inner fabric.

Sculpted wooden beams are seen at the top of the doorways leading to the entrance hall and the sanctum. In style they resemble the wooden doorways found at the Shwe-zigon.

The rear gateway has been partially bricked up to prevent cattle straying inside.

Main entrance gate, interior. Original, brick seated figure in niche. The vaulted ceiling retains much of its painting. (DS)

Two restored figures flanking entrance to inner corridor. Triple arch formed by stone and brick voussoirs, originally concealed by frescos.

The flooring of the entrance hall is glazed sandstone, while that in the interior is glazed brick. Both are coloured green.

Sanctum

Three gilded brick Buddhas standing against the rear wall are the focus of devotion and were likely added sometime before the 18th century. The central one is shielded by the coils of a vast snake, perhaps symbolizing the episode when the Buddha was shielded from a storm by the hoods of a snake-king during his 6th week at Bodh Gaya, following his enlightenment. (This incident is usually depicted with the Buddha seated). The coils of the serpent are shown on the base, with the tail winding up the wall.

Three skylights illuminate the images in the whitewashed interior. The sanctum probably featured originally a single seated Buddha, like the Kubyauk-gyi (Myinkaba), or perhaps a triad of Buddhas, like the Pahto-thamya. The walls were almost surely once covered in frescos.

The doorjambs of the shrine were whitewashed centuries ago, attested by several 16th-century horoscopes. Other horoscopes in the entrance hall are 15th century, although one is dated to 1694.

Sculptures within the Corridor and Entrance hall

Stone sculptures were placed in scores of niches, on both sides of the inner corridor and in the barrel-vaulted entrance hall. These were removed to the museum in the late 1980s, and nearly all were replaced by gypsum replicas. Seventy-one niches now hold 69 reproductions. Most were placed in their original locations, but some are out of position.

The sculpture in the entrance hall ranged widely over episodes in the Buddha's life, recalling the themes in the four halls at the Ananda. Each hall at the Ananda had sixteen figures, but here there were only ten. (Only one sculpture was missing from the ten niches). These scenes from the life of the historical Buddha Gotama, set the stage for the sculpture around the sanctum which focusses on the Buddhas that preceded him.

The sculptures lining both sides of the corridor are dedicated to the theme of the 28 Buddhas. The historical Buddha named Gotama was preceded by twenty-seven Buddhas whose biographies closely reflect that of Gotama, such as royal parentage, an encounter with Mara, and achieving enlightenment beneath a special tree. The only Buddha to be shown standing is Dipankara, the Buddha who prophesizes the birth of Gotama. Each Buddha is represented twice.

The first is shown before enlightenment, in the meditation-gesture, seated upon a high base, ornamented with small figures relating to the life of each individual Buddha. Then the Buddha is shown in the earth-touching gesture, signifying his enlightenment.

As we face the sanctum, the series runs clockwise in the correct sequence, beginning on the outer wall, to the right of the shrine door. The first Buddha, Tanhankara, is placed in a niche on the far right, bordering the corridor. The second and third Buddhas are missing but the fourth, Dipankara, is on the side wall (east). The series continues around the rear wall and finishes with the 14th Buddha, Sumedha, before crossing over to the outer wall (east). These then continue in a clockwise fashion, alternating also with Buddhas in the earth-touching gesture. Gotama, the last Buddha, appears toward the middle of the other side wall (west), followed by the depiction of his enlightenment, flanked by Brahma and Sakka, according to Luce.

The remaining five niches (west and north wall) were filled with standing and seated Buddhas. Luce was unable to relate these to the overall schema, but they may connect to some of the events associated with the Seven Weeks. (The only omission is the sixth week where Gotama is shielded by the hoods of the snake-king). If these remaining sculptures are not linked to the iconographic programme as a whole, then this suggests that they were inserted randomly at the time, or that some fiddling occurred before Luce's day.

Snake-hooded Buddha and flanking Buddhas.

The Frescos

The sorry condition of the Nagayon's murals does little justice to their quality and importance in the art of Pagan. The frescos require a good torch and some patience, but our inspection will seem less hapless if we recognize that the ancients must have had a hard time too.

The indefatigable Luce and his Burmese colleagues laboured with the tiny Mon ink inscriptions and identified most of the scenes. They range widely over the Pali canon, from *jatakas*, through *suttas* (sermons) and sections from the biography of the Buddha. There was a preference for a clockwise direction in general, but this was not completely adhered to. The most impressive compositions are high on the walls but their condition is miserable. There is no strict beginning or end to the murals, unlike the design for the sculptures.

The style of the Nagayon paintings broadly relates to that of the Kubyauk-gyi (Myinkaba) but is less mannered and somewhat fresher in feeling. Once the paintings have been restored, it will be easier to assess the place of the Nagayon's murals in the development of Pagan's art.

The sanctum outer wall

Small *jatakas* are painted in the area surrounding the niches containing sculpture on the sanctum wall. The series begins with the first tale on the south, or rear wall, a short distance east of centre, and proceeds in a clockwise fashion, concluding on the south face. Luce identified at least 284, with their Pali names and a short description in Mon.

The panels above the top row of *jatakas* are much larger and illustrate subjects drawn from a variety of sources, including the *jatakas*. These are about three metres in height and the longest is nearly four metres. Luce found no order or sequence, but perhaps the direction was clockwise, to judge from the numbering of the *jatakas*. Some panels repeat certain *suttas* from the *Digha Nikaya* that are found on the small register above. One *sutta* extends into at least three panels. The *jatakas* that Luce identified begin with 509 and include 510, 515, 533, 544, proceeding clockwise. Each story is contained in a single panel, but sometimes has multiple captions. A few episodes from the life of the Buddha were probably drawn from the *Nidanakatha*.

The most dramatic composition surrounded the central niche on the rear of the sanctum and depicts the attack of Mara. This panel measures over eight metres in length and is the longest example at Pagan. The battle with Mara also occurs on the rear wall of the sanctums at the Abeyadana and the Kubyauk-gyi (Myinkaba).

Above these large panels are much smaller depictions, each presenting one of the Buddha's sermons. The series begins above the entrance to the shrine, and proceeds clockwise, that is, first to the wall on the left (east). It starts with 34 *suttas* from the *Digha Nikaya*, followed by those from the *Majjihma Nikaya*. The scenes are standardized, with a single seated Buddha shown in the earth-touching or teaching-gesture. These panels are nearly a metre high.

Outer Wall of Corridor

Between the windows and niches of the outer wall are small framed paintings of the Buddha preaching his sermons. Luce read 186 names and tentatively identified their sources in the Pali canon but felt that the panels did not adhere to a clear order.

The upper section of the walls has large panels over a metre in height and over two metres long. Some scenes are taken from the *Khuddaka Nikaya* and the *Nidanakatha*. *Jatakas* that Luce could read, going in a clockwise direction beginning on the left wall (east) are: 531, 449, 276, 514, 532, 537. All extend into at least two panels, except no. 276. That *jataka* no. 537 is the last tale before the famous set of ten (nos. 538-547) can hardly be coincidental, but the last ten do not seem to be given special prominence. The single *jataka* from the last ten (no. 544) occurs on the inner wall, where it appears immediately next to *jataka* no. 533.

Those planning these frescoes deliberately chose to only highlight certain *jatakas* (the large panels), unlike most temples that showed the entire series. The reasons for this selection are unknown, but it implies that certain tales were more popular than others, at least for these artists or patrons. It is also clear that there was little importance attached in presenting these *jatakas* in the correct sequence.

Opposite: Dancing figure, outer shrine wall, plinth.

ABEYADANA

Highlights

★ Frescos

Date: 11th-12th centuries

The Abeyadana is known for its frescos featuring Mahayana imagery, contrasting with the Theravada themes found in other early temples, such as the Pahto-thamya and the Nagayon. The temple's founding is associated with Kyanzittha's queen in legend, but no firm evidence supports this. The temple, crowned by a bell-shaped stupa, probably dates to the late 11th or early 12th century.

Visit

The Abeyadana is located off the main road leading south of the Walled City, shortly beyond Myinkaba village. It is near the Nagayon and can also be combined with the So-min-gyi stupa.

The founding of the temple is mired in myth. The *Glass Palace Chronicle* claims that the temple was built by King Kyanzittha's principal queen, or Apayatana, a modification of 'Apay-ratana' (Pali), or 'Beloved Jewell.' Luce noted two much later ink inscriptions in the entrance hall that further associate Kyanzittha with the temple. However, no inscriptions survive from the time of the temple's construction, so we cannot be sure of the patron or its date.

The *Chronicle* also reports that the queen's daughter wished to marry a king of Pateikkara, identified by Luce with a location in eastern India (now Bangladesh). He concluded that her mother must also have been from eastern India, and that her homeland explains

Rear view of the Abeyadana.

The Hindu god Shiva upon his bull, shrine wall, west.

the iconography and style of the painting. These multiple shaky assumptions illustrate how the *Chronicle* has muddled our views of ancient Pagan.

Seventy niches inside the corridor and sanctum were intended for sculpture, but only a handful survived into the 21st century. In style, they resemble those in the Nagayon, Kubyauk-gyi (Myinkaba) and the Ananda. They have now been removed to the Pagan Museum.

Exterior

The temple faces north, like the nearby Nagayon. Both have similar plans and are roughly the same size, but the Abeyadana feels more intimate, perhaps because it lacks a wide compound and imposing gates. Each side has three windows, reduced from the Nagayon's five, enhancing a sense of compactness. Sloping roof terraces support a bell-shaped stupa surmounted by an octagonal spire made up of separate umbrellas. The umbrellas are linked by vertical bands, similar to the spire at the Pahto-thamya and those found on miniature stone stupas from eastern India.

Rather horrible new cement sculpture has replaced the original double-bodied lions on the entrance hall roof. The lowest terrace has miniature stupas, while the second has urns. Stairways to the terraces, skylights and glazed ornament found at the Nagayon are nowhere in evidence here. There are also no stone voussoirs or rows of header bricks, as we see at the Nagayon. In this way it is similar to the Pahto-thamya, another early temple. The analysis of such features may help to determine a more reliable chronology of the temples.

Roughly seventy-percent of the exterior stucco survives, but the cusped pediments above the windows are rigorously plain compared to even those at the Nagayon and have little connection to the flamboyant examples at the Kubyauk-gyi (Myinkaba). On the other hand, the perforated brick windows beneath the pediments scream for attention, delicately ornamented with raised floral designs as fresh as the day they were applied. The finesse required to balance these bricks within the empty window space, edge to edge, would test anyone's dexterity, let alone patience.

Mara attacking on his elephant, shrine wall, rear. (Courtesy Lilian Handlin)

Entrance Hall

The side and rear walls of the entrance hall were covered with *jatakas*, but today only traces survive. The series consists of eight tiers beginning on the top of the north wall, as we face the outer door. Damaged frames to the left of the doorway contained scenes serving as a preamble to the *jatakas*, but these are virtually all gone. Immediately to the right of the doorway is a frame depicting the standing Buddha Dipankara, followed by the first *jataka*. Dipankara also begins the great *jataka* cycle at the Kubyauk-gyi (Myinkaba).

The Pali title is recorded for each birth-story, together with a brief description of the action and the number of the *jataka* within its division (*nipata*, Pali). The series runs clockwise around the walls and concludes on the north wall where it began. The number of *jatakas* may have totalled the same as the unglazed plaques at the East and West Hpetleik stupas, 550, rather than the usual 547, but Luce was unsure since much of the painting was missing.

The Sanctum

A large seated Buddha takes up much of the the rear wall, flanked by two disciples. The three are heavily restored but the surrounding stucco and base are original. The throne back, adorned with *kinnara*, *kinnari*, and rampant lions, recalls similar examples from eastern Indian art and a description of a throne in Kyanzittha's palace inscription. Four seated male figures appear within the base, their feet dangling over a semi-circular horizontal band. Such breaks in symmetry add a welcome spontaneity.

Only one sculpture was found in the six niches inside and little of the painting remains, apart from rows of figures faintly discerned high on the walls below the cloister vault. On the wall next to the entrance can be seen one seated Buddha, his left hand raised in the direction of a seated, bearded figure, an unusual subject.

The wide walls preceding the sanctum were once covered with seated figures and dancers at the bottom. Intrusive painting includes two kneeling male figures holding flowers that are virtually identical to two figures found in the same location at the Pahto-thamya. These are probably from the 14th-16th centuries, or possibly earlier.

Outer Wall of Sanctum

The front wall of the sanctum is dominated by an enormous arch. To the sides are two wide niches, once containing recumbent brick and stucco figures featuring the Dream of Maya and the Death of the Buddha, on the left and right, respectively. Sixteen narrow niches surround the outside of the sanctum originally filled with stone sculpture.

The top half of the sanctum is encircled by seven painted horizontal registers, consisting of numerous seated Buddhas, white

This niche once held a brick sculpture depicting the Death of the Buddha, paired with the Dream of Maya, in the niche on the opposite side of the shrine entrance. (DS)

stupas, a floral band, and a row of red-robed Buddhas. Above
the wide niche on the right are figures honouring the death of the
Buddha, including a row of Brahmas. Over the niche on the other
side are females, one of whom holds a child in her lap, an unusual
theme. She is perhaps Maya, holding the Buddha, an unprecedented
depiction.

Each of the trefoil niches is elaborately ornamented with stucco,
as if making up for the simplicity of the outside pediments. Between
the niches are tall, thin stands supporting roundels. Midway up the
shaft are four-armed bodhisattvas, seated upon lions and elephants.
These stands may represent real objects used in ritual contexts, or
perhaps they were simply fanciful creations.

The seventeen roundels feature deities belonging squarely to the
Hindu tradition. The gods on the side walls face toward the sanctum
entrance, while those on the rear wall turn to the wall's central niche.
To the right of the entrance (west) the series starts with the three
major Hindu gods, Brahma, Shiva, and Vishnu. On the opposite
wall (east) are represented the three great River Goddesses of India,
the Ganges riding upon her crocodile, Sarasvati upon her goose, and
Jumna upon her tortoise. Other deities on the same wall probably
depict Indian directional deities, such as Agni on his goat and Indra
on his elephant. Hindu deities were also part of Mahayana Buddhism
prevalent in eastern India, but this is the clearest expression of these
themes at Pagan.

The most spectacular composition is on the rear of the shrine,
depicting the defeat of Mara riding an elephant, which charges on
the left of the central niche and flees in defeat on the right, in the
opposite direction.

*Woman and child, shrine wall,
front. (Courtesy Lilian Handlin)*

Bodhisattva next to makara
*with gaping mouth, upper row,
outer corridor.*

Outer Wall of Corridor

Each side of the passage leading to the outer corridor
was once painted with a standing bodhisattva. These
mirror other bodhisattvas found on the walls inside
the porch, but all these figures are badly weathered.
Above one of the bodhisattvas in the inside passage
are six horoscopes, the earliest dating to 1602. The
location of these bodhisattvas is similar to that at the
Kubyauk-gyi (Myinkaba).

The original focus of the outer walls were
sculptures within two parallel rows of niches that
were surrounded by some of the richest mural
painting at Pagan. Each painted niche on the lower
half of the wall displays four, two-armed bodhisattvas.
They sit with their right leg raised and generally hold
weapons and wear boots. Above them are other seated
bodhisattvas, with their right leg pendant. Some hold
circular lotuses and are likely Avalokiteshvara, while
others are Manjushri, who balances a palm-leaf
manuscript on a blue lotus, two of his common
attributes.

The top half of the wall contains standing two-
armed bodhisattvas, also holding weapons. Only one

*Two tantric deities in
caves, outer corridor, rear.*

Ascetic in cave, outer corridor, east.

holds a lotus. Above them are long lotus stalks supporting seated Buddhas shown in the teaching-gesture, beneath which are bearded laymen and crowned individuals offering devotion. Luce estimated that there were 36 bodhisattvas in all but some have been lost, especially on the north and west walls.

Figures in Caves

Dividing the two upper and lower sections of the wall is a band of small figures depicted in individual caves. Each wall has thirty (east, west, south) and there were probably thirty along the north wall giving a total of 120, but most of these are lost. At least some, perhaps fifteen, are Buddhas, shown with various hand gestures, while another fifteen or so are dressed as monks engaged in diverse activities. Some of these scenes have been connected to *jatakas*, but this seems doubtful, in view of the context. Another group appears to feature two-armed bodhisattvas. Another ten or so seem to be the consorts of bodhisattvas, known as Taras, most with two arms but others with four or even six.

By far the largest group, almost thirty, depict ascetics living in caves. They are emaciated and their hair is usually piled up in two buns, resembling ascetics in much of Indian art. Some are shown conversing with people or with animals, such as a monkey or a deer. Some wear a strap around their waist that winds around a raised leg, an aid to meditation often seen in Indian art. These ascetics perhaps are part of a group of semi-legendary Buddhist figures called *siddhas*, and associated with supernatural accomplishments, a theme known to eastern India and especially popular in Nepal and Tibet.

Another group are so-called Tantric deities, roughly equally divided between male and female. These figures manifest various terrifying aspects, such as standing upon a corpse and holding various weapons. Some are animal-headed. These diverse personages are placed in no obvious order, with monks, Taras, ascetics, and Buddhas in neighbouring caves, like a single community.

The precise identities of these figures remains enigmatic, but they raise issues critical for understanding the civilization of Pagan. For example, was a specific text or iconographic manual from eastern India, Nepal or Tibet responsible for this imagery? Or did the artists and patrons pick and choose themes from a variety of sources, such as from artists' sketch-books brought to Pagan from India or other countries, with no deep understanding of their meaning? The seventeen Hindu gods represented in the roundels raise identical questions.

The enigmatic role of Mahayana Buddhism at Pagan is underscored by the juxtaposition of prominent bodhisattvas and *jatakas* with Pali captions. Were the sharp distinctions made today between the Theravada and Mahayana divisions important for the ancients? For example, the terms Theravada and Mahayana never occur in inscriptions at Pagan. Pagan's residents likely absorbed a variety of influences, from Sri Lanka, eastern India and perhaps Nepal and Tibet. However, as noted elsewhere, the general religious tone at Pagan was Theravada Buddhism, as evidenced by the copious quotations from the Pali canon recorded in ink inscriptions. Equally, the *jatakas*, are widely considered by modern scholars to be associated with the Pali Theravada tradition. Indeed, they are rarely represented in eastern Indian art where the Mahayana flourished, but are commonplace at Pagan. Nevertheless, *jatakas* with Pali titles in the entrance hall of the Abeyadana coexist with Mahayana depictions, Tantric deities and Hindu gods. Were Theravada believers in the entrance hall automatically transformed into Mahayanists and Tantrics after passing from the hall to the sanctum? Pagan's residents clearly did not form the distinctions we do today.

Bodhisattva holding sword, upper row, outer corridor.

If Mahayana Buddhism played a truly significant role at Pagan, then at least some of the numerous stone inscriptions would have revealed this. It seems most likely that the lavish painting which included multi-armed bodhisattvas and even Tantric figures were all regarded simply as Buddhist, auspicious, and infused with merit. Thus, Mahayana subject matter was probably borrowed from eastern India and combined with Theravada material in ways that scarcely make sense from a modern perspective that draws a hard line between these two divisions of Buddhism. This borrowing from eastern India was not so much an absorption of Mahayana beliefs, as a cultural and artistic appreciation.

SO-MIN-GYI

Date: 11th-12th centuries

The stupa is celebrated for its glazed panels ornamenting its terraces. The lively figurative work proves that artists in clay competed in ingenuity with painters and sculptors, especially when freed from the formal constraints of depicting *jataka* tales. The earliest dated glazed work is found at the Shwegu-gyi, 1131, but glazing certainly started earlier and continued into the Konbaung period (1752-1885).

Visit

The So-min-gyi stupa is located south of Myinkaba village and can be visited together with the Abeyadana and the Nagayon. Unlike many stupas designed with median stairways, the terraces at the So-min-gyi are unconnected with each other and access to the top was therefore never intended. The square terraces are crowned by an octagonal base supporting the large dome. Thick raised bands originally surrounded the base of the dome whose tapered summit was also encircled by ringed bands. Small corner stupas on the top terrace are original, though greatly restored, but there is no firm evidence for the shape of similar stupas now found on the lower terraces. Each terrace is topped with a row of rounded crenellations, like the Shwe-san-daw and Mingalazedi. The spire of the stupa was

The stupa's glazed figurative work encircling the terraces is unique. The temple was restored recently and a new hti *installed in a grand ceremony in 2002.*

destroyed long ago. The monument was restored recently by the Department of Archaeology and a ceremony celebrating the raising of a gilded spire, or *hti*, was held at the end of 2002.

The So-min-gyi is the only stupa at Pagan to display rows of glazed ornament encircling each terrace. Many glazed segments are missing, but enough remains to give the sense of its original appearance. All of the surrounding brickwork would have been covered with stucco, thereby enhancing the effect of the glazed work which was inserted into continous shallow registers. The pieces vary in length but the longest are 66 cm. The height is about 20 cm and the thickness is between 7-10 cm. The edges on the long ends of each individual glazed segment are fashioned with a pronounced slant, thereby ensuring a firmer fit with its neighbour.

Within connected frothy lotus bands are seen male dancers and drummers, tortoises, lions, birds and monkeys, three-headed elephants, floral medallions, and shell patterns. Prominently displayed on the recessed corners were the faces of large ogres. The tops of their faces are glazed but their jaws were originally formed by stucco placed over the ends of stone tenons set deeply within the brick fabric. The stucco has flaked off so the ogres are missing the lower part of their face, unexpectedly enhancing the sense of the macabre.

Examples of the glazed ceramics are in the museums of Pagan, Yangon and Mandalay, while other pieces are now deposited in Berlin (Museum für Indische Kunst), removed by Fritz von Noetling, in the late 19th century.

Horse within a band of foliage.

Three-headed elephant.

Surviving glaze on this small bird contrasts dramatically with the underlying surface.

SEIN-NYET-AMA & SEIN-NYET-NYIMA

Date: c. 12th-13th century

Such a pairing of temple and stupa is rare at Pagan, as if the ancient architects had the the foresight to realize that visitors today would not benefit from viewing these two different building types in one glance. The spire of the stupa was spoiled in the 1975 quake but was sensitively repaired in 1977-1978. The ancient names of the monuments are unknown, but today the temple is called Sein-nyet-ama (elder sister) and the stupa is Sein-nyet-nyima (younger sister).

Visit

This impressive duo dominates the landscape on the major road leading south of the Walled City, after leaving Myinkaba village. To capture both monuments in a single photographic frame is easiest from outside the walls. The entrance from the road actually faces the rear of the temple.

Stupa drum rataining spectacular original stucco ornament. Four Buddhas in the teaching-gesture are within niches on the cardinal directions. Restored corner stupas. (PP)

The temple

The temple faces east and its entrance hall is directly aligned with
the stupa. Its plan is designed around a solid core, with prominent
doorways on the sides and rear. We can spot that it is a 'late' temple
because doorways appear on the sides and rear of the sanctum. For
'early' temples there were no doorways but windows, like the
Nagayon and the Kubyauk-gyi (Myinkaba), dated to 1113.

The exterior has lost roughly 80% of its stucco, but the
best remaining examples are on the façade and on the pilasters
surrounding the rear door. Its lace-like quality can be associated
with work from the second half of the 12th century, such as the
Sulamani, 1183, or the Kubyauk-gne (no. 1391), dated to 1198.

The wide barrel-vaulted hall leading to the main shrine is lit by
the main door and four windows. The little fresco work remaining
on the ceiling reveals a pattern of squares and circles confined
within separate borders.

The poorly preserved wall painting on both side walls once
boasted a complete series of *jatakas* contained in eleven tiers. These
are identified below in weathered Burmese ink inscriptions. The
series begins at the top of the south wall in the southeast corner (on
the left as we enter), and winds clockwise around the entrance hall.
Each tier contains roughly fifty *jatakas*. The name of each and its
action is briefly described, such as, 'The Buddha-to-be being a lion'.

*The Sein-nyet-ama temple, left, and
the Sein-nyet-nyima stupa, right,
were built together on an east-west
axis, a rare pairing.*

Seated Buddha in the teaching-gesture within cusped niche. Stupa drum, west side. A kirtimukha *frieze encircles the drum.*

Roughly hewn stones bind the surface of the wall to inner fabric. North entrance hall. (DS)

Above the tiers of *jatakas* are the Twenty-Eight Buddhas but without identifying inscriptions.

The shrine doorway is defined by a large arch missing nearly all of its stucco, except at the far right where a lively *makara* chases a lion. Inside is a solid core encircled by a corridor covered in a three-quarter barrel vault. On the front and rear sides are large restored Buddha images set into deep niches, with only small traces of the original painting. The other sides of the core were once adorned with huge painted Buddhas, with only traces remaining in the shallow frames. The interior was covered with a light tan-coloured wash, similar to the Dhammayan-gyi and other temples.

In the corridor can be seen large stones embedded in the walls used to bind the facing with the inner fabric. The best examples are on the north side where half dozen or so roughly hewn sandstone pieces are visible near the door.

Let into one corner of the entrance hall is a stairway providing access to the three roof terraces where spectacular views of the adjacent stupa unfold. The spire of the temple was restored in the 1990s based on conjecture alone.

The Stupa

The graceful shape of the bell-shaped dome and its rich stucco ornament make this one of the finest surviving stupas at Pagan.

The architects omitted the median stairways, witnessed on many large stupas, such as the Mingalazedi or the Shwe-san-daw. This lack of access suggests that circumambulation occurred at ground level, if at all. The spire was badly damaged in the quake of 1975 but repaired sensitively.

The dome encased a smaller stupa that was once partially visible by a large exposed cavity on the southeastern side. The age of the encased monument cannot be determined. Over fifty percent of the original stucco survives.

Four niches set into the dome at the cardinal directions are filled with seated Buddhas whose hands are in the teaching-gesture. Each niche takes the form of a miniature temple, complete with a pediment and crowned by a tower. This tall device links the base of the dome with the summit, surmounted by a register of sloping lotus leaves. The shape and ornamentation of this dome is found throughout Pagan (nos. 1507, 1518)

Perhaps the finest sculpture at Pagan is found among the twelve figures placed on the corners of the three terraces. Each is made of carved brick covered with a thick layer of stucco moulded by hand. The lowest terrace was reserved for bird-like (?) ogres. The most impressive example is on the left, after exiting the temple. It sits majestically, with a great snarl and holds a double three-pronged weapon in its left hand. The next level has lions, while the figures on the top terrace were probably giant birds, to judge from surviving fragments.

Ogre, brick and stucco,
north-west corner, first terrace.

EAST AND WEST HPETLEIK

Date: 11th century

The *jataka* tiles housed here are counted among the most exciting and engaging in all of Southeast Asia. Also, the series is the among the earliest at Pagan.

Visit

The two adjacent stupas are found in the southern end of the archaeological zone. The one on the left is the West Hpetleik, while the East Hpetleik stands on the right. The two were constructed slightly off axis, although they were built to the same breadth. Both stupas are based around a solid, square, brick core, surrounded by a corridor once covered with a three-quarter barrel vault, surviving only on the East Hpetleik. This layout is unique for a stupa at Pagan.

The entrance to the East Hpetleik was probably a minor entrance originally. The principal ancient entry led from a narrow porch on the opposite side, designed with eight niches for sculpture (missing since the temple's discovery in the late 19th century). It is today engulfed in vegetation and difficult to approach. The main entrance to the second stupa was either on the north, indicated by a narrow porch, or on the east.

The stupa on the right is capped by a plain, square block, a form perhaps derived from Sri Lanka, while the corresponding crown on the other is segmented into recessed vertical divisions, some still with

East Hpetleik. Modern surrounding wall and cement roof. The stupa is designed with four niches in the cardinal directions and a square top. It is missing its original finial. The principal entrance was on the opposite side, on the east.

original stucco. Examples of these two distinctive stupa types are found all over Pagan, but their pairing here is proof that the architects deliberately juxtaposed styles. The finials to both stupas are missing. Four vertical niches on their drums once contained Buddha figures, similar to the Sein-nyet-nyima stupa and many others.

The drum of the West Hpetleik contained small terracotta votive plaques with long tenons on their reverse sides, designed for secure insertion into the building's fabric. Each depicts a standing Buddha, with both arms raised at the elbow, the hands upheld near the shoulders, a form of the teaching-gesture rarely found at Pagan. Plaques can still be seen *in situ* in an unrepaired cavity on the north side.

The Jatakas

The corridors of both stupas were filled with rows of unglazed *jataka* plaques. The standard Pali *jataka* series from Sri Lanka totals 547 tales, but here three extra *jatakas* were added (nos. 497-499), raising the total to 550. The three extra tiles probably reflect a Southeast Asian, Burmese or Mon variant. Other ceramic series and painted examples adhere to the standard number although the ordering of the last ten *jatakas* is somewhat different at Pagan.

Each tale is identified with an inscription on the top and its Pali name followed by its number. Luce and his colleagues determined that the sequence of the *jatakas* was designed in a counter-clockwise direction, another unique feature among the *jataka* tiles at Pagan. It is also the only surviving large series of *jatakas* that is unglazed.

East Hpetleik (stupa on the right)

The series begins on the inner face of the east corridor, running from top to bottom in four parallel tiers. It proceeds north, in a counter-clockwise direction. The last *jataka* on the inner face is no. 490, which ends on the bottom tier on the south side. The series then skips to the outer face of the corridor, contained within two parallel rows of niches, beginning on the bottom tier and ending on the top. It starts on the east wall, with *jataka* no. 491. The last ten *jatakas* were accorded more than a single plaque. A few surviving tiles belonging to the Vessantara *jataka* are each numbered '550'. On the outer wall, on the western side, are a dozen or so plaques featuring the various tortures in hell. Many are labelled, such as 'False Weights Hell', presumably intended for those engaged in monkey business in the market place. One of the best shows a shower of spears raining down on three helpless kneeling figures.

Top: Three jatakas *(nos. 497-499) were added to the Hpetleik series, creating a total of 550, deviating from the standard 547 in the Pali canon. Therefore, the top* jataka, *no. 540 in the canon, is incised with the number 543. The bottom* jataka, *no. 534 in the canon, is labelled no. 537. West Hpetleik, outer corridor, east side.*

Above: A small group of hell scenes are found to the left of the modern entrance, East Hpetleik. (DS)

West Hpetleik (Stupa on the left)

The direction of the tiles in the West Hpetleik is also counter-clockwise and starts within the east corridor, inner side, top row. Here there are three parallel rows and not four, such as we have at the East Hpetleik. The last *jataka* on this face of the corridor

Jataka *inscribed with number 539, or no. 536 in the Pali canon.*

Detail from jataka *no. 537.*

was 340. Luce was not sure where the remaining *jatakas* (341-550) began on the two rows of niches making up the outer corridor wall but felt that it went from top to bottom. Luce noted that all of the *jatakas* once on the outer wall (210 tiles, or *jatakas* 341-550) were lying loose, awaiting to be re-inserted.

This stupa differs from its companion by having an outer wall on the east face dedicated to tiles; today's entrance is on this side. The outer wall is divided into two rows of parallel niches, and its tiles repeat the same *jatakas* contained within the inner corridor, beginning with 493 and ending with 500. It starts in the north, from the bottom tier upwards and goes south, or in a clockwise direction, unlike the other plaques. The series ends on the far left, top row, as we enter the stupa today. The last ten *jatakas* appear to have been assigned only a single plaque, unlike in the neighbouring stupa. Reasons for repeating a part of the series on this wall cannot be readily explained.

Many of the plaques in both stupas were reinserted in the early 20th century into the wrong niches and some were incorrectly placed in a clockwise direction. Also, some loose plaques from one temple strayed into the other, another fact bemoaned by Luce.

Tiny inscriptions have been incised in the stucco separating the top and bottom rows of *jatakas* (the corridor we first see as we enter the West Hpetleik). These Mon glosses recap the story for the tiles. Only one inscription survives on the left half of the wall but many can be detected on the right, with some difficulty. It is unknown why these captions were placed here; they may have served a didactic purpose. The inscription above tile numbered 502 has been translated by Luce, "The bodhisattva was King Siviraja. He gave ... six hundred thousand ... every day. He gave as a gift ..."

Little can be added to Luce's description of the tiles, "There is nothing stilted, formal or exaggerated; and not overmuch that is conventional or repetitive. One would call them realistic, but for their constant simple dignity and grace. Calm, not dramatic nor theatrical, they tell their story and have done." (Luce, I, 266). Note the intricate detailing, such as the incised patterning in garments. The compositions are more complex and livelier than the later glazed *jataka* series, such as at the Ananda or the Dhamma-yazika. They are far removed from the crude unglazed examples belonging to the Shwe-san-daw and perhaps connected to the reign of Anawrahta (1044-1077). The Hpetleik tiles probably date to a period between the Shwe-san-daw tiles and the rise of the great glazed series, beginning with the Ananda. A date in the late 11th century is therefore possible.

The Kyauk-sa-ga-gyi Temple

A remarkable building across the dirt road from the two Hpetleik shrines is the Kyauk-sa-ga-gyi (no. 1029). It is probably an early temple, from the late 11th or 12th century. It has been heavily restored but its stone sculpture is among the finest, especially a seated Buddha in the teaching-gesture. There were originally eleven stone images and some were removed to the museum. Recently, U Thein Lwin uncovered in the surrounding area a handful of terracotta votive plaques nearly a metre in height, the largest in Burma. These appear to be made from the same mould used for plaques at the Maung Di stupa found between Yangon and Twante, and bear the name of Anawrahta.

East Hpetleik, niches containing jataka *plaques. (DS)*

Standing Buddha and disciple (?) inside Kyauk-sa-ga-gyi Temple (no, 1029). (DS)

Between the rows of tiles is a stucco register incised with Mon captions found only in the West Hpetleik outer corridor, near modern entrance. Top: Jataka *531 and 502 (below). (DS)*

NORTHERN GROUP

UPALI THEIN
HTILOMINLO
KUBYAUK-GYI (WETKYI-IN)
SHWE-ZIGON
KYAUK-KU-UMIN

UPALI THEIN

Date: 1793-1794

The Upali Thein was used as an ordination hall where monks were inducted into the Buddhist community. The frescos date to the late 18th century when Pagan saw a wave of new construction and refurbishment. The subject matter of the murals focuses largely on ordination, the life of the monk, and the historical Buddha.

Previous pages: Visible up and down the Irrawaddy, the glistening Shwe-zigon Stupa is the principal focus for the northern group of temples.

Visit

The Upali Thein lies on the north side of the Pagan-Nyaung-U Road leading between the Walled City and the Shwe-zigon stupa. A nearby landmark is the huge Htilominlo, on the opposite side of the road. The long building faces east in the centre of a modest compound, with narrow gateways on two sides. The hall is illuminated by the principal entrance in the east, two median doorways, and a fourth in the rear.

The monument and its paintings suffered greatly during the earthquake of 1975, and stout metal ribbing inside now reinforces its walls. The seated Buddha on the pedestal at the rear is restored, but

Rear view of Upali Ordination Hall.

its surrounding painting is largely original, together with roughly
60% of the wall murals. The barrel vaulted ceiling is hipped at both
ends and is dominated by four large square floral designs ingeniously
entwined together, reminiscent of the ceiling frescos at the Ananda
Temple Monastery. Only about 35% of the ceiling painting survives.

These murals were done roughly ten years or so after those at
the Ananda Temple Monastery and about thirty years following the
dated paintings at the Shwe-zigon stupa.

The Proud Donors

An ink inscription outside the temple above the window on the
north side records that the paintings were started on March 4, 1793,
and completed a year later at a total cost of 1,920 *kyat*. A short
inscription located inside, within the window chamber on the left
(south), records that the hall was founded in 1794, or in the Burmese
era, 1156 ('1156 *ku thein tin*').

The donors were unnamed but they were most likely the
husband and wife painted on both sides of the short passageway
leading into the hall. Each points their finger toward the interior,
as if exclaiming, "Look what I have donated!" They are idealized,
without individualization, since realism was not a concern of the
artists. From the faint ink inscriptions next to the donors, the word
for ordination hall ('*thein*', Burmese) can be made out.

Donor pointing toward the interior of the hall, entrance passage.

Buddha Medhankara, setting out (bottom) and enlightenment (top).

The Wall Paintings

The walls are divided into three horizontal
registers of roughly equal size. The uppermost
features the 28 Buddhas, each master beneath the
specific tree connected with his enlightenment
and identified by ink inscriptions in Burmese
below. In the row beneath are the same
individual 28 Buddhas setting out on their
spiritual quests, riding their different mounts,
such as horses and elephants, and accompanied
by male attendants in procession holding lamps.
In the caption below, these auxiliary figures are
called '*nats*', the traditional Burmese 'spirits';
these characters are always referred to as 'gods',
or *devas* in the Pali sources. In each composition
the demon Mara is shown on the right as a well-
appointed courtier, defiantly holding aloft his
opened right hand, as if to say, "Halt! Abandon
your spiritual quest right here."

A formulaic inscription in Burmese below
identifies each scene: "Maydinkaya [Medhankara,
Pali] on horseback in the forest and *nats* show
lighting [with torches]." Medhankara is the
second Buddha among the 28. The series starts
immediately to the right of the doorway and
proceeds clockwise. The Buddha Gotama
appears to the left of the doorway as the last
in the sequence of 28.

Left: Nats *holding torches.*

Right: A Buddha departing by elephant, rear wall.

The lowest register depicts the historical Buddha delivering sermons at important monasteries in eastern India during the annual rainy season. This theme was not popular in the ancient period but enjoyed considerable favour by the Konbaung age. These episodes were first summarized in a 5th-century Pali text, the *Manoratthavilasini*, but the inspiration for later painters were more likely later recensions of this work. There were in total 44 rainy seasons, but the Buddha returned over twenty times to one monastery, in Savatthi. The scenes do not proceed in a strictly sequential way in the hall, unlike the other themes that are in correct order and go clockwise. For example, the caption beneath the scene closest to the door identifies the scene as a brahmin village where the Buddha spent his eleventh rainy season after his enlightenment (note two bearded and turbaned figures representing Indians).

Buddha passing a rainy season within a monastery.

How A Humble Barber came to be Ordained

Behind the central Buddha is a deep, recessed doorway with a long painted panel featuring four monks seated before a king. The two-line inscription below reads: "Four monks arrived from Sri Lanka: Shin Mahasa, Shin Anuruddha, Shin Buddhaghosaka, and Shin Upali. With King Anawrahta presiding and Shin Upali as the chief, they established the Upali Thein [Upali's ordination hall]." King Anuwrahta (1044-1077) is none other than one of the founding kings of ancient Pagan. This 'historical' painting demonstrates the enduring role ancient Pagan kings played in the cultural life of Burma for nearly a millennium. The references to Sri Lanka also highlight the connections between this Buddhist island and Burma, especially in the minds of people in the later period.

The Upali mentioned in the inscription was ordained at the time of the Buddha. A lowly barber, he belonged to the same clan as the Buddha and joined the order with a group of friends, including the king. It was agreed that Upali would be admitted first, since it would promote equality and humility if a former barber entered the monkhood first and thereby acquired greater seniority, however trifling. The seated monks hold palm-leaf manuscripts, and Upali is probably the slightly larger monk to whom the others are turning for guidance. Anawrahta is on the far left.

The monk Anuruddha, like Upali, was an important disciple of the Buddha. The monk Mahasa cannot be identified, but Buddhaghosaka is likely Buddhaghosa, the famous author of the *Visuddhimagga* and Pali commentaries who flourished in Sri Lanka during perhaps the 5th century and who is considered important in the transmission of Buddhism to Burma. In the chronicles and in Pagan inscriptions, Anawrahta is not associated with a mission that brought texts directly from Sri Lanka. This scene therefore probably represents a conflation of characters in an imaginary setting. Upali's presence is explained by his close identification with ordination and monastic discipline in the Pali canon.

King Anawrahta, left, and Monk Upali, right, rear chamber.

No Ordinary Inheritance

On the right of the hall (north wall) within a recessed door is a scene of the Buddha seated before monks in a monastery at the time of the ordination of his son, Rahula. The Buddha sits on a high throne before his senior monks, the young lad being led to his ordination by the hand of a senior disciple. The Buddha's son was encouraged by his mother to request his inheritance – the right to become a universal ruler. Instead the Buddha bestowed upon him a gift without measure, admission into the religious order.

On the opposite side of the window chamber are shown more monks. The inscription below identifies the scene as a discussion between Sariputta, one of the Buddha's chief disciples, and a prominent brahmin named Punna. He converted to Buddhism and became a monk, together with 500 of his clansmen. His fame attracted Sariputta who in the mural is shown exchanging words with Punna (*Rathavinita Sutta, Majjhima Nikaya*). The inscription mentions the Weluwon (Veluvam, Pali) monastery, in Yasagyo (Rajagaha, Pali), near Bodh Gaya. That Anuruddha, Upali and Punna are mentioned together in the first chapter of a Pali text influential in Burma, the *Buddhavamsa*, may explain why all three are represented in the hall's murals.

In the opposite window chamber (south) appears a group of five monks reading from palm-leaf manuscripts. The capiton reads, "Five monks thwarting Mara through presenting a resolution at the monastery chapter."

Central Buddha, restored with original painting. (PP)

Ordination of the Buddha's son, side chamber.

HTILOMINLO

Date: C. 12th-13th centuries

The Htilominlo dominates the northern plains of Pagan and rivals the Sulamani, the Gawdaw-palin and the Dhammayan-gyi in size. It is known chiefly today for its fine stucco ornament.

Visit

The temple lies midway between the Walled City and the Shwe-zigon on the Pagan-Nyaung-U Road. It can be visited together with the 18th-century Upali Thein ordination hall situated across the road. Today's approach to the temple is from the north side, but its principal entrance faces east. No inscriptions relate to the founding of the temple, but the *Glass Palace Chronicle* claims that the temple was built by Zeyatheinhka (1211-1235). According to the *Chronicle*, the king's father erected a white umbrella amidst his five sons and declared that the umbrella would tilt toward the one who deserved to be his successor. It fell toward Zeyatheinhka, the youngest son, and he built the Htilominlo, which was also said to resemble the Sulamani. The temple probably dates from the last quarter of the 12th or first quarter of the 13th century, but even those approximate dates are uncertain. The Htilominlo never fell out of worship, judging by later ink inscriptions and refurbishing. Its history most likely therefore parallels the other mammoth temples at Pagan.

It is a two-storied temple, following the same design of the Sulamani, Thatbyinnyu, and Gawdaw-palin. The upper floor has an

The Htilominlo, its compound wall and gateways. Visitors today enter on the north side but the principal ancient entrance is on the east (on the left in the photograph).

encircling corridor with four seated Buddhas facing outward, the chief one on the east face. It is unusual since it has a single inner floor separating the bottom storey from the top. This inner floor, or entresol, has a vaulted encircling corridor but it was not intended to be entered and is windowless. It cannot be seen from the exterior. It was used to perhaps lighten the mass. The square upper terraces have the standard axial projections and large stupas at the corners. The *shikhara* was repaired long ago and now has a finial whose shape is based on conjecture.

Restored Buddha, principal shrine, east face. The walls retain much of their original tan wash. The ceiling frescos are also original.

Exterior

The temple sits within a large compound with four massive gateways. The monotony of the high enclosure wall is relieved by a row of simple cross-shaped designs, formed by recessed bricks. Construction techniques are well in evidence here, since roughly half of the temple's exterior stucco is missing. Left exposed are regular rows of header bricks and also a continuous string of thin grey stone blocks at the tops of the walls. The headers and stones were used to bind the outer facing to the inner fabric. The rich and intricate stucco surrounding the numerous doorways and pilasters is starkly juxtaposed against the plain surface of the walls. Next to each central doorway at ground level are large niches intended for seated images, a convention also found at the Ananda and the Shwegu-gyi temple, dated 1131. Today there are new sculptures in the niches.

The Htilominlo is also remarkable for its glazed ornament, on the base and around all of the roof terraces. Many are in the ubiquitous green but others are two-coloured, green and yellow. The latter is

Secondary entrance, north face.

Painted Buddhas added at the end of the 14th century by Monk Anandasura, north corridor, near modern entrance. (DS)

used as an accent on the green background. The technique was not perfected since the yellow rarely adhered properly to the surface. The same two-coloured combination was used more successfully at the Sulamani.

Interior

The interior was subject to constant refurbishment, beginning after the capital shifted from Pagan to Ava in the 14th century and all of the major Pagan temples experienced limited use. An influential donor was a monk named Anandasura whose bold, red ink inscriptions appear at most of the major temples in connection with painted, seated Buddhas intrusively added to corridor walls. His exact dates are unknown but a horoscope dated to 1376 protrudes over one of his Buddhas in the north corridor of the Htilominlo. He therefore must have flourished sometime before the last quarter of the 14th century. His short inscriptions are generally a one-line formula, "This is the donation of Monk Anandasura." Also within the corridors were added a number of painted series featuring the 28 Buddhas, some with labels likely dating to the 15th or 16th centuries. Inscriptions from 1442, 1625 and 1639 also record refreshing the Buddha images at the temple. Large painted Buddhas were added in the Konbaung period (1752-1885), resembling those at the Sulamani. Two elephants were painted on the east face, one named One Tusk Rogue dedicated in 1759, and another named Flying Contempt (Than Tun, 1996). Many 17th-18th century horoscopes are visible high on the walls in the north corridor.

The best preserved ancient painting is within the ceiling vaults where about 70 percent is still intact, albeit faint. The principal pattern consists of roundels filled with five small circles, a design also found at the Gawdaw-palin. The walls themselves retain about 60 percent of their original painted surface. Vast areas were covered originally with a plain light coloured wash. These broad areas were then framed by standard horizontal registers at the base and at the top of the wall and on the pilasters. There were no murals with Buddhist subject matter, so it would be a mistake to think that much original figurative painting was covered in a later refurbishing. This same is true of other enormous, late temples, such as the Sulamani and Dhammayan-gyi.

Seated Buddhas are the focus of each of the entrances, restored but retaining their complex ancient surrounds. The upper sections reveal the probable appearance of stupa finials. In the three minor entrance halls are two small chambers whose function is unknown but which were most likely used for storage.

The principal entrance hall is an impressive space, dominated by the huge restored Buddha. The painting surrounding the Buddha may date from the Konbaung period, and most of the stucco ornament appears to be original. A seven-line ink inscription on the right side of the hall at knee-level is dated to 1764 and records an unspecified 'good-deed' by Mr. Kyaw Son and his son and daughter's families. Their humble hope is to achieve '*nibban*' (nirvana). In the entrance way are large horoscopes in characters perhaps belonging to the 14th century, together with Pali prayers organized into different shaped compartments. Other horoscopes are dated between 1472 to 1640.

To one side of this hall is a large, standing, gilded wooden Buddha with his palms raised and facing outward. This image was said to have been fished out of the Irrawaddy a number of years ago and then established in the temple. The idea of recovering wooden images in rivers and then establishing them for worship appears now and then in Burmese folklore. Significantly, in the last hundred years or so there are a number of *nat* myths centring on 'spirits' inhabiting a tree trunk that is floated down river, brought to light by Bénédicte Brac de la Perrière.

Buddhas added over original tan wash, depicting the 28 Buddhas. Entrance hall, south. (DS)

Pali prayers, east entrance porth, added over the original tan wash.

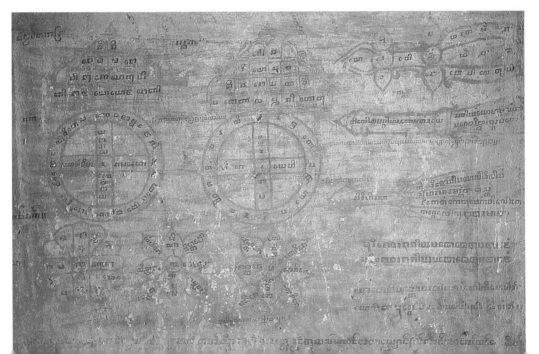

KUBYAUK-GYI (WETKYI-IN)

Highlights

★ frescos

★ Mara's demons

★ jatakas

★ Eight Great Events, Seven Weeks

Date: 13th century

The temple's 13th-century murals make a dramatic contrast with the earliest Pagan painting from a hundred years or so before. Solid core monuments usually have a vaulted corridor encircling the entire sanctum, but the corridor here only surrounds the sides and rear. The top of the tower toppled long ago, and the temple was further damaged in the 1975 quake. It was conjecturally rebuilt in the 1990s. It was one of the few temples vandalized by Europeans in the 19th century, losing much of its fresco work in the entrance hall.

Visit

The temple is visible off the Anawrahta Road leading south from Nyaung-U and borders the village of Wetkyi-in. It can be combined with the Alopyi (no. 374), situated between the Kubyauk-gyi and the Walled City. The Alopyi has important early period painting.

The Kubyauk-gyi is best viewed from the side, since its façade is now thick with souvenir shops. A low wall with gateways in the east and west encloses the temple. The wide entrance hall faces east and contains the principal seated Buddha. The temple is based around a solid brick core, but is unusual since the encircling corridor does not include the front of the shrine. There are doorways on the sides and the rear, faced with double pediments. The tower does not have the ordinary curved shape but is pyramidal, similar to the Mahabodhi

Entrance and compound gate.
Conjecturally restored finial.

Temple. The surface of the entrance porch was renovated at some
point and can perhaps be associated with an eleven-line inscription
dated to 1488, seen on the right. The corridor encircling the solid
core has restored Buddhas, with original painting on their surrounds.
The interior was never planned with figurative painting but was
covered in a tan wash that is divided into large panels defined by
painted frames. At the tops of the panels are pairs of birds, facing
one another. High on the walls are a handful of horoscopes, many
dated to the 17th-18th centuries.

Glasgow Evening Times, 1899

The deep vertical incisions on the left wall in the entrance hall
are grim reminders of the rapacity of a German art thief named
Th. H. Thomann who succeeded in removing a number of frescos
from Pagan in 1899. The local British officer deported the team
and recovered some material, but not before some crates escaped
to Europe. Some of Thomann's collection was purchased by the
Hamburg museum in 1906. The missing sections from this temple
were thought to be in Hamburg, but their whereabouts are still
unknown. However, four glass plate negatives taken by Thomann
were discovered thirty years ago in the Hamburg museum and
after enlargement, Luce and a colleague on a "working holiday"
painstakingly deciphered the now missing ink glosses from these
photographs (Ba Shin, Whitebread, Luce, 1971). The large gaps
from the lower walls reveal the extent of the damage. Despite the
theft, roughly half of the original frescos survive on the walls.

Towards the rear of the left wall are large sections covered with
a red coloured wax, used by Thomann to remove the frescos, with
the help of newspaper. Beneath one panel was noted a section from
the Saturday edition of the *Glasgow Evening Times*,
March 18, 1899, a paper that the German group
probably acquired in old Rangoon. (Than Tun, 1996).

The Frescos
Defeat of Mara

The most striking painting surrounds the restored
central Buddha at the rear of the hall and features
the attack of the demon Mara and his army. This
subject matter complemented the central Buddha
shown in the earth-touching position which signalled
the defeat of the demon king.

Scores of grotesque figures and bizarre animals
are shown attacking from the left and fleeing on the
right. Mara appears twice, riding upon his elephant.
On the left he is seen with his bow, one of his key
attributes. On the right he rides with his consort,
three figures grasping the legs of the elephant,
catching a ride in the rout. The elephant on the left
is in profile but on the right it faces outward, a
convention found elsewhere at Pagan and also in
early Pala sculpture (see the famous Jagdishpur stele
in Bihar).

Restored principal Buddha.

*Mara's demons in defeat,
rear wall of entrance hall.*

Ceiling ornament in the central hall.

Some demons have large ferocious masks on their stomachs, a convention that was probably inspired by Pala manuscripts where Mara's demons are also sometimes pictured in the same way. It is also found in early Pala sculpture (Jagdishpur stele) and was a part of Indian art from the beginning of the first millennium.

The ceiling retains about seventy-five percent of its original painting. The ceiling is dominated by the Buddha's footprints, surrounded by quatrefoil frames containing seated Buddha images. Behind the front wall is a spectacular painted arch, with lively aquatic creatures chasing winged lions at the ends. Next to the painted pilasters are a handful of compositions depicting probably Mogallana's defeat of the snake-king Nandopananda and the Buddha's defeat of Alavaka, an ogre. On the side walls, just inside the entrance, is a *kinnara* and *kinnari*, isolated against a plain background to tremendous effect.

Side Walls

The side walls feature hundreds of *jatakas* framed by the 28 Buddhas and other scenes from the Buddha's life. The *jatakas* were arranged in eleven tiers, but now many of the lower rows are missing, having been removed in 1899. In the centre of each wall was a large panel showing the Buddha, surrounded by rows of seated figures, some of whom are ascetics. On the right side of the hall we can clearly see where this important panel was hacked off, leaving the surrounding *jatakas*.

Makara chasing fanciful lion, bottom of arch, front wall of the entrance hall.

The *jatakas* on each wall are set within 272 squares, to make a total of 544. The series begins on the left wall (south), on the top row. They proceed from left to right. They then continue to the row beneath, going from left to right. The last *jataka*, at the bottom right (no. 272), was painted again on the north wall where the series continues on the top row, on the left. The identities of the *jatakas* on the lost bottom rows were reconstructed on the basis of the antique photographs in Hamburg.

Each tale is identified by ink glosses below, beginning with its name followed by an abbreviated description, such as "Prince and King", or "Son of a Fuel Gatherer." This is followed by the number of the *jataka* within the 22 chapters (*nipatas*, Pali) into which all 547 *jatakas* were divided in the Pali canon. The presence of only 544 frames, three less than the number required for inclusion of all of the *jatakas*, suggests that completion of the series was sacrificed for symmetry.

Evidently some ancient fiddling with the series occurred, since a few frames are left empty and four frames from the bottom row on the south side contained scenes from the Buddha's life, beginning with the sight of the dead man and ending with the casting of the bowl into the river at Bodh Gaya. The last *jataka* that can be identified by an inscription is no. 537 (niche 530). The series seems to have continued, from niche 531 to 544, but the glosses of these missing panels could not be read fully. These last niches presumably were intended for the last ten *jatakas*. Perhaps the omission of certain *jatakas* was deliberate in order to accommodate the most important last ten, the painters having realized that the 544 niches were three short of 547.

The 28 Buddhas
Above the *jatakas* on both walls are two rows of seated figures representing the 28 Buddhas. The series begins on the south wall, near the door, and then continues on the north wall, also near the door. This deviation from a clockwise direction was perhaps

Jataka *scenes from left wall (south). Top row: nos. 80, 81,82. Bottom row: nos. 102, 103,104.*

Jatakas in small niches surrounding partially missing central panel. The vertical incisions were made by Thomann in 1899, but he failed to remove all of the frescoes. (DS)

designed to give greater focus to the more important last four Buddhas, since they are closer to the central image and not shunted into the corner. Each Buddha is described in two separate lines. The top names the Buddha and provides biographical information, such as the tree under which his enlightenment occurred. The bottom line refers to the prophesy. The captions for the twenty-fifth Buddha on the north wall (the fourth frame from the left) reads:

"Top line: Kakusan (Kakusandha) Buddha blossomed at the *kutkuiw* tree (*Albizzia lebbek*). His stature was 40 cubits. His life span was 40,000 years."

"Lower line: The future Buddha, then King Khema, dedicated monastic robes and eye salves; and having become a monk, received the prophecy (Luce, I, 396)."

In the bottom register the kneeling figure making offerings before a seated Buddha is probably the king.

Life Scene Panels

The *jatakas* on each wall were bounded by eight panels featuring scenes from the Buddha's life. Only six remain today from the original sixteen, but the missing ones are recorded in Thomann's old photographs. Each was identified with a Burmese gloss. Four are visible on the right wall and only two on the left.

Right Wall (North)

Those on the right wall focused on the Seven Weeks that the Buddha spent at Bodh Gaya, beginning with his enlightenment, represented on the far right, near the entrance. The adjacent panel shows the Buddha standing and gazing at the Bodhi Tree (Week 2). On the other side of the *jatakas* are the seated Buddha sheltered by the Snake King (Week 6), and the Buddha seated beneath the Rajayatana Tree (Week 7). The four panels beneath these are missing. The last in the sequence appeared on the far right, below the Buddha obtaining enlightenment. This depicted a deity, Brahma Sahampati, who implored the Buddha to share his doctrine with the world. This episode comes immediately after the seventh week in the *Nidanakatha*, the ancient Pali text most likely responsible for this theme of the Seven Weeks at Pagan.

Left Wall (South)

The eight panels on the left wall covered a number of subjects, mostly drawn from the Eight Great Events, such as the First Sermon at Sarnath, the Taming of the Nalagiri Elephant, and the Descent from the Heaven of the 33 Gods. The only two remaining are on the left portion of the wall. The one closest to the entrance shows the Taming of the Nalagiri Elephant, followed by the Division of Relics by Dona which occured after the Buddha's death.

Opposite:
Kakusandha, 25th Buddha, right wall, north.

SHWE-ZIGON

Date: 11th-12th centuries

The Shwe-zigon stupa is a must-stop for Burmese pilgrims, ranked equally with the Ananda. Founded in the 11th or 12th century its countless renovations and additions reflect the entire history of the nation. Enshrined inside the stupa is thought to be a tooth of the Buddha from Sri Lanka and a forehead bone. It is difficult to sift fact from myth, since no surviving sources from the time refer directly to the contents of the stupa or even its patrons. The *Glass Palace Chronicle* records that Anawrahta (1044-1077) finished the first three terraces, and that Kyanzittha (1084-1112) completed the dome, but nothing can be confirmed. The stupa and auxiliary *nat* shrines are major religious attractions, and therefore the Shwe-zigon is ideal for observing modern devotional practices.

Visit

The stupa is situated just west of modern Nyaung-U, off the main paved road leading to the Walled City. It is best visited early in the morning or as the sun sets, since its open compound is hot and blinding at mid-day. During its annual winter festival the surrounding fields are packed with locals and pilgrims purchasing everything from toothbrushes to huge glazed jars floated down river from above Mandalay.

    The history of the Shwe-zigon is pieced together from both inscriptions and chronicles. It begins in the 11th century and

The stupa from the south, long modern corridors lead to the compound. Irrawaddy river in distance.

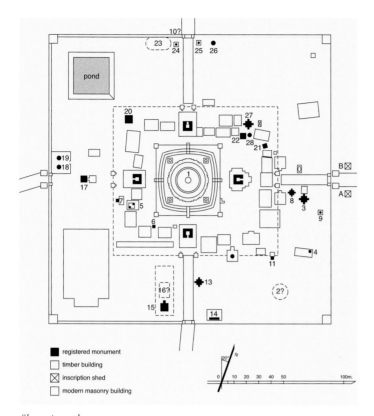

Shwe-zigon plan.

Site plan, Scores of auxiliary shrines, rest houses, and pavilions were added over the centuries inside the stupa compound. The four temples adjacent to the stupa and aligned to the cardinal directions belong to the ancient period.

Glazed stone jataka *plaques are placed in niches among the terraces.*

continues up to the present day, with new additions and refurbishing. Epigraphs suggest that the name of the stupa, or the area in which it was built, may have been called 'The Land of Victory', or Jayabhumi (Pali). The *Glass Palace Chronicle* records the enshrining by Anawrahta of the forehead bone of the Buddha that he removed from an ancient stupa in the Pyu capital of Shri Kshetra, together with a tooth-relic given by the ruler of Sri Lanka. The *Chronicle* further attributes the three lower terraces to his patronage, while the stupa's completion is assigned to Kyanzittha. But none of this information can be corroborated. An inscription by Kyanzittha is today found at the Shwe-zigon, but it is not a formal donation of the stupa, nor does it mention Anawrahta. However, its presence there strongly argues for his involvement in the construction of the stupa, and is one more reason to date the monument to his reign. Burmese inscriptions from the 13th century onwards testify to the donation of lands for the upkeep of the stupa, such as one in 1381 dedicating some 'servants', a bullock and a cow, and land containing toddy-palms. The great King Bayinnaung (1551-1581) left an inscription in Mon, Pali and Burmese on a bell now kept in a locked room near the eastern entrance. This king gilded the Shwe-zigon completely and also offered the bell, weighing 3,429 kg, in 1557.

Gilded metal Buddhas are found in each of the four ancient temples in the compound.

Below: A detail of the left hand. East temple.

The latest major stone inscription belongs to King Hsinhpyushin (r. 1763-1776), an early Konbaung period (1752-1885) king who ruled in Ava, near Mandalay. A special shrine in the Shwe-zigon compound was made to contain the inscription that is dated to 1768. The main purpose of the inscription was to record the replacement of the metal finial (*hti*) said to be established by Kyanzittha five hundred years earlier. This almost certainly was untrue, but its belief at the time reveals the connection Konbaung kings wished to make with ancient Burma. The inscription also repeats the legend that Anawrahta enshrined the tooth relic and the forehead bone. The new finial was constructed in a special pavilion within the palace at Ava. This eleven-tier spire is meticulously described, with the exact amounts of iron, copper and gold used in each tier, as well as some of the 998 precious stones ornamenting the *hti*. In addition, lands said to be dedicated to the stupa by specific ancient Pagan kings were renewed.

East Entrance

The enormous outer compound wall measures over two hundred square metres, competing in size with the Ananda. Most visitors today approach via the east corridor but access from the other three directions is also possible. High above the souvenir vendors on the walls are modern painted panels recounting the story of the Buddha's life, together with the history of Pagan. King Anawrahta, for example, is shown escorting from Lower Burma the captured Pali canon on the back of an elephant, thereby establishing Theravada Buddhism in his realm. These quasi-historical scenes are drawn from the *Glass Palace Chronicle* and reveal how legendary history is perpetuated in the popular imagination. The long hallway itself was dedicated in 1948.

To one side of the corridor stands a life-size elephant, two wooden tusks embedded in its whitewashed brick core and handsome glazed ornaments dotting its headdress. Just outside the entrance to the compound wall are the two small shrines containing the undated Mon stone inscriptions by Kyanzittha. The text does not refer directly to the stupa, but its presence here helps to prove his connection with the monument. The entrance is marked by two shrines placed to either side of the walkway and guarded by two seated stone figures. On the southern side are unusual ten-armed stone figures. Just inside the inner compound is a new building on the left containing the famous inscribed bell belonging to Bayinnaung. A little beyond and facing the stupa is an entire room dedicated to a replica of a standing wooden figure said to be discovered recently and thought to represent the monk, Shin Arahan, King Anawrahta's Buddhist preceptor. A copy is now worshipped, protected by glass. Legends are formed in this way and over time are added to the uncontested 'facts' associated with monuments, often migrating into modern-day history books and popular guides.

The Four Buddhas of this Age

Facing each of the corridors and aligned to the stupa's median stairways are four identical temples, complete with original towers (*shikharas*). Although each is heavily restored, they may belong to the time of the stupa's original construction or perhaps a little later. Similar temples may have stood originally around the Shwe-san-daw stupa, but the surviving structures differ from each other. Traces of Pagan-period murals are found only in the ceiling of the western shrine, which include the 28 Buddhas. Inside the four shrines are single tall metal images representing the four Buddhas of this era, ending with the historical Buddha Gotama. These are not cast bronze but are made up of gilded metal sheets attached to a concealed metal skeletal frame. At regular intervals numerous small metal pins connect the edges of the sheets to the frame. Since the hands of the four figures are attached separately and perhaps reflect repairs, it is probably wise to pass over their iconographic significance until scientific tests determine if the hands are the same age as the rest of the figure. Indeed, until a study can verify the approximate age of the images it would be premature to attribute any of the four to the Pagan period. Large bronzes used as principal objects of worship inside temples would be unique for ancient Pagan, another reason for caution in attributing these to the early Pagan period. It is more likely that the chief objects of veneration in these four temples were seated Buddhas, made of brick and covered with stucco.

The Stupa

The stupa is not only among the largest at Pagan, but it also is the only stupa made of stone, not brick. The *Glass Palace Chronicle* records that the stupa enshrines specific relics (see above) but in reality we have no idea of its real contents. The dome rests on an octagonal terrace supported by three square terraces, each divided into ten separate recessed sections and connected by a median stairway on all sides. At the corners of the terraces are large urns and stupas. The heavily restored double-bodied lions at the corner on the lowest terrace and the crocodiles at the bases of the steps are likely much later additions. The dome, finial, and crowning metal *hti* reflect innumerable refurbishings over the centuries.

Structure containing stone inscription, dated 1768.

Spire and hti.

Glazed stone jataka *plaque, ground floor terrace.*

Two details from the ancient wooden door panel within the compound, east side.

The Jataka tiles

Placed into niches on the three square terraces are green glazed plaques. Incised beneath each scene is the name of the story in Pali and its ordinal number. Artists at Pagan generally followed the standard Pali collection of 547, but here at the Shwe-zigon the *jatakas* numbered 550. The same number occurs on the unglazed plaques at the Hpetleik stupas. Luce believed that the series of 550 stemmed from an early Mon convention that was later supplanted at Pagan by the standard Pali collection of 547, derived from Sri Lanka. There are differences, however, between the Hpetleik series and those at the Shwe-zigon, although the last ten *jatakas* have the same names and numbers. At the Shwe-zigon the last ten are only accorded a single plaque, unlike those at the Ananda and the Mingalazedi where each of the last ten stories is presented over numerous tiles.

The series begins on the east face, to the left of the median stairway, and progresses in a clockwise fashion, following the same disposition as at the Mingalazedi. The last plaques on the top terrace end on the east side. Many plaques are missing and many are out of their correct serial order. Moreover, over thirty *jatakas* are repeated, either in duplicate or even in triplicate, sometimes placed in adjacent niches or far from one another. No ready explanations account for this disorder, but it cannot be blamed entirely on modern fiddling, since plaques are repeated. There are a total of 597 niches and 420 surviving plaques, but almost certainly all of the niches were once filled. That the designers had 47 more niches than the 550 *jatakas* may suggest why duplicate and triplicate plaques were installed, to fill the gaps created by having too many niches. On the other hand, a total of 67 surviving plaques were duplicated and triplicated, twenty more than the 47 needed to fill all of the niches. Even with

more study, this question may forever remain an enigma. Such a design flaw is not found in the Ananda or the Mingalazedi. All of the plaques appears to be carved from stone and then covered with a green glaze, according to the unpublished findings of Dr. Aung Bo of the Myanmar Ceramic Society.

Wooden doorway

The most remarkable survival at the Shwe-zigon is the doorway which once belonged to the temple on the north side. Over four metres tall, it was salvaged in 1922 and is kept in a small hall near the eastern entrance. The two separate vertical sections are joined together in the modern display and would have opened and closed like double doors. It is made up of panels fastened to the wooden frame by wide metal strips. Dancers and musicians are placed in the small bosses, each framed by rich floral ornament. In style they are reminiscent of the sculpted wooden lintels at the Nagayon. They are the only ancient doorways to have survived and make an instructive contrast with the Konbaung period doorways at the Ananda and the Shwegu-gyi. No such doorways have survived in eastern India.

Shrines in Compound

Numerous shrines and buildings crowd the compound, dating from the Konbaung period up to the present day. These were usually established by wealthy families from throughout Burma and resemble those around the Shwedagon in Yangon in modern times. Some are open-air wooden pavilions in traditional Burmese style,

The Great Departure, east side of the compound.

*Modern Reclining Buddha,
north side of compound.*

while others are brick structures blending European and Burmese
elements. These largely date to the 1920s and 1930s and are
contemporary with the three corridors in the Ananda compound.
Among the latest is an art-deco style building on the north side,
dated with an inscription to 1948.

On the east side a wooden porch attached to the ancient temple
boasts wooden figures based on the life of the Buddha, such as the
Four Great Sights (the old man, the sick man, a corpse and an
ascetic). The Buddha is shown mounted on his horse, together with
the demon Mara dressed as a courtier. Make sure not to miss the
spooky corpse! More intricate carving in other shrines also depict
scenes from the Buddha's life. Some of the best woodwork is found
in the Yoke-son Tazaung, on the south side of the compound. In the

*Small shrine, northeast
corner of stupa compound.*

southeast section of the compound is a huge metal
hti, said to be the one replaced by the Konbaung
king Hsinhpyushin. On the southern side of the
compound a modest bell is ornamented with a
scene inspired by the Hindu epic, the *Ramayana*.
At the top the demon Ravana sits in a celestial
chariot, beside Sita, the abducted beauty and wife
of Rama. The Hindu myth never enjoyed the same
popularity in Burma as it did in other Southeast
Asian countries, but it was somewhat popular in
the Konbaung period. The bell is dated by an
inscription to 1912 and records its donation by a
woman and her family, and cost in *kyat*.

On the northern side is a short, reclining
Buddha, now within a cage, like a trapped bird.

Pilgrims insert an arm through the narrow bars, and if their extended hand can touch the Buddha's robe then they can expect to return to Pagan in three years. Be sure to try it! Nearby is a modern seated figure placed in a small pool of water. This is the Buddhist saint Upagupta (Pali) who is known in Burma as Shin Upagok. He was believed to be an advisor to King Ashoka in India and over the centuries migrated into Pali lore in some parts of Southeast Asia (Strong). He is usually shown seated, gazing upward and with his right hand in his bowl held on his lap. His shrine also appear at the Shwedagon in Yangon. Upagupta was also represented nearly a thousand years earlier at Pagan, at the Kubyauk-gyi (Myinkaba), conferring with Ashoka. One 19th century shrine in the northeast corner contains a figure of a kneeling figure (no. 21). Facing the stupa is a tall wooden pillar, crowned with a giant goose, or *hin-tha* (Burmese), together with standing deities near the base. Ancient stone footprints of the Buddha and a single footprint from the Konbaung period are also found in the compound. Two stone lions from the ancient period are located outside the compound, on the western side.

Nat Shrines

One of the most revered set of *nats* in the country is also located here, housed in a modest new building in the southeast corner of the compound. One popular guide reports that the original *nats* were stolen by a collector and are now in Italy, but this is untrue, adding to the misconception that Pagan has been plundered by Westerners. Morever, the 37-*nats* are all of 20th century date. However, to one side of the shrine is Pagan's finest surviving ancient wood sculpture.

Above left: Hin-tha (Goose) on the pillar, northeast corner.

Above right: Figure at the base of hin-tha *pillar, northeast corner.*

Bell with Sita and Ravana seated together on the top. Cast in 1912. U Thein Lwin, Department of Archaeology. (DS)

It stands 2.65 m and is said to represent Sakka, since he appears to hold a thunderbolt, one of his common attributes in India. However, Sakka normally carries a conch at Pagan, not a thunderbolt. Sakka, known as Thagyamin in Burma, is chief of the 37 *nats*. The detailed drapery work in the lower garment is exquisite, still visible beneath heavy new gilding.

Other *nat* shrines fill the compound, but only one features all 37 deities. The most popular contain two huge seated stone figures, a father (Shwe-myo-zin) and his son (Shwe-zaga). Devotees make cash offerings, often stuffed into an outer garment covering their lower parts. Other male and female *nat* shrines are found within the enclosure also.

Konbaung Murals

One prominent whitewashed building in the northeast corner was built to contain an enormous stone inscription dated to 1768. The inscription records the renewal of the *hti*, the restoration of the stupa and the rededication of donated lands to the stupa by the King Hsinhpyushin. The murals were almost certainly completed at the same time and therefore are an important landmark in Konbaung painting that has been overlooked. The top rows present the 28 Buddhas, identified with Burmese captions, with rows of figures beneath them. The building is normally locked, but you can peek through the grated door. Only a decade or two separates this work from the Upali Thein and Ananda Temple Monastery, but the difference in style is dramatic. Next to it is a much taller brick temple from the ancient period, probably the 12th century (no. 20). A similar one is in the northwest corner (no. 27). A number of other Konbaung temples and stupas are in the compound and also outside the walls, some with painting inside, but none with dated inscriptions (nos. 3, 8, 911, 13).

Gilded stone nat, *Shwe-myo-zin, west side.*

Right: Mural in structure housing stone inscription, dated 1768. Top row: One of the 28 Buddhas. Bottom: Devotees.

Opposite:
The Shwe-zigon is the only large stupa at Pagan constructed in stone. (DS)

KYAUK-KU-UMIN

Date: 11th-12th centuries

Remote and tranquil, the Kyauk-ku-umin temple evokes old Pagan in the pre-modern period. It is also the only important temple carved partly from the living rock, and with subterranean chambers probably used for meditation.

Visit
The Kyauk-ku-umin is located a long stone's throw from the bank of the Irrawaddy, some two miles northeast of Nyaung-U. Reaching the temple requires a special effort and is best accomplished with a local guide familiar with the dirt tracks. If you set out from the Walled City by taxi, then budget at least two hours total, going and coming. No inscriptions are associated with the founding of the temple nor is it tied to any popular legends. The modern Burmese name translates as 'Stone Temple and Tunnels'. The temple's sculptures are now in the museum and in storage, but their style suggests an early date for the structure, perhaps to the second half of the 11th century or early 12th century.

The temple is not visible from the river, since it is "sunk in a romantic gully strewn with fossil wood and pebbles bright like jewels", in Luce's inimitable words (Luce, I, 288). A flight of modern steps takes us down to a wide area in front of the edifice.

The Kyauk-ku-umin is built partially within an escarptment. The stone façade conceals its brick fabric. The doorway arch was reconstructed long ago.

The exterior is faced with carved stone placed over a brick core, following the same fashion as the Nanpaya. The only section carved from the living rock is at the rear of the shrine. The arch in the central porch collapsed long ago but was reconstructed. Three large perforated stone windows are framed by pilasters with unusual designs. The wall is ornamented with a floral register below and at the top with a standard frieze of *kirtimukhas*. There is an upper brick storey containing a narrow vaulted corridor lined with small empty niches whose purpose is unknown. Above are two rectangular terraces crowned with a new stupa.

The Doorway

The two door jambs consist of three recessed sections composed of hundreds of small pieces. Many of the designs and figures are unique at Pagan, but it has long been recognized that the doorway has connections with the art of eastern India. Such a similarity lends weight to the belief that artists' sketch books were used at Pagan, perhaps brought to Burma by Indian artists. The paired guardian figures at the base are adorned with huge earrings ornamented with a horse and an elephant, a motif only found here. The female standing upon a foliated crocodile and holding a small vessel is the mythical personification of the River Ganges in north India. The goddess on the other side is missing her mount, but it was almost certainly a tortoise, a combination identified with north India's other sacred river, the Jumna. These two river goddesses are often paired at the bottom of doorways in north India, in both Hindu and Buddhist shrines alike. Above the two goddesses are winged *kinnaras*, or human-birds, holding long stringed instruments. In the vertical registers alternating lions and geese are set within thick floral ornament.

Door jamb with Ganges goddess at right, standing upon a crocodile.

The Interior

Against the rear wall is a large Buddha, now restored, but originally made of brick and covered with stucco. Its base is nearly 3 metres high, echoing the dimensions of the interior. To either side of the

Above: Elephant earring on guardian.

Above right: A kinnara.

Ornament on pier.

Buddha are rows of fragmentary painted seated Buddhas from the ancient period. The hall is dominated by two large piers faced in stone and forming immense arches. The dramatic open spaces created by these arches is somewhat reminiscent of the wide section facing the Buddha in the Shwegu-gyi temple dated to 1131. Each pier is adorned at the base with intricate floral ornament. A total of fifty-three niches set into the ground floor walls in three vertical tiers were intended for stone images. All of the surviving images, 36 in number, were taken to the Pagan museum following a theft in 1988. One of the sculptures soon surfaced at an auction in New York but thanks to the sharp eyes of a scholar the standing Buddha was saved from the block and returned to Burma. Despite this celebrated theft, few ancient artifacts from Pagan have entered the international art market. The sculpture may have been established in a narrative sequence, going in a clockwise direction from the entrance, but the original disposition of all of the images is not easy to determine. The most unusual sculpture depicts the seated fasting Buddha, paired with two standing men poking the Buddha's ears with rods,

Buddhas high within the shrine. (DS)

discussed in the Painting and Sculpture chapter. One sculpture showing the death of the Buddha was noted in the late 19th century but went missing long ago. High on the walls of the interior are carved seated Buddhas, each with small flanking attendants. In one corner of the hall is an inscription with two dates, 1188 and 1270, but it was evidently brought from elsewhere.

To the sides of the Buddha are entrances to the dark tunnels running deep into the mountain. There are several small chambers leading off these passages, likely used for meditation. In one of them was found over twelve wooden standing male figures sculpted with crowns and jewellery. Many similar examples were found throughout Pagan and one or two are on display in the Pagan museum. Inside the underground tunnels the watchmen normally set up candles. However, should a wind arise you would be stranded in the dark, so it is best to take your own torch. It would also not be a happy place in the event of an earthquake, however auspicious and ancient.

A small handful of artificial excavations with small simple unadorned cells exist throughout Pagan where the landscape is suitable. These are normally not part of a temple, like we have here, yet their presence helps to prove that rigorous no-nonsense type of meditation occurred at Pagan. These subterranean chambers were surely a contrast to the lavishly ornamented temples and rather comfortable monasteries. Caves like this are still used by monks in certain monasteries in Burma.

On the plateau after climbing out of the ravine is a small temple name Yat-sauk (no. 124). Its Buddha is restored but on the wall are rows of *jatakas* and a painted inscription dated to 1220 that mentions a monastery with a rest house and a school.

Restored central Buddha.

CENTRAL GROUP

SHWE-SAN-DAW
LOKA-HTEIKPAN
DHAMMAYAN-GYI
SULAMANI

SHWE-SAN-DAW

Date: C. 11th century

The Shwe-san-daw is thought to enshrine a sacred hair relic of the Buddha presented to King Anawrahta (1044-1077) by a conquered ruler of Lower Burma. The tremor in 1975 was particularly cruel to the stupa, since its modern spire was cast down all five terraces. It remains on the ground where it landed, a poignant reminder of the Buddhist notion of impermanence.

Previous pages: The vast Dhammayan-gyi dominates the surrounding plain. It is the only major temple whose tower has been left unrestored.

Visit

The whitewashed Shwe-san-daw is visible throughout much of the countryside south of the Ananda. It lies a short distance off the main paved road and can be combined with the nearby Loka-hteikpan.

It is probably one of the earliest stupas at Pagan since terracotta votive tablets with Anawrahta's name were discovered long ago in a relic chamber. The bell-shaped dome, together with ascending terraces and median staircases, was the preferred design for the most important stupas at Pagan, such as the Shwe-zigon and the Mingalazedi. Somewhat similar in design is the early Mon Thagya Stupa in Lower Burma in the town of Thaton, probably from the 11th or 12th century and originally adorned with unglazed and un-inscribed *jataka* plaques which are much larger and more sophisticated than those from the Shwe-san-daw.

The Shwe-san-daw is one of the earliest large stupas at Pagan.

The tall tapering drum ends in a number of thick ringed bands and is now crowned with a new metal spire, or *hti*. The dome itself rests on two receding octagonal terraces that are in turn supported by five concentric square terraces linked by median stairways on all sides. The dome has been renewed with fresh stucco over the ages, but traces of original stucco are found among the terraces. Today we can easily enter the walkways encircling the upper terraces from each of the four stairways but that was probably not possible originally. A victim of the last earthquake, the former spire rests forlornly on the modern walkway surrounding the stupa.

On the corners of some terraces are seated stone male figures, while other stone fragments lie around the base of the stupa; their original locations are uncertain.

At the corners of the base were large brick lions with split bodies. Only the example on the northeast corner has survived. This tradition continued throughout the Pagan period and similar lions occupied the same position at Mingalazedi. Later, these lions were replaced at some stage by the motif of the man-lion (*manuthiha*, Burmese). Examples can be seen at the 19th-century Kyauk-taw-gyi facing the lake in Amarapura.

Over twenty small unglazed terracotta *jataka* plaques are associated with this stupa. None are inscribed with captions so it is difficult to positively identify specific scenes. They were originally placed within the small niches among the ascending terraces. Their rather crude figural style is in sharp contrast to the magnificent unglazed examples from the Hpetleik stupas, a difference in quality that remains unexplained. Two examples are on display at the museum.

The Shwe-san-daw, left, at sunset. (PP)

Reclining Buddha, brick and stucco, c. 17th-18th century.

The Compound

The stupa's ruinous compound wall originally had gates on each side. Within the compound and oriented to each of the stairways are four temples (nos. 1564, 1566, 1567, 1569). Their plans are different and it is unlikely that they were all built at the same time. The ones on the north and south are in ruins and in thick brush, but the two once stood in the spacious courtyard. The most interesting is on the north side. Inside are four restored seated Buddha figures placed back to back on a high platform. They are made completely in brick and were once covered with stucco. Unlike other brick images placed against a flat wall surface these figures were fully three-dimensional, with many of the bricks cut to fit the shape of the figures. The figures likely represent the historical Buddha and his three immediate predecessors.

Modern stupa spire thrown down in the 1975 quake.

The temple on the south side is of different design and its entrance faces the gate. Inside the temple on the west, adjacent to the long building housing the reclining Buddha, is an enormous stone base once intended for an image that is now missing.

The remains of this temple's splendid dome can be seen from the terraces of the stupa. On the eastern side of the stupa but off axis is another temple containing three stone Buddha figures. The central image probably dates to the 14th century or later and resembles a sculpture in one of the entrance halls of the Dhammayan-gyi which is perhaps linked with an ink inscription dated to 1343.

Reclining Buddha

A huge recumbent Buddha is found in the long building facing the stupa (no. 1570). The structure probably belongs to the Konbaung period (1752-1885) or somewhat earlier, since its location interrupts the compound wall, strongly suggesting that it was added after the wall become derelict centuries earlier. The Buddha is made of brick, covered with stucco, and is now and then refreshed with new paint. The interior is dominated by rows of flamboyant trees, probably symbolizing the twin *Shala* trees (*Shorea robusta*) between which the Buddha expired. The other notable large reclining figure at Pagan is at the rear of the Manuha temple and that too likely belongs to the Konbaung epoch or slightly earlier. Large reclining Buddhas are somewhat rare in the ancient period in Burma.

Feet of the reclining Buddha and surrounding frescoes.

Temple in compound with reclining Buddha inside, c. 17th-18th century. (DS)

LOKA-HTEIKPAN

Date: 12th century

The Loka-hteikpan temple can be likened to Cinderella, a neglected beauty awaiting discovery. Its murals depict a wide range of subjects drawn from the Pali Buddhist tradition. Most of the scenes are identified by Mon and Burmese captions.

Visit

The temple lies beside a wide dirt path intersecting with Anawrahta Road, near the Shwe-san-daw. Most visitors speed by this modest shrine without realizing its importance. A watchman with a key is usually napping outside beneath a tree.

The Loka-hteikpan contains some of Pagan's most engaging painting, despite its unpretentious exterior.

The combined use of Mon and Burmese ink captions led Luce and others to date the temple to no later than c. 1125, a transitional period before Mon was replaced by Burmese at Pagan. The glosses were published in 1962 in a monograph on the temple by Ba Shin, a colleague of Luce.

The central Buddha sits on a wide base near the rear wall in a hollow central shrine capped with a cloister vault. Unlike many other early temples, it was not designed with a solid core or an enclosed sanctum. A windowless entrance hall faces north. The best stucco survives above the windows, but roughly 70 percent is lost. A stairway at one side of the sanctum leads to the roof. On the corners of the square terraces are restored miniature *shikharas* and stupas. The top of the central *shikhara* tumbled centuries ago, so the design of the spire is conjectural.

The Frescos

The temple's diverse compositions and subjects are thematically linked. The focus is on the historical Buddha, Gotama, and his previous lives, both within the *jataka* series and the lineage of 28 successive Buddhas. The painting on the side walls is planned very differently, creating a striking asymmetry unusual at Pagan.

The painters drew exclusively from Pali sources, with no overtly Mahayana elements, such as bodhisattvas with multiple arms. While the overall context remains Theravada, certain iconographic features, are drawn from eastern India, an area influenced by the Mahayana faith. For example, the infant Buddha is shown standing on a row of pots, a feature in some illustrated palm-leaf manuscripts from India.

Some hasty touch-up work took place after the 1960s, judging from pre-restoration photographs in Ba Shin's book. Conservation work was later undertaken by the Department of Archaeology, 1993-1994. The extensive, rich murals at the Loka-hteikpan remind us of how much great painting has been lost at Pagan over the centuries.

No further painting was added to the temple, apart from a number of dated horoscopes in the entrance hall, many from the 16th century.

Restored Buddha, with the Eight Great Events painted on the rear wall. (DS)

A disciple, rear wall.

Kinnara, rear wall.

Mara's elephant in defeat, rear wall.

Rear Wall (South)

The seated Buddha in the centre of the hall symbolizes the defeat of Mara and the Enlightenment, and the painting on the rear wall is directly linked to the other major events in the Buddha's life. Two vertical rows on the sides contain scenes associated with the Eight Great Events. Maya is shown giving birth, the infant emerging from her right side, his hands clasped in homage in a fashion also known in manuscripts from eastern India. Above is the Miracle at Savatthi where the Buddha replicates himself, followed at the top by the Descent from the Heaven of the 33 Gods.

At the bottom of the other tier is the Presentation of Honey from the monkey. In the middle is the First Sermon at the Deer Park. The last panel shows the Taming of the Nalagiri Elephant, sent to kill the Buddha by his wicked cousin. Above is a long horizontal register containing Mara's army, attacking on the left and retreating on the right. A multiple-armed Mara sits astride his elephant.

The topmost register is nearly all missing, but was in tolerably good condition in 1960. Seven panels dealt with the death of the Buddha. In the centre was the recumbent Buddha lying on his right side. On the left stood the brahmin Dona who intervened among the seven Malla kings who fought over the Buddha's remains after his death. On the right was the distribution of these relics. At both ends were two frames, each containing two unidentified stupas.

The border surrounding the Buddha features two lively *kinnaras* poised at the top of the throne, their feathery tails trailing off into the nimbus. Kneeling below are the disciples, Sariputta and Mogallana, on the left and right, respectively, touched up in restoration. On the right of the frame is Brahma holding a white umbrella, matched with Sakka blowing his conch on the other side. None of the scenes on the rear wall are identified with captions, unlike the other walls.

The four sections of the cloistered ceiling are joined by a square frame in the centre filled with a lotus. The Buddha's footprints appear in the ceiling of the entrance hall.

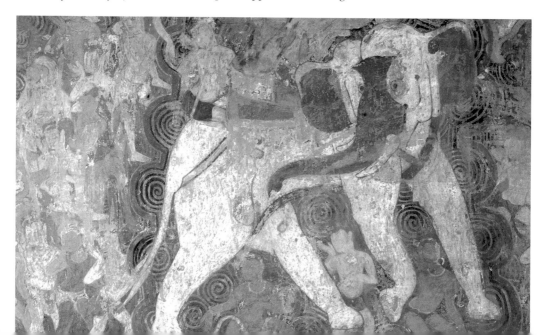

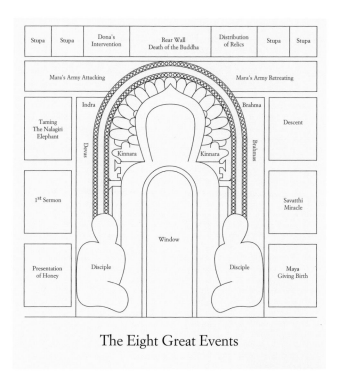

The Eight Great Events

| Stupa | Stupa | Dona's Intervention | Rear Wall Death of the Buddha | Distribution of Relics | Stupa | Stupa |

Mara's Army Attacking · Mara's Army Retreating

Indra · Brahma

Taming The Nalagiri Elephant · Descent

Devas · Brahmas

Kinnara · Kinnara

1st Sermon · Savatthi Miracle

Window

Presentation of Honey · Disciple · Disciple · Maya Giving Birth

Maya giving birth to the Buddha, rear wall.

Left: Rear wall plan, south.

Right: Rear wall. Right side. Lower panel: Birth of the Buddha, Middle: Miracle at Savatthi, Top: Descent from the Heaven of the 33 Gods. Mara's elephant in top horizontal register. (DS).

Brahma holding umbrella, rear wall.

Left Wall (East)

This is perhaps one of the grandest compositions among all the frescos at Pagan. The central scene is identified with Mon and Burmese ink inscriptions, the only location in the temple where both languages exist side by side in the same register. Centre stage is the Buddha seated upon Sakka's stone throne within a seven-tiered pavilion. The Buddha preached from this special seat to his mother and others residing in the Heaven of the 33 Gods, ruled by Sakka. The teachings were Buddhist philosophy, or the last division in the Pali canon, or *Abhidamma*. A Mon ink caption states that the Buddha sits "in the Vejayanta pavilion of Sakka . . . and preaches the seven books of the *Abhidamma* to the gods, beginning with his mother, who lives in the 10,000 universes." This is also abbreviated in Burmese. Behind is a flamboyant Red Choral tree, also specified in the Pali canon. To the sides are two small pavilions, housing deities.

Two stupas appear at the top. The one on the right is identified in a Mon gloss as the Dussa

The Buddha enthroned on Mount Meru, centre. Left wall, east. (DS)

Detail from above scene to left of Vejayanta pavilion. (DS)

stupa where Ghatikara, a Brahma, enshrined the robes of the Buddha after he discarded them on abandoning the palace. To the left is the famous Chulamani stupa, marking the site where Sakka enshrined the Buddha's headdress that he removed to begin his career as an ascetic. The Mon caption reads, "The Holy Lord Metteyya . . . worships the Chulamani ceitya (stupa)." Metteyya is the Buddha of the Future, believed in Burma to manifest himself 5,000 years after the death of the Buddha. A Mon epigraphist felt that it did not refer to the enshrinement of the Buddha's headdress but to his collar-bone (*knan ko*, Mon) that Sakka sent to the king of Sri Lanka, according to the *Mahavamsa* (cited in Griswold). This tradition was known at Pagan, since it is recorded in one of the ink inscriptions at the Kubyauk-gyi (Myinkaba). Below these stupas are scenes of gardens with rectangular lotus ponds, possibly representing two parks said to be in Sakka's heaven. To the side of the Buddha are rows of two standing figures, two deep. At the back are three-headed Brahmas, while other gods are in the front.

Below the seated Buddha is Mount Meru,
the centre of the Buddhist universe, with the
Buddha's ascent and descent on the right and
left, respectively. The seven pillar-like objects
on either side represent the seven mountains
surrounding Meru and separated by oceans,
indicated by four fish swimming in wavy water
at the base. On the right in a pavilion is the
earthly king named Pasenadi who was a noted
patron of the Buddha. The standing Buddha is
shown twice, looking back to his friend the king
and then again ascending. On the left side
the Buddha descends, accompanied by the
umbrella-wielding Brahma. No inscriptions
identify these scenes.

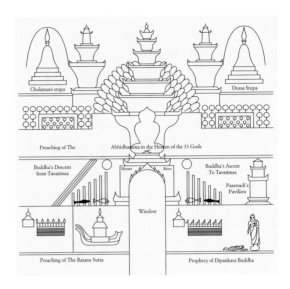

Left wall diagram.

The horizontal register below and to the
right of the window depicts the standing
Buddha named Dipankara, who is the fourth
Buddha in the series of 28. He stands before the prostrate hermit
Sumedha, the scene identified by a Burmese gloss below. Dipankara
is important, since he prophesizes that Sumedha will become
Gotama in a future birth. To the left of the window the Buddha
rides in a boat in the Ganges river on his way to Vesali where he will
deliver a sermon designed to rid the city of plague and famine. This
is drawn from the *Ratana Sutta* in the *Khuddakapatha*. The scene is
also captioned in Burmese. Scenes in Vesali after his disembarkation
are on the left, bordering the wall. The boat scene may relate to a
mural in one of the window chambers of the Kubyauk-gyi temple
(Myinkaba) which is uncaptioned.

*The Buddha descending from the
Heaven of the 33 Gods, left wall.*

The jatakas, *right wall, south. (DS)*

Right Wall (West)

The other side wall and the murals in the entrance hall are dedicated to the 547 *jatakas*. In the Pali canon the *jatakas* are divided into 22 books (*nipata*, Pali), of which the last contains the most venerated, a series of ten (nos. 538-547). The designers here focused on the last ten and represented the previous 537 by selecting a tale taken from each book, usually the first within that division. The first twenty books are represented in two rows at the top of the wall, beginning on the upper left and going from left to right and continuing on the second row in the same direction. The *jatakas* on these two rows are all identified with Mon glosses stating the number of the division (*nipata*), its name and a brief description. For example, the *jataka* beginning the second row, on the left, has the following Mon caption: "11th Book, Matuposa Jataka, the Bodhisattva was king of elephants." The third row begins with no. 537, the final tale before the revered last ten, which also proceed from left to right. This *jataka* and all the remaining ones have captions in Burmese. Since each of the last ten involve multiple scenes the descriptions are lengthy.

Entrance Hall

The last two *jatakas* (546, 547) skip to both sides of the entrance hall. As we enter the temple, the wall on the right (west) is given over to no. 546. The last *jataka*, the Vessantara, is on the opposite wall (east). These long stories were arranged in eight rows, of which only the top six survive. The action moved from left to right, top to bottom. The last *jataka* also goes from top to bottom but the depictions and the captions begin at the left and proceed to the right, in the reverse direction to those on the opposite wall. These last ten *jatakas* follow the sequence of the Pali canon. Other *jataka* series at Pagan depict the same tales, but in somewhat different order.

Front Wall (North)

The wall facing the central Buddha image is devoted to the 28
Buddhas. The first in the series begins with the first Buddha on the
left at the top. The 22nd Buddha ends the third row from the top,
on the right. The three large niches to the right of the door present
three Buddhas (23, 24, 25) in descending order. To the left of the
door at the top is the 26th, followed by the 27th. The last niche on
the bottom is Gotama, but the inscription is too effaced to decipher.
Most of Mon inscriptions are legible and give the name of the
Buddha and the specific tree under which he obtained
enlightenment, such as "The Lord Buddha Konagamana blossomed
at *pran* tree [*udumbaa*, Pali, *Ficus glomerata*]." At the entrance, just
above the door, is a seated figure within a pavilion, perhaps the
Buddha of the Future, Metteyya.

Why Mon and Burmese Ink Inscriptions?

The presence of both Mon and Burmese captions within the
same temple underscores the notion that artists at Pagan had many
different illustrated models. These were probably long cloth scrolls
illustrating common episodes accompanied by Mon or Burmese
captions, closely resembling the actual murals. Such models must
have been necessary, since not even a team of artists could evoke
from memory all 547 *jatakas*, including their written descriptions.
This explains why the two top rows of *jatakas* are captioned in
Mon and the ones below in Burmese. That Mon artists did the top
two rows and Burmese did the bottom rows is unlikely. Only one
instance occurs in the entire temple where both languages appear on
the same register to describe the same subject. This is the description
of the principal seated Buddha on the left wall (east) where he
preaches in the special heaven. This example suggests that for scenes
of great importance one language was translated into another or that
possibly two models of the same subject were available and both
captions were copied.

Cloister vault in the sanctum.

Scene from jataka *no. 543, right wall.*

DHAMMAYAN-GYI

Date: 12th century

The Dhammayan-gyi is the largest temple at Pagan, dominating the plains southeast of the Walled City. The inner corridor was bricked up at the time of its construction for reasons which are still unknown, creating one of Pagan's chief enigmas. The top of the temple tower was in ruins long before the quake in 1975, and it has wisely never been restored. Intrusive painting was added from time to time, beginning as early as the 14th century.

Visit

The Dhammayan-gyi can be combined with the nearby Sulamani, but if time forces you to choose, I would suggest the Sulamani for its excellent 18th-century painting. Also, the Dhammayan-gyi is the only large temple still home to bats, so a disagreeable odour discourages lingering.

Today the major approach to the temple is from the north, passing first through one of the enormous gates fixed at each cardinal direction in the compound wall. The temple plan is modeled on the cruciform design of the Ananda, that is, with four entrance halls of equal dimensions. Like the Ananda, two concentric corridors were designed to surround the central core, but the inner corridor and the numerous passages leading to it were bricked up from the beginning, as mentioned above. Today the principal focus is on the east, with a large seated Buddha set inside the core. The inner corridor was entirely sealed, so we cannot be sure if similar images were planned for the other three sides, such as we have at the

An aerial view from the east. The Dhammayan-gyi is the only large temple at Pagan whose tower has not been fully restored.

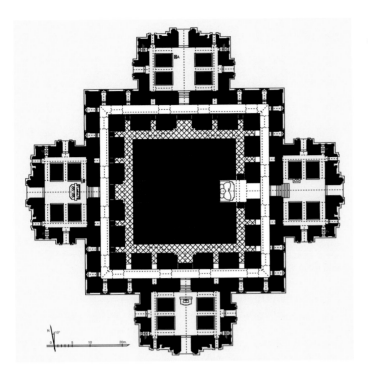

The inner corridor was bricked up, for reasons which have never been explained. Cross-hatching indicates the bricked up corridor.

Ananda. There was no provision for stone sculpture, another indication of the temple's late date. In the early temples at Pagan, stone figures set into niches were the rule, such as at the Nagayon, Abeyadana and the Ananda.

The other Leviathans at Pagan, the Htilominlo, Sulamani, Thatbyinnyu, and Gawdaw-palin, were all are designed with a separate second storey featuring a large Buddha. The Dhammayan-gyi differs from this model and rises in a series of receding square terraces. The two lowermost terraces have sloping roofs, like the Ananda. The top was crowned by an enormous *shikhara* which has never been restored.

A Burmese inscription found inside the north entrance hall is dated to 1165 and lists bonded servants, including female singers and dancers. It also includes a dedication of a monastery, 48 cattle, a garden, a water tank and paddy fields. It concludes with a chipper imprecatory note for those allowing the temple to fall into ruin: "may the rice and curry they eat, the water they drink, the house they live, poison them!." Since this inscription does not mention the construction of a temple or list the name of any temple, it cannot be safely used to establish the date of the

Two-storied monastery in compound. Regularly spaced holes in brick indicate where wooden beams were once placed, forming the flooring. (DS)

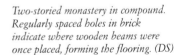

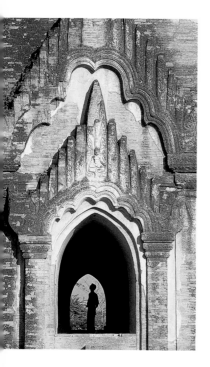

Doorway with pediments, south face.

Dhammayan-gyi. Another shorter inscription added later on the same stone (east side) records the dedication of five bonded individuals in 1220.

Two more 13th-century Burmese stone inscriptions are found in the west entrance hall. One belongs to 1205 when King Sithu requested the head of the 'Dhammaram', (the Dhammayan-gyi), to build a temple to the west side of the Dhammaram. This donated temple cannot be identified today, but this is the earliest reference to the Dhammayan-gyi temple itself. That Dhammaram, meaning Peaceful Abode for the Buddha's Teaching, was the ancient name is supported by an ink inscription in the east hall, dated to 1343, recording a dedication in the temple of that name.

An Enigma

Luce suggested that the inner corridor was bricked up by invading troops from Sri Lanka to humble the Burmese king, but new research, bolstered by common sense, indicates there was no invasion from that island kingdom (Aung-Twin, 1998). The *Glass Palace Chronicle* reports that the temple was never finished, but blames it on the ruthless and brutal reign of Narathu (1169-1170), the successor of Alaungsithu (1113-1169). This is another example of how the *Chronicle* probably recorded local legends that likely had little to do with the original history of the monuments. Luce also recorded an old legend claiming that a monk who was an alchemist-magician walled himself in.

The walls inside the blocked up inner corridor were completely painted, suggesting that the corridor was bricked up during the final stages of construction. Perhaps the engineers felt the temple would be unable to support the massive weight of the tower unless the inner corridor was filled with brick, but the real reason for filling the inner corridor with brick is probably forever lost to us.

Exterior

The exterior resembles the Ananda and the Thatbyinnyu, with two horizontal divisions in the walls, each with numerous windows. Large cut stones embedded deeply into the walls and visible where the stucco has flaked off help secure the outer facing to the fabric of the building. Only ten percent or so of the stucco remains. Huge cusped arches above the entrance ways are surmounted with standard, vertical flame-like elements. The one on the south side is perhaps the best preserved, a male figure holding two lotus stalks, shown seated above an impressive *kirtimukha*. By each entrance are small niches once containing sculpture, a feature at the early Ananda and Shwegu-gyi.

In the corners of the vast square terraces are miniature replicas of temples and stupas, but even early in the 20th century these were never in good repair. Unlike all of the other major large temples, the Dhammayan-gyi has no decorative ceramic ornamentation. Each terrace is divided into seven recessed registers, diminishing in size and providing a smooth transition to the *shikhara*. Some idea of the Dhammayan-gyi *shikhara* can be gleaned from the restored Sulamani, despite its somewhat distorted contour.

The Entrance Halls

The four entrance halls and both inner corridors were completely painted in a light tan wash at the time of construction. Dark, multi-coloured decorative bands surround the doorways and mark cornices and base mouldings. This contrasts with the interiors of early temples that are filled entirely with stone sculpture and murals of Buddhist subjects and decorative motifs, such as the Kubyauk-gyi (Myinkaba), dated to 1113.

Horoscopes in black pigment were painted directly over this very layer of wash in the north entrance hall. Look for four circles, divided by symmetrical lines, in the vault between the two piers on the right. The lower one on the right is the earliest and is dated to 1305.

The entrance halls and inner corridor are filled with later, intrusive painting. These begin as early as the 14th century, with Buddhas donated by the monk Anandasura who was active in Pagan sometime before 1376 (see the Htilominlo temple for his dates). Long boats are painted over some of the Buddhas, proving that there were repeated additions. Two painted elephants appear in one of the window chambers on the north side, with captions identifying the pair as two elephants married to the same king-elephant (*jataka* no 541). One wife was jealous of the other, and in a future life she conspired to kill her late husband but then later died of a broken heart. This *jataka* was popular throughout the Buddhist world, appearing at the gateways of Sanchi and at Ajanta in India. The elephants perhaps date to the 15th-16th centuries, as may the ogres on the principal doorways.

In the east entrance hall is a seated stone Buddha, partially restored in cement and painted in red splotches. The face is largely original, however. (See photo on page 93) A ten-line ink inscription nearby is perhaps the dedication of this image by a court official, dated to 1343, over a century after the foundation of the temple. This inscription also records the name of the temple as Dhammaram, just as in the stone inscription from the previous century. If this inscription is associated with this Buddha, then this figure is an important dated example in the history of Burmese sculpture. A similar Buddha is found in one of the shrines facing the Shwe-san-daw and one in the east-facing temple at the Dhamma-yazika.

Double-sided screen, entrance hall, west.

Later painted Buddhas, entrance hall, west. (PP)

The east face is the only side to retain the temple's original main inner sanctum, now occupied by a restored Buddha but flanked by late 18th or early 19th-century painting (two disciples, with rich foliage). We can see how the inner corridor was completely bricked up by examining the side walls of the shrine.

Four small stones projecting from the rear wall of the hall originally would have helped secure the large standing figures made in brick. In one corner is a staircase leading to the upper terraces.

In the south hall is a later large Buddha image, but the original painting framing the arch leading to the corridor is probably the best preserved. The west hall has a large double-sided screen. The outer face contains two images, and the inner one has a recumbent Buddha. None of these figures belong to the original time of construction but were part of later refurbishing. The floor of the western entry is paved with small flagstones, unlike the other halls in brick. A fragmentary later painting depicting a temple or pavilion is seen on one of the piers.

Inner Corridor

The inner corridor begins after stepping over a massive, no-nonsese stone threshold. Just inside on the floor are stone cups, meant for swinging wooden doors. The flooring is glazed brick, reminiscent of the Nagayon.

Inside the corridor, high on the inner wall, are the bricked up semi-circular openings with painted surrounds. That the tan coloured wash was painted over these openings is another indication that the inner corridor was sealed at the time the temple was finished.

Monastery in Compound

An ancient monastery sits in the compound corner, to the side of the modern entrance. It is largely in ruins but it reveals how the upper floor of two-storied monastic units were constructed with timber beams inserted into the brick walls at regular intervals. Only the holes for the wooden beams are seen today. In the centre was an inner chamber. The compound gateways are good places to inspect the complex nature of Pagan vaulting.

Opposite: View from the east.

SULAMANI

Date: 1183

The Sulamani weighs in with other Pagan Leviathans, such as the Thatbyinnyu and the Gawdaw-palin. It is about 15 years junior to the Dhamma-yazika stupa, finished in 1197-1198, which probably represents the last gasp of gigantic construction in the city. The tower was damaged in the 1975 quake and restored with less than perfect proportions. The hoisting of its gilded finial, or *hti*, was the focus of national attention in September, 1998. The corridors boast perhaps the most inventive and engaging 18th-century painting in Burma.

Visit
The Sulamani can be combined with the nearby Dhammayan-gyi temple. The approach to the temple today is from the west, but its ancient entrance is on the opposite side. Shops lining the modern entrance mar the view intended by the architects, so it is wise to scoot to one of the other three sides for a proper appreciation.

The temple's stone inscription is located inside the northern entrance hall and is dated to 1183. The original ancient name of the temple is unknown, but its present name stems from '*chulamani*' (Pali), or the jewelled-headdress that Gotama removed upon

The Sulamani, dated to 1183, is an important landmark in understanding Pagan's development. The tower and finial are restorations. (DS)

Glazed insets dramatically accent
exterior, entrance hall, south. (DS)

abandoning the palace. It is believed to reside in a special heaven
where it is worshipped by the gods.

The two-storied design is reminiscent of the Thatbyinnyu,
Gawdaw-palin and Htilominlo, its massive solid core encircled by
a corridor from which numerous passages open to the exterior. The
smaller upper storey mirrors the plan below, with a large Buddha
seated within a central chamber facing east. Prominent stairways
leading to the upper terraces are in both side corridors.

Roughly 40 percent of the original exterior stucco survives, much
of it fresh as the day it set. Stone blocks and rows of header bricks
binding the facing of the wall to its inner fabric are visible where the
stucco has flaked off.

Below the lavish pediments over the doors are small niches once
probably containing seated figures, an early convention found at the
Shwegu-gyi and the Ananda. Miniature stupas above allow us to
imagine the design of ancient, large stupas that have not survived
in their entirety.

Glazed ceramic insets accent the base of the temple and the
upper terraces and glisten in the setting sun. Many of the tiles are
coloured both green and yellow, a combination that probably began
sometime in the second half of the 12th century. The earliest dated
glazed tiles are in solid green colour and are seen at the Shwegu-gyi,
dated to 1131. The same two-coloured tiles are used at the
Htilominlo, but the yellow has adhered far less well.

*Makara with gaping mouth,
chasing a fanciful lion.*

Central figure within the doorway pediment, south face.

Refurbishing

The Sulamani was subject to constant refurbishment after the capital shifted from Pagan to the Ava area in the fourteenth century. All of the major temples entered a period of limited use and were subject to intrusive painting, offered as acts of devotion. Ink inscriptions from as early as 1299 and 1317 point to refreshed brick sculpture and painting additions. (Than Tun, 1996). The ubiquitous monk Anandasura was also active at the Sulamani, witnessed by his one-line inscriptions in red ink. Few works can be seen from this early period, however. The ogres painted on the major doorways may date to this early phase, but they could also be considerably later.

Painting belonging to the time of construction in 1183 is mainly in the vaulted ceilings where roughly 40 percent survives. The walls, however, were covered originally with a light tan wash framed by painted corner pilasters and registers at the tops and bottoms, resembling the interiors of the Thatbyinnyu, Dhammayan-gyi and all of the later large temples. This treatment is readily appreciated in the main modern entrances where large ogres have been painted over the tan wash. It is therefore a mistake to think that any later painting covered earlier figurative murals.

The central brick Buddha images and the smaller ones within the corridors were repaired by the laity between 1927 and 1929, recorded in many ink inscriptions on the nearby walls. Much of this was organized by an energetic monk name U Thathana.

The most commanding painting was added to the corridors and entrance halls by multiple donors between October, 1778 and April, 1779. (Than Tun, 1996). This occurred before King Bodawpaya (1782-1819) whose reign saw the building of the Ananda Temple Monastery and Upali Thein ordination hall. Murals from the Konbaung period (1752-1885) at Pagan were generally part of a single commission, with all of the painting in each monument conforming to a uniform programme. The walls of the Sulamani, however, reveal no connected subject matter, since multiple donors commissioned different paintings at various times. Much of the Sulamani painting was done some ten years after the Shwe-zigon murals dated to 1768, but the style looks forward to the later murals, such as those at the Ananda Temple Monastery. The decade following 1768 perhaps signalled a fundamental shift in painting at Pagan.

The Sulamani painting also affords the best opportunity to witness the underlying grids used to make compositions symmetrical. Similar grids from the ancient period are visible now and then throughout Pagan. Many dated ink inscriptions record donations at the temple, but more study is required before the donations can be connected to the scores of compositions.

Ogre with green and yellow glazed insets, west.

West Corridor (Modern Entrance)

The west corridor today forms the temple's entrance, but it was originally at the rear.

A lengthy inscription in Pali and Burmese to the left of the central seated Buddha is dated to 1778. A large painted reclining Buddha further to the left represents the master's death at Kushinagara in India, identified in a tiny inscription near the Buddha's feet ('Kusannaram'). The two identical *Shala* trees, flanking the Buddha, are as they are described in the Pali texts. The figures closest to the Buddha express their grief with their hands over their faces, but others, more enlightened, are shown unperturbed, a distinction made in Buddhist art from a very early time.

Small ogre at the south face.

A shorter inscription on the right side of the corridor belongs to Maung Hpyu, described as a rich man wishing to obtain nirvana. He donated a Buddha sheltered by the snake-king Muchalinda and the Buddha residing at the Jetavana Monastery. Many of these are within this corridor, but others are perhaps throughout the temple. The inscription is placed next to a huge seated Buddha and a kneeling disciple.

North Corridor (Side)

The first painting on the outer wall of the corridor is a large seated Buddha flanked by two disciples. An adjacent eleven-line inscription dated both in the Burmese and the Buddhist Era equates to 1778. The donor was named Nandasila from Inwa (modern Ava). He also says that it was painted with yellow, red and multiple colours and was done by an artist ('*panchisaya*', Burmese).

The walls of the entrance hall are filled with late 18th-century painting. The lengthy inscription high on the eastern wall records the rebuilding of Buddha images in 1779 by a monk named Vimala. This monk also dedicated paintings showing the Buddha shielded by Muchalinda, the Buddha converting the five ascetics at Sarnath, the 28 Buddhas and possibly the Seven Weeks, painted in

White King Elephant, north corridor, 18th century.

Buddha sheltered by Snake King, north entrance hall, c. 18th-19th century.

various colours, according to the inscription. The scene at Sarnath is immediately below and to the right, the five new disciples kneeling in a row. The Muchalinda composition is likely on the other side of the wall, while the Seven Weeks is probably on the east side of the temple.

Another inscription records a date of 1885 when foreigners of different religions ruled Burma and the Buddhist community was then weak. The rebuilding and painting was undertaken to restore the Buddhist faith. The English had taken the palace at Mandalay in 1885 and the country was officially annexed in the following year.

In one of the doorway chambers before the stairway are two magnificent tuskers, each with captions. The one on the right loosely translates, "The King Elephant, the White Elephant, beauteous for all to behold." The companion painting on the opposite side is identified as, "The Elephant looking like a Black Cloud." These can be dated by an ink inscription to November 6, 1778 (Than Tun, 1996).

At the end of the corridor is another large seated Buddha next to a reclining Buddha. A long inscription placed between them high above cannot be made out. The disciple next to the Buddha is identified by a caption as Sariputta.

East Corridor (Original Entrance)

The principal Buddha is restored, but 18th-century painting on the side walls of the deep chamber are devoted to the seven-week period that the Buddha spent at Bodh Gaya, already a popular theme in the ancient period. It is possible that this composition can be associated with the inscription of 1779 in the north entrance hall. The first week commemorates the enlightenment (1), represented by the central brick Buddha. The other weeks begin on the right wall, starting with the Gazing at the Bodhi tree (2), the Jewelled Walk (3), and the Jewelled House (4). The remaining weeks on the opposite wall start with the Buddha resting beneath a Goatherder's Tree (5), followed by the Buddha protected by the hoods of the snake-king (6), and the last week where the Buddha is given four bowls by the World Guardians and offerings by two merchants (7). Each of the weeks is captioned in Burmese. Immediately following the seven-week period, the deity named Brahma Sahampati persuades the Buddha to share his doctrine with the world. Holding a circular wreath, the artists wisely placed this delightful figure toward the front of the wall, near the Goatherder's Tree, out of chronological sequence, and labelled 'Thahanpati', (Burmese).

South Corridor (Side)

The most spectacular painting at the Sulamani takes up one entire side of the south corridor. The massive composition is divided into six unequal divisions, with each segment captioned in Burmese. The mural probably belongs to the late 18th century, but no donative inscriptions have yet been identified.

The top row shows the 28 Buddhas, going from left to right, each with his own specific tree identified with a caption. The last scene on the right shows the Buddha taming Alavaka, a master-demon, (*yakkha*, Pali). This important episode has no formal connection to the 28 Buddhas, but it sets the stage for the register below devoted to the forty-five years the Buddha wandered and stayed in various monasteries in north India. This theme was never significant during the earlier Pagan period but grew important by the 18th century. It is also prominent at the Upali Thein. The next register shows the Buddha in the centre, Sariputta and other disciples on the left and Moggallana and others on the right. The fourth row shows monks and nuns who achieved enlightenment during the lifetime of the Buddha, 45 men on the left and 13 women on the right. The fifth row is taken up by lay men and women who reached the same stage

Restored central Buddha. Theme of the Seven Weeks painted on side walls, c. 18th century. Devotee applying gold leaf. Shrine, east.

A fragmentary 18th-century painting, porch, east.

of enlightenment during the lifetime of the Buddha. The bottom row depicts scenes from the Buddhist hells and is very fragmentary.

Beside this huge composition are scenes based on everyday life in Burma, such as three boats pulling a barge during a festival. The cartouches contain songs. The remainder of the corridor is painted with numerous Buddha figures, all probably from the late 18th or early 19th century. Two lively monkeys frolic whimsically about a wooden pole

The Sulamani Monastery
Sharing the compound wall and northern gateway with the Sulamani temple is an open-air monastery likely dating to the 13th or 14th century (no. 745). It stretches a full 134 metres long, with nearly 80 cells and a brick-lined drainage channel leading to a shallow pond. It has not been restored and is worth a peek.

Frolicking monkeys, south corridor.

Disciple of the Buddha,
c. 18th-19th-century, south corridor.

Brahma Sahampati, included within the Seven Weeks, east.

Procession of donors, south corridor, c. 18th-19th-century.

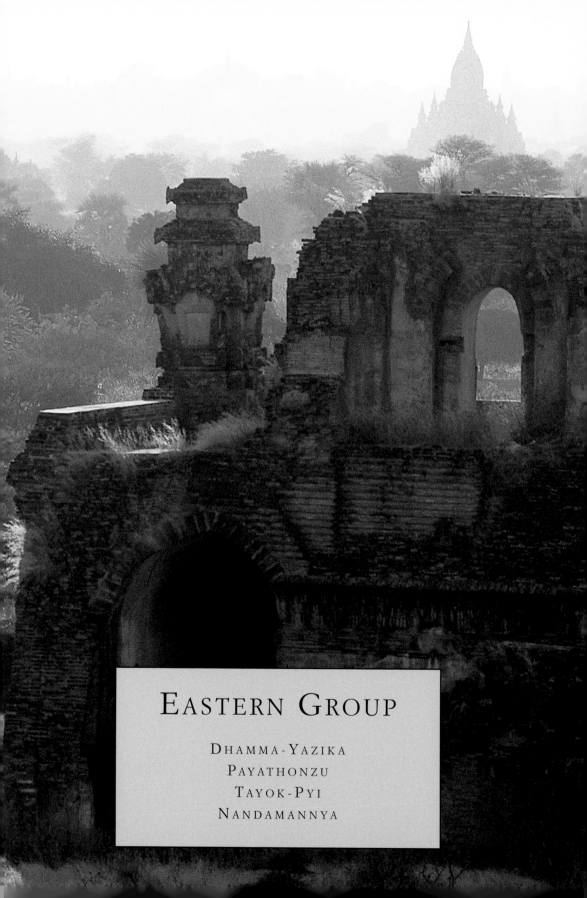

EASTERN GROUP

DHAMMA-YAZIKA

PAYATHONZU

TAYOK-PYI

NANDAMANNYA

DHAMMA-YAZIKA

Previous pages: The remote area lying to the east of the Walled City witnessed a tremendous expension in the late 12th and 13th centuries. Monuments in this area also suffered the least at the time of the 1975 quake.

The Dhamma-yazika was one of the last great stupas constructed at Pagan. Its pentagonal plan honours the Four Buddhas of the Present Era and the Buddha of the Future, Metteya.

Date: 1197-1198

Five-sided stupas are found nowhere within the Buddhist world except in Burma and at Pagan. They are dedicated to the historical Buddha, Gotama, his three predecessors and the Buddha of the Future. The Dhamma-yazika is among the largest stupas at Pagan, weighing in at approximately six million bricks, based on estimates of the stupa's volume. It was completed in only two years. It also represents one of Pagan's last vast building projects, since the 13th century saw few large monuments. Its relics from Sri Lanka highlight the important role that this Buddhist island played in the religious life of Pagan. The stupa was virtually deserted until it was completely renovated in the mid-1990s.

Visit

The glistening dome of the Dhamma-yazika is a landmark in the southern part of Pagan near the settlement known today as West Pwasaw. Numerous narrow dirt roads lead there, and it is impressive from every angle, especially in early morning or late afternoon sun. The Dhamma-yazika can be combined with the southern or eastern groups of temples.

This unusual five-sided plan honours five principal Buddhas: the historical Buddha Gotama, his three predecessors, and the Buddha of the Future, Metteyya. These five Buddhas are important in Theravada countries, but Burma is the only country to develop a

five-sided monument to commemorate this grouping. These five Buddhas were perhaps in worship as early as the Pyu period, suggested by two stone slabs at Shri Kshetra depicting five seated Buddhas in a row, beneath a stupa. That the Pyu knew of the four Buddhas preceding Metteyya, is proved by an inscribed silver casket in the national musuem, Yangon.

Relics from Sri Lanka
The founding of the stupa is recorded in a broken stone inscription now located within the temple on the east face. The ruling king, Narapatisithu, sought an auspicious site in 1196 to preserve precious relics he received from the king of Sri Lanka. He spotted a column of vapour arising from the earth, with the girth of a palmyra tree, and noted the location with an iron nail. Work on the stupa began the next year at this location, and was finished in 1198. The inscription does not mention any of the five Buddhas specifically but is dedicated to the "five Holy Ones born in this *kalpa* [present age, Pali]". The king gifted 1,000 robes for monks, and donated to the stupa 500 bonded Burmese, 500 Indians and agricultural plots throughout the realm. The stupa's name in the epigraph is Dhammarajika.

No inscriptions identify any of the Buddhas within the five temples, and so therefore we cannot be sure which individual Buddhas were believed to be in the five shrines. Nor does the Pali canon associate the five with specific directions. An ink inscription dated to 1695 records the refurbishment of an image of the Buddha Kakusandha in the temple on the east face and the raising of a new finial on the stupa, together with horse and cart races. (Than Tun, 1996). The seated Buddhas themselves were in ruinous condition before their restoration in the the 1990s. There are sixteen five-sided monuments at Pagan, but the majority are temples, not stupas. One is found at Sale. In these examples too we cannot be sure which direction each Buddha was assigned, if any (Pichard, 1991).

Temple on stupa platform, west side.

The stupa in 1985, before its restoration in the 1990s. (DS)

Detail of temple wall.

Exterior

The stupa sits within an enormous fifteen-sided walled compound planned with five gateways. Each entrance to the compound leads directly to five identical temples abutting onto the base of the stupa. The only temple oriented to a cardinal direction is on the east. Three pentagonal terraces support the massive dome. No ready access to the terraces was planned, suggesting that circumambulation was never intended, at least among the terraces. A modern stairway is provided for visitors.

A small portion of the dome's original stucco had survived, but was destroyed in the recent restorations. The new stucco, however, is faithful to the original in its design and placement. Patches survive within the terraces, but the corner stupas on the top terrace have been entirely resurfaced. Weathered stone lions with riders guard the stairways on the third terrace. Large brick urns were at the corners of the two lower terraces, while large stupa-shaped structures were reserved for the top, similar to the arrangement at the Mingalazedi. All have been renovated.

The Jatakas

A complete set of 547 *jataka* stories was planned for the three square terraces. The niches total 601 but only 371 tiles are installed today. Each of the first 537 *jatakas* is represented by a single plaque, with a caption below listing its name and ordinal number in the standard Pali series. The last ten *jatakas*, the revered Mahanipita, were placed on the higher terraces and each tale was accorded a number of tiles,

A complete set of jataka *tiles filled hundreds of niches within the terraces.* Jataka *no. 339. (DS)*

resembling the series at the Ananda and the Mingalazedi.

Many of the tiles, if not the majority, have been re-installed haphazardly, so it difficult to be sure of the correct order, unless a number of plaques appear together in right sequence. The series likely began to the left of the temple facing east and proceeded clockwise, winding its way up the terraces. The starting-point would mirror that at the Mingalazedi that also began on the east face, immediately to the left of the median staircase.

The Five Temples

These identical temples gives an idea of the type of stucco work used in royal sponsored work at the end of the 12th century. That a temple

dedicated at exactly the same time, the Kubyauk-
gne, (no. 1391), used quite different stucco designs
is an indication of Pagan's diversity. Comparision
with the Kubyauk-gyi (Minkaba), dated to 1113,
reveals how many of the basic motifs continued,
but their treatment lacks a sense of proportion and
strength by the end of the century.

A long lancet-like motif rises on all four sides
of the *shikharas*; at the bottom are two-armed
figures holding lotuses that meander to the apex
of the tower. All of the temples were renovated
throughout the ages, mostly with intrusive
painting, probably beginning in the 14th century.
Only two temples are open to the public.

The stone inscription recording the principal
dedication of the stupa is located a few steps
beyond the doorway within the temple on the east
face. A new metal figure has replaced the former
Buddha in brick. Small portions of the grid used by the original
painters are just visible on the rear wall, high on the right. Also
inside the shrine is a large gilded stone Buddha sitting on a huge
stone base. It resembles a stone Buddha in the entrance hall at the
Dhammayan-gyi, perhaps dated by a nearby inscription to 1343. Its
stone base is also similar to one found in a temple facing the Shwe-
san-daw where another stone Buddha relating to these is housed. It
is tempting to suggest that these rather rare stone bases were
contemporary with these possibly 14th-century images. Original
painting survives on the walls and especially on the vaulted ceiling.
Many later inscriptions are sprinkled here and there about
the temples.

A Buddha seated beneath a large tree is
painted over the original mural work on the
left side of the entrance arch (see page 75
bottom, for photo of this painting). This
instrusive work probably dates to the 14th
century and is one more indication that
the principal temples probably fell into
limited use after the capital shifted to
Ava in the first half ot the 14th century.

The other temple open to view also
retains much original mural work. A
monk named Wut Thein left a five-line
ink inscription on the left wall, dated
to 1735, recording his repairs to three
Buddhas that were damaged by robbers.
These were painted in red and yellow,
continues the inscription. Another
inscription by the same monk appears
in the eastern temple, dated to the same
year, and refers to unspecified repairs;
the object was likely the Buddha he
restored in that temple.

Jataka *tile no. 85.* (DS)

*The pentagonal plan is unique to
Burma. Only the temple on the east
faces in a cardinal direction.*

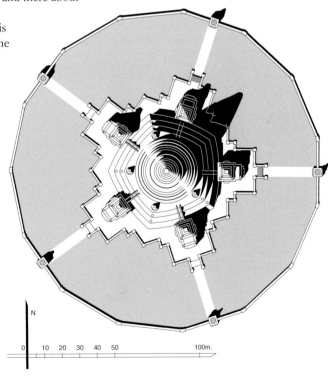

PAYATHONZU

Highlights

★ mural painting

★ prepatory outlines for murals

★ unique triple-shrine

Date: 13th century

The 13th-century murals at the Payathonzu represent the last flourish of Pagan painting. How the ancient artisans set about their work can be understood by examining the partially finished sections. Its unique ground plan unites three separate temples with a single corridor.

Visit

The Payathonzu is only steps from the main road and can be combined with the nearby Tayok-pyi. No surviving stone inscriptions speak directly of its construction, but it was probably erected in the thirteenth century when this area of Pagan experienced a building boom. Three shrines joined by a common corridor is a unique configuration at Pagan, but the design of each individual temple conforms to similar 13th-century monuments, if not earlier.

Typical late Pagan stucco patterns on the exterior have weathered badly, leaving only about 15 percent. The new tower finials are completely conjectural, since their original summits collapsed before the 20th century. A small chamber on the façade and one within a porch may have served for storage, reminiscent of those in the outer halls at the Htilominlo. The exterior was completely finished, but much of the interior painting was left unfinished for unknown reasons. It suggests that the painters began their work after the exterior work was completed, or at least well advanced. The central

The triple temples of the Payathonzu joined by a single corridor. Restored finials.

brick Buddhas in each shrine were
restored in the 1990s.

Frescos

Two of the temples are filled with
murals, but in one (on the west)
painting was never started, nor inside
the modest entrance hall of the central
temple. The sections that were never
begun probably represent the last step
in preparing the wall surface before
the application of grid lines
and preparatory drawings. This is
confirmed by late 14th-century

*Previous Buddhas severing their hair,
modelled on the life of Gotama,
the 28th Buddha. (DS)*

horoscopes painted directly over the prepared blank surface in the
unfinished temple. Large, partially finished wall surfaces are rare at
Pagan but can be found now and then, such as at temple no. 1244
with an exposed grid. The two sanctums have retained about 80
percent of their wall painting and about 60 percent on the vaulted
ceilings.

How these 13th-century artisans organized the interiors differs
greatly from the earliest Pagan temples, such as the Kubyauk-gyi
(Myinkaba), the Nagayon or the Pahto-thamya, from the late
eleventh or early twelfth centuries. For example, the later painters
strove to make the flat wall surface appear layered and three-
dimensional, somewhat in the fashion of the celebrated ancient
murals at Pompeii where an even more exaggerated sense of *trompe
l'oeil* was achieved. This sensibility is most clearly expressed by the

*Restored Buddha in central shrine,
looking toward the side shrine on
the east.*

8

Ceiling ornament in the side shrine. (DS)

Makara and ogre in the side shrine, rear wall.

painted pillars in each of the sanctum's corners. Such columns served no structural purpose, but simulated a sense of being within a room with complex interior space. Further enhancing the sensation of depth and progression were boldly overlapping motifs and figures. For example, large man-birds, or *kinnara*s, are placed directly over rows of miniature Buddhas. Earlier generations of Pagan painters were usually reluctant to have their compositions stray far from their frames, seeing the wall as merely a surface for presenting illustrations. By the 13th century, the flat walls were viewed as a challenge, to be brought alive with freshly conceived designs and patterns.

The unbridled imaginations of later artists at Pagan also created new motifs with remarkable complexity and whimsy. For example, a small rectangular frame within a side wall shows a long snake emerging from the mouth of a *makara* that in turn is surrounded by four cavorting figures (see photo on page 86). This rich composition requires close inspection to appreciate fully, since it is confined within a space no wider than 10 cm. Indeed, from a distance, this inventive detail is lost. This penchant for intricacy is absent in early Pagan painting. Many of these motifs are new to the late 12th or 13th century and are found nowhere else in the Buddhist world. It is uncertain if these changes in Pagan's pictorial art reflected foreign influence or if it was a strictly internal development, or a combination.

Unfinished Painting

Partially finished painting in the corridor leading from the central temple to the shrine on the right (west) allows us to peek into the workings of the ancient ateliers. One composition centres on a pavilion, surrounded by kneeling, crowned men. The figures were probably first created in lead pencil, seen among the figures at the top who are faintly outlined. Below sit figures revealing the

next step in the process, where the pencil outlines were more sharply
defined in blank paint. The dark, red background surrounding the
outlines of the figures was applied at about the same time. The last
sections, such as the faces and patterning within the garments, were
never finished. Other paintings, in various degrees of completion,
can be detected in this corridor. Some panels in the other side
temple (east) appear to be finished, but closer inspection reveals that
many details were left undone, such as the addition of the faces.

The Central Shrine

Painting was never started in the temple's entrance hall. The light
coloured smooth surface is exactly how the painters left it in the
13th century, before a grid or preparatory sketches were undertaken.
Inside the sanctum is a subtle emphasis on the Buddha's triumph
over Mara. For example, the small demon perches on top of the false
pilasters on the rear wall and releases an arrow toward the seated
Buddha. Also, a Buddha in the earth-touching gesture is seen at the
top of all of the arches, signifying Mara's defeat. The most inventive
work is contained on the false pilasters in the corners, with couples
and groups of figures. Indeed, this ranks among the finest of Pagan's
13th-century painting.

Side Temple (East)

The narrow entrance hall is devoted to the *jatakas* and other scenes
but a symmetrical organization was impossible, owing to irregular
openings in the walls. Large panels placed amidst the *jatakas* depict
the Taming of the Nalagiri Elephant, the Descent from the Heaven
of the 33 Gods and the Birth of the Buddha. In a deep pointed niche
are also episodes from the Buddha's life, such as the Presentation
of Honey, the Buddha's First Sermon at Sarnath and probably the
Miracle at Savatthi. The *jatakas* seem quite crudely executed
compared to the painting in the sanctum; none are labeled. The
28 Buddhas appear at the top of the wall.

The emphasis in the sanctum is on the Buddha's First Sermon,
since the painted Buddhas above the arch are in the teaching-gesture,
contrasting with those in the earth-touching gesture in the central
shrine. Panels next to the outer doorway and on the other side of the
temple highlight the 28 Buddhas, seated beneath diverse trees. Below
each tier are small figures illustrating the lives of the individual
Buddhas, focusing on the moment when they severed their hair,
signalling their quest for enlightenment. A panel in the corridor
leading to the central shrine features the Buddha gazing at the
Bodhi tree.

Other important temples in the vicinity
of the Payathonzu include the Lemyathna
(no. 447) and it monastic complex and the
Thambula temple (no. 482).

*Partially finished painting,
in corridor. (DS)*

*Taming of the Nalagiri Elephant,
entrance hall, side shrine. (DS)*

Payathonzu temple plan.

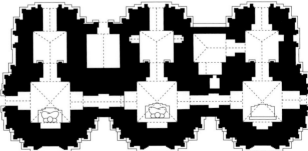

N 3°

0 1 2 3 4 5   10m.

TAYOK-PYI

Highlights

★ Stucco work

★ Frescos

★ Monastery

Date: 13th century

The Tayok-pyi is among the larger temples in the eastern zone, with impressive murals and stucco ornament. A ruinous monastery within its wide compound walls suggests the temple's importance. The Tayok-pyi was constructed sometime before the mid-13th century, since an ink inscription dated to 1248 was added later to the interior.

Visit

This eastern area of Pagan was densely populated with monuments, beginning in the late 12th century and peaking in the 13th century. The extent of this building boom can be appreciated from the terraces of the temple. Also, this area of Pagan is the best place to see unrestored monuments, inasmuch as the pace of rebuilding has been somewhat slower here. The temple is a short distance from the Payathonzu, on the opposite side of the dirt road.

The tower was entirely restored, with a conjectural finial. Glazed insets glisten in the afternoon sun. Entrance hall projects on the right. From the south.

Exterior

The temple is built around a massive central core, faced with restored seated Buddhas oriented to the cardinal directions. The wide entrance hall faces east. Two narrow staircases lead to the upper chamber which is a mirror image of the one below, only reduced in size. The tower was entirely rebuilt in the 1990s.

The plan is characteristic of later Pagan architecture, with wide and deep entrance halls on the rear and sides that intersect with the inner corridor. The earliest surviving temples at Pagan have no side or rear doors, and the outer wall is pierced only by windows, such as the Nagayon or the Pahto-thamya. Small windows placed next to the doorways at the Tayok-pyi are a feature of later, large temples at Pagan (nos. 37 and 744).

Roughly sixty-percent of the stucco survives, especially impressive among the double-arched pediments in the middle of each wall and over the entrance. The lower arch is formed from the tails of two *makara* placed at both ends. New motifs were introduced in the later Pagan period, such as a split-bodied squatting lion at the base of corner pilasters. Also common in the later period are vertical or horizontal registers, ornamented with tiny concentric raised circles.

South entrance.

The foundation and the terraces are accented with small green and yellow glazed ceramic insets, creating a glistening profile. The first dated temple using tiles in this way is the Shwegu-gyi, from 1131, but the tradition certainly started earlier. Some of the rounded crenellations contain green glazed sandstone plaques. Covering stone with a green glaze is found at the Shwe-zigon, for the *jataka* plaques, but this technique is rare at Pagan.

The side wall of the sanctum. (DS)

Frescos

The entire wall surface is filled with figurative painting, unlike many later temples at Pagan whose walls were covered in a light tan coloured wash, such as the Dhammayangyi and the Thatbyinnyu. Important themes include the 28 Buddhas, the Eight Great Events and the Seven Weeks at Bodh Gaya. The walls retain about 40 percent of their murals, while the ceiling about 50 percent.

In the entrance hall the 28 Buddhas are found at the top of both walls. Much is missing below, but there were perhaps seven principal compositions on each wall, centred on standing or seated figures. The episode of the Buddha gazing at a Bodhi tree (the second week at Bodh Gaya) can be made out on the left wall, and on the right is a crowned figure in a pavilion. Traces of the Buddha's footprints can be seen in the ceiling.

Inside the corridor on the outer wall surrounding the sanctum are large compositions devoted to the 28 Buddhas, shown with their individual trees, and identified with Burmese ink inscriptions. They run in a clockwise direction. On the inner wall are scenes from the life of the Buddha, drawn from a variety of Pali sources and with lengthy Burmese captions. On the south side is a composition devoted to the Buddha's invitation to Vesali to fight a plague begun by demons (*Ratana Sutta*). Other episodes cover the Buddha's preaching in Rajagaha and the donations of King Pasenadi in Kosambi.

The entrance halls on the sides and rear showcase scenes from the Eight Great Events and the Seven Weeks. Each hall has a total of four scenes, two on each side. The most impressive perhaps is on the north side and shows probably the Savatthi Miracle, next to the Buddha gazing at the Bodhi tree. Similar subjects are found within the side and rear halls in other temples from the 13th century, such as the nearby Lemyathna temple (no. 447) in Minnanthu.

Buddha Gazing at the Bodhi Tree, north entrance hall.

Later Ink Inscriptions

A ten-line inscription in the deep window chamber in the northwest corner is dated to 1248 and records a donation by a minister. Close by is a horoscope date to 1316. Another donation is within a window on the north face and is dated to 1291, together with a horoscope dated to 1302.

Bold inscriptions in red ink by the monk Anandasura appear on each of the rear and side doors. Painted inscriptions by this monk appear widely throughout Pagan and usually follow the same wording: 'The Elder Monk Anandasura's Donation'. In most cases, he donated large painted Buddha images within the corridors of temples whose walls were originally free of narrative figurative painting, such as the Htilominlo and the Dhammayan-gyi. A dated horoscope at the Htilominlo suggests that he flourished during the 14th century. His usual intrusive Buddhas are not found in corridors of the Tayok-pyi, but perhaps placing his customary inscription in a temple was considered an act of merit. However, large ogres are painted within each of the doorways and in proximity to this monk's inscriptions, tempting one to think that Anandasura may have been responsible for them. The ogres are certainly later than the construction period of the temple, and they are found at many of the most prominent temples at Pagan, also associated with Anandasura's donations.

The unrestored single-storied monastery (no. 540) in the compound reveals typical vaulting techniques. Its missing wooden porch would have faced in the direction of the temple. Two ruinous mounds in the compound were much smaller monastic buildings (nos. 541-542).

Crowned figure within a pavilion, main entrance hall. (DS)

The Miracle at Savatthi, west entrance hall. (DS)

NANDAMANNYA

Date: 13th century

The Nandamannya is known chiefly for its 13th-century painting and for an engaging rendering of Mara's three seductive daughters. The simple single-storied temple is crowned with a stupa dome, a combination popular in the 13th century.

Visit

The Nandamannya is located some ways north of the Payathonzu and Tayok-pyi and is visible on the right side of the road, proceeding from the direction of Minnanthu village. Its ground plan appears symmetrical, but the eastern façade extends slightly more than the other three. This widely used plan in the 13th century is often capped with a large stupa-dome, a reminder that the usual architectural distinctions between temple and stupa were often blurred at Pagan. The missing summit has been conjecturally restored. The surviving stucco amounts to about 25 percent.

Temple entrance from southeast.

Interior

The interior shares a similar organization with the Payathonzu, except the Buddha image is placed against the rear of the shrine. The Nandamannya is designed with six large painted panels, two at the entrance and two within each window chamber, similar to the Payathonzu. There is also the same use of the cloister vault, with the ceiling painting accenting the four equal divisions. Roughly 80 percent of the interior murals survive. A temple nearby and to the northeast has a similar interior and can be easily visited (no. 585).

The Buddha has been restored and repainted, but little else has been re-touched. The tree above the Buddha is a vibrant, dark green, a colour added to the painter's palette by the 13th century. Two disciples flank the

Buddha, probably Sariputta and Moggallana, on the left and right, respectively. The ceiling has scores of seated Buddhas painted in alternating square and circular frames, centred on a large, intricate lotus roundel. Just below the ceiling are the 28 Buddhas arranged in a row. Beneath each is the figure of the Buddha-to-be severing his hair, as Gotama did upon abandoning the palace.

Large painted arches frame the window chambers, with false pillars in each corner, much like the interior at the Payathonzu. The two vertical rows include scenes from the Eight Great Events and the Seven Weeks at Bodh Gaya, such as Gazing at the Bodhi tree and the Descent from the Heaven of the 33 Gods.

The panels at the entrance feature two seated Buddhas, with flames issuing from their haloes, surrounded by 32 Buddhas, each beneath a tree. These may refer to the Miracle at Savatthi. The two panels in the window chamber on the right depict the Enlightenment and the First Sermon. The latter scene shows at the base the Wheel of the Law flanked by two deer, symbols of the Buddha's First Sermon at the Deer Park in Sarnath. The scene is unusual, since the Buddha's hands are not in the teaching-gesture, but rather the earth-touching gesture signifying his enlightenment. The window itself is bordered by narrow panels presenting the Birth of the Buddha and a standing figure, likely a bodhisattva. An aquatic scene below is filled with fish and crustaceans. The Birth scene does not fit with the surrounding imagery and diminishes the symmetrical nature of the interior, but its placement here suggests that subjects were perhaps juxtaposed with some freedom.

The Buddha, with a procession of Mara's daughters, window chamber, south daughters.

Restored central Buddha, cloister vault and doorway on right.

Stucco head, exterior.

Right: Fanciful ornament on side wall.

Fish and crustaceans on the window chamber, north side.

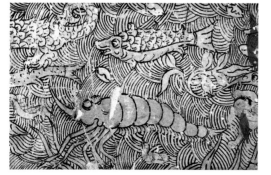

'Let us entice him in all possible ways'

The pair of panels inside the opposite window chamber signal the defeat of Mara's three daughters, Tanha, Arati and Raga (Pali), who allegorically represent Desire, Aversion and Lust, respectively. After the Buddha defeated Mara during his first week at Bodh Gaya, the demon's daughters offered to help their father by winning the Buddha over to the world of attachments. This occurs in the fifth week at Bodh Gaya, according to most Pali traditions, such as the *Nidanakatha*. The earliest painted example of this incident is probably at the Pahto-thamya.

Without the benefit of modern psychology, the trio reasoned that since men's tastes differed they would therefore each assume a hundred different guises, "as virgins, as women who had not borne children, who had given birth to one child, or who had two children, or as women in middle age, or as elderly women. Let us entice him in all possible ways." (*Nidanakatha*, 106). This is the background behind the procession of diverse women appearing on the lower register, some quite young and others as 'elderly women', bent over steeply with exposed breasts; one even seems to require a stave to support herself. Earlier scholarship labeled this scene as 'tantric', due to the partial nudity, but this is not the case. The Buddha sits unperturbed in a temple setting, his right hand lowered.

The opposite panel, on the right, features the seated Buddha in the same position. Mara discharges an arrow, standing in a chariot, at the

base. The demon is shown again in the same register seated with his consort on a dais, his three daughters kneeling before him. They are shown defeated, ill-proportioned and half-clad, resembling the 'elderly women' on the opposite wall. These 'hags' perhaps reflect a legend reported in the *Nidanakatha* that claimed that the Buddha cursed the elderly daughters and forced them to remain as hags forever, "with their broken teeth and grey hair." (*Nidanakatha*, 106). The ancient compiler dutifully notes this story but adds that this episode is only legend, since the Buddha would never contemplate such a spiteful act. The *Nidankatha* is centuries earlier than Pagan, but this colourful story surrounding the 'hags' may have survived in Buddhist folklore. If so, the three elderly women seated before their father are probably pleading with him to resolve their predicament and turn them once again into beautiful women. Such depictions of Mara's elderly daughters are rare in Buddhist art. Whatever the interpretation, the stakes were high for playing a seductress.

A stone inscription dated to 1248 sits inside the porch, but it was taken there some time ago and does not relate to the temple. Opposite the Nandamannya is an extensive underground monastery, the Nandamannya-umin (no. 583). Its subterranean cells suggests a form of meditation stressing isolation, also seen at the Kyauk-ku-umin.

Mara, right, and his daughters, left. Detail from panel, window chamber, south.

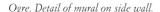

Ogre. Detail of mural on side wall.

Watercolour. Colesworthy Grant, c. 1855.
View of the Bupaya stupa bordering the Irrawaddy.
(Courtesy The Oriental and Indian Office Collection, British Library)

ACCOMMODATION

Hotels and Resorts

Hotel staff can arrange horse-carts, bicycle rentals, private taxis and guides. All rooms are air conditioned, with hot water. Rates usually include a buffet breakfast. Less expensive hotels are located in New Pagan and in and around Nyaung-U.

Thiripyitsaya-Sakura Hotel

This hotel was the first built at Pagan, in 1972. Outdoor dining area overlooking the river. Luxury suites with river view, plus bungalows in spacious acreage. Pool. Located immediately outside the Walled City, bordering the river.
Tel. 95 1 255 333 (Yangon), 95 2 67289-90 (Pagan)
E-mail: thiri@myanmar.com.mm
www.myanmars.net/thiripyitsayahotel

Bagan Thande Hotel

Newer rooms enjoy stunning views of the river. The old British Circuit House is set within the grounds, constructed for the visit of the Prince of Wales in 1922 and a setting for a short story by W. Somerset Maugham. Perhaps the best place to a enjoy a 'sundowner' and enjoy the view of the river. Outdoor dining with nightly puppet shows. Bungalows. Pool. Situated behind the museum, within the Walled City.
Tel. 95 1 703 992 (Yangon), 95 2 67144 (Pagan)
E-mail: thande@myanmar.com.mm
www.baganthandehotel.com

Bagan Hotel

Memorable evening pageants feature men with flaming torches and others disguised as elephants, enlivened with a dramatic sound track. If flamboyant Hollywood musicals from the 1930s are your thing, then don't miss it. This show can also be combined with a hearty diner buffet. The architectural ambience is inspired by motifs from the monuments. Two ancient temples within the grounds. Pool. Behind the Gawdaw-palin and inside the Walled City.
Tel. 95 1 249 622 (Yangon), 95 2 70145-6 (Pagan)
E-mail: baganhotel@myanmars.net
www.myanmars.net/baganhotel

Activities

Excursion to Mount Popa

This extinct volcano is home to one of Burma's most auspicious *nat* centres. It is about 50 kilometres from the Walled City, or a little over an hour by private taxi. The lush semi-tropical setting is a sharp contrast to the plain below.

At the base of the mountain is the *Popa Mountain Resort*, with breathtaking views, especially at sunset. This boutique resort has an excellent restaurant, also with a view. Staff can organize walks and horseback riding. If you are 'templed-out', then this is the place for you. Bungalows. Pool.
Tel. 95 1 202 071-73 (Yangon), 95 62 70365-7 (Pagan)
E-mail: woodland@mptmail.net.mm

Ballooning

Reservations for '*Balloons Over Pagan*' can be made in the lobby of the Bagan Hotel, and information about this balloon service is available at all of the major hotels.
Tel. 95 1 652 809 (Yangon)
E-mail: balloon@myanmar.com.mm
www.balloonoverbagan.com

Lacquer ware and souvenirs

The best place to witness the multi-step production of lacquer is *Moe Moe Lacquer Shop*, in New Pagan, facing a roundabout on the main road leading south of the Walled City. For one-stop souvenir shopping, try *Shwe War Thein Handicraft Shop*, near Tharabha Gate, in Taungbi village.

Boat Trips

Small motorized launches are available at the jetty beyond the Mahabodhi temple and the Government Lacquer Ware Museum. Individual boatmen offer hourly rates, which are negotiable. Best times are in the morning or early evening.

Travel agents in Yangon

Y & A Tours
Tel. 95 1 210 728
E-mail: info@discover-burma.com

Good News Travels & Tours
Tel. 95 1 246 788, Mobile 95 9 501 9044
E-mail: good-news@mptmail.net.mm
www.goodnewsofmyanmar.com

Licensed guide for Pagan

Moe Aung Lwin ('Moe')
Tel. 95 1 534 003, 722 052
E-mail: moeandwin@mptmail.net.mm

GLOSSARY

Sanskrit (S); Pali (P); Burmese (B)

Arimaddanapura (P). 'City of the Crusher of Enemies'. This was the formal name for Pagan in the ancient period, used in inscriptions.

Avalokiteshvara (S). A principal bodhisattva, associated with compassion. Lokanatha (P), Lokanat (B).

Bodhi tree Tree under which the Buddha obtained his enlightenment in Bodh Gaya, India. It is a pipal tree (*Ficus religiosa*), or *ashvattha* (S), *assattha* (P).

Bodhisattva (S) An 'Enlightenment Being'. A being capable of enlightenment but who remains in this world to assist others. The historical Buddha is also called a 'bodhisattva' before he achieved enlightenment. Bodhisatta (P), baw-di-that (B).

Brahma (S, P) A Hindu deity absorbed into Buddhism, as a devotee to the Buddha. Byan-ma (B).

Deva (S, P). God. Nat (B). 'Celestials' in the Buddhist pantheon.

Garuda (S) Part human, part bird, garuda is the vehicle of the Hindu god Vishnu. Galon (B).

Gautama (S) Personal name of the Buddha. Gotama (P).

Glass Palace Chronicle A comprehensive history of Burma, composed in Ava in 1829.

Guha (S, P) A temple. Gu (B).

Hamsa (S, P) A goose. Hin-tha (B).

Hti (B) The metal finial placed at the summit of a stupa.

Indra (S) A Hindu deity absorbed by Buddhism, as a devotee to the Buddha. Sakka (P), Thagya-min (B).

Jataka (S, P) 'Birth-Story'. The Buddha's 547 former lives in which he demonstrated his selfless dedication to others, in animal or human form. Zat (B).

Kinnara (S, P) Part bird, part human. It is often matched with a female, or kinnari. It originated in India and was popular throughout Southeast Asia. Kein-naya (B).

Kirtimukha (S) 'Face of Glory'. This ubiquitous motif in Indian art was introduced throughout Southeast Asia. Bilu-pan-shwei (B).

Mahanipata (P) The last ten jataka stories and the most revered in Burma.

Mahayana 'Great Vehicle'. A major division within Buddhism that stresses the role of the bodhisattva. It arose some 500 years after the Buddha's death and was practiced in India and throughout the Far East.

Maitreya (S) The Buddha of the Future. In Burma this Buddha is thought to appear 5,000 years after the death of Gotama. Metteyya (P).

Makara (S) A mythical sea-creature. A motif introduced throughout Southeast Asia from India. The head resembles a crocodile and it is often depicted with a foliated tail.

Mara (S, P) The demon-king who thwarts the Buddha's progress to enlightenment. Man Nat (B).

Mon The Mon occupied southeastern coastal Burma before the rise of Pagan civilization. The Mon are found today in southeast Burma.

Mudra (S) A gesture made with one or both hands, denoting certain activities or events, such as the Buddha's Triumph over Mara or his First Sermon in the Deer Park.

Nat (B) A 'spirit'. Indigenous spirits worshipped in Burma. The most celebrated is a group numbering 37.

Pagoda An English word used in Burma used often to describe either a stupa or a temple.

Pyu The Pyu occupied large parts of central Burma before the advent of the Burmans in the 9th century. A principal Pyu city was Shri Kshetra. There are no Pyu today in Burma.

Shikara (S) Superstructure of a temple.

Sima (P) Ordination hall for Buddhist monks. Thein (B).

Stupa (S, P) A Buddhist structure containing relics which are often thought to be the corporal remains of the Buddha. Relics, however, can include any objects that are considered auspicious, such as precious stones or images of the Buddha. The Burmese term for stupa is zedi, derived from caitya (S, P), a concept related to the stupa.

Sutra (S) A sermon delivered by the Buddha. Sutta (P).

Theravada (P) 'Speech of the Elders'. A broad division of Buddhism found in Southeast Asia and Sri Lanka. The sacred canon is composed in Pali.

SUGGESTED READING

Aung-Thwin, Michael, *Pagan: The Origins of Modern Burma,* Honolulu, 1985

_____ *Myth and History in the Historiography of Early Burma,* Singapore, 1998

Ba Shin, *The Lokhahteikpan,* Rangoon, 1962

Bautze-Picron, Claudine, *The Buddhist Murals of Pagan,* Bangkok, 2003

Blurton, T. Richard, Isaacs, Ralph, *Visions from the Golden Land,* London, 2000

Bode, M. *The Pali Literature of Burma,* Rangoon, l909

Boudignon, Francoise, 'La ruse dejouee: un histoire, des images', *Aseanie,* 4, 1999

Brac de la Perrière, Bénédicte, 'Royal Images' in their 'palaces': the place of the statues in the cult of the 37 nats', in *Burma: Art and Archaeology,* London, 2002, eds. A. Green, T. R. Blurton, London, 2002

Brown, Robert L, 'Narrative as Icon: The Jataka Stories in Ancient Indian and Southeast Asian Architecture,' in *Sacred Biography in the Buddhist Traditions of South and Southeast Asia,* ed. J. Schober, Honolulu, 1997

_____ 'Bodhgaya and Southeast Asia' in *Bodhgaya,* ed. J. Leoshko, Bombay, 1988

Cooler, Richard, 'Principal Monuments', in *Grove Dictionary of Art,* 23, Oxford, 1996

Covington, Richard, 'Sacred and Profaned', *Smithsonian,* September, 2002

Cox, Hiram, *Journal of a Residence in the Burmhan Empire,* London, 1821

Eade, J. C. 'Early Burmese Horoscopes,' *Etudes birmanies,* Paris, 1998

Epigraphia Birmanica, Rangoon, 1-3, 1919-1923

Frasch, Tilman, *Pagan: Stadt und Staat,* Stuttgart, 1996

Fraser-lu, Sylvia, *Splendor in Wood,* Bangkok, 2001

Galloway, Charlotte, 'Relationships between Buddhist text and images of the Enlightenment during the early Pagan Period,' in *Burma: Art and Archaeology,* eds. A. Green, T. R. Blurton, London, 2002

Grave, P., Barbetti, M. 'Dating the City Wall, Fortifications and the Palace Site at Pagan' *Asian Perspectives,* 40, 1 (2000)

Green, Alexandra, 'Narrative modes in late seventeeth to early nineteenth-century Burmese wall paintings,' in *Burma: Art and Archaeology,* eds. A. Green, T. R. Blurton, London, 2002

Griswold, A., Review of Lokahteikpan by Ba Shin, in *Artibus Asiae,* 33, (1971)

Guillon, Emmanuel, *L'armee de Mara au Pied de l'Ananda,* Paris, 1985

Guy, John, 'A dated Buddha of the Pagan period' in *Indian Art & Connoisseurship: Essays in Honour of Douglas Barrett,* ed. John Guy, Middletown, 1995

_____ 'The Mahabodhi temple: Pilgrim souvenirs of Buddhist India', *The Burlington Magazine,* June, 1991

Herbert, Patricia, *The life of the Buddha,* London, 1993

_____ 'Burmese cosmological manuscripts' in *Burma: Art and Archaeology,* eds. A. Green, T. R. Blurton, London, 2002

Hudson, B., U Nyein Lwin, U Win Maung, 'Digging for myths: archaeological excavations and survey of the legendary nineteen founding village of Pagan', in *Burma: Art and Archeology,* eds. A. Green and T. R. Blurton, London, 2002

_____ 'The Origins of Bagan: New Dates and Old Inhabitants', *Asian Perspectives,* 40, 1 (2000)

Lieberman, Victor, *Strange Parallels: Southeast Asia in Global Context, c. 800-1300,* I, Cambridge, 2003

_____ 'How Reliable is U Kala's Burmese Chronicle? Some New Comparisons', *Journal of Southeast Asian Studies,* XVII, 2, (1986)

Luce, G. H., *Old Burma-Early Pagan,* 1-3, Ascona, l969

_____ Ba Shin, 'Pagan Myinkaba Kubyauk-gyi Temple of Rajakumar', *Bulletin of The Burma Historical,* Commission, 11, (1961)

_____ Pe Maung Tin, *The Glass Palace Chronicle,* Rangoon, l960

_____ *Inscriptions of Burma,* 5, Rangoon, l933-1956

Lujan, R., P. Pichard, 'Painting' in *Grove Dictionary of Art,* 5, Oxford, 1996

Murcott, Susan, *The First Buddhist Women: Translations and Commentary on the Therigatha,* Berkeley, 1991

Nidanakatha, The Story of the Gotama Buddha, translated by N. A. Jayawickrama, Oxford, 2000

Pal, Pratapaditya, *Art of Nepal,* Los Angeles, l985

_____ 'Fragmentary Cloth Paintings from Early Pagan and Relations with Indo-Tibetan Traditions', in *The Art of Burma: New Studies,* ed. D. Stadtner, Bombay, 1999

Pichard, Pierre, *Inventory of Monuments at Pagan,* 1-8, Paris, 1992-2001

_____ 'Ancient Buddhist Monasteries', in *The Buddhist Monastery,* eds. P. Pichard, F. Lagirarde, Paris, 2003

_____ 'A Distinctive Technical Achievement: The Vaults and Arches of Pagan,' in *The Art of Burma: New Studies,* ed. D. Stadtner, Bombay, 1999

_____ 'Pagan Newsletter', Pondicherry, 1982-1986

_____ 'Pagan', in *Grove Dictionary of Art,* 23, Oxford, 1996

_____ *The Polygonal Monuments of Pagan,* Bangkok, 1991

Pranke, Patrick, 'The 'Treatise on the Lineage of Elders' (Vamsadipani): Monastic Reform and the Writing of Buddhist History in Eighteenth-century Burma', Unpublished dissertation, University of Michigan, 2004, new edition.

Shorto, H. L. 'The devata plaques on the Ananda basement', in *Essays Offered to G. H. Luce,* ed. Ba Shin, Ascona, 1966

Stadtner, Donald, 'The Three Jewels at Pagan', in *In the Footsteps of the Buddha,* ed. R. Ghose, Hong Kong, 1998

_____ 'A Fifteenth-century Royal Monument in Burma and the Seven Stations in Buddhist Art,' *The Art Bulletin,* 73,1 (1991).

_____ 'King Dhammaceti's Pegu', *Orientations,* February, 1990

_____ 'The Art of Burma' in *Art of Southeast Asia,* M. Girard-Geslan, et al., New York, l998

Strachan, Paul, *Imperial Pagan,* Honolulu, 1991

Strong, John S., *The Legend and Cult of Upagupta,* Princeton, 1992

Symes, Michael, *An Account of an Embassy to the Kingdom of Ava,* London, 1800

Than Tun, History of Buddhism in Burma, 1000-1300, *Journal of the Burma Research Society,* LXI, 1-2. (1978)

_____ *Bagan Let-thit and other papers compiled by Dr Than Tun for the 80th Birthday of Ludu Daw Ah Mar,* Mandalay, l996

_____ 'Pagan Restorations', *Journal of the Burma Research Society,* (l976)

Trainor, Kevin, *Relics, Ritual and Representation in Buddhism,* Cambridge, l997

Win Than Tun, 'Myanmar Buddhism of the Pagan Period (AD 1000-1300)', Unpublished dissertation, National University of Singapore, 2002

Woodward, Hiram, Jr. 'Influence and Change: Burma and Thailand in the Twelfth and Thirteenth Centuries,' *Arts of Asia,* 24, 2 (March-April, 1194)

Yule, Henry, *Mission to the court of Ava in 1855,* Reprint, Oxford, l968

INDEX

PAGAN

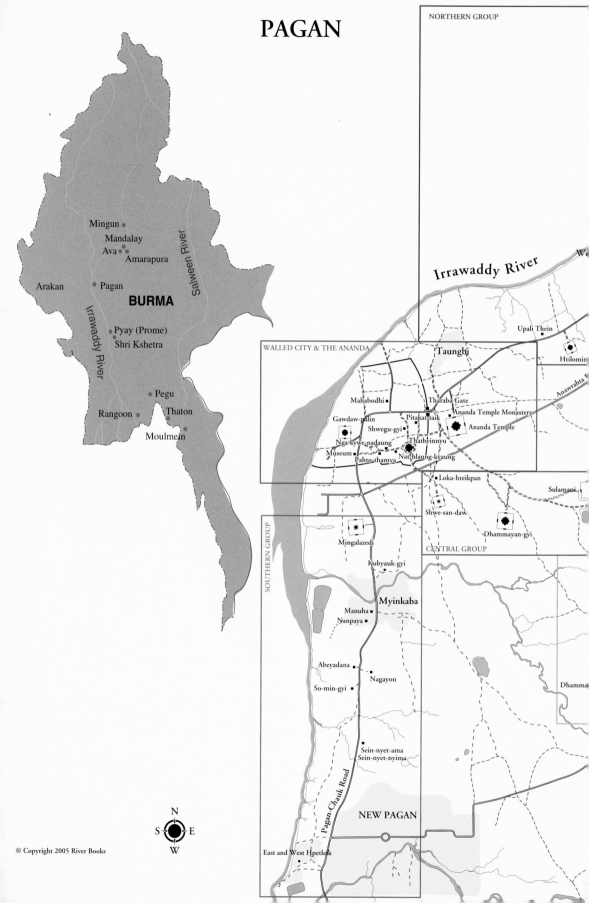

NORTHERN GROUP

Irrawaddy River

W

Upali Thein

Taunghi

Htilomin

WALLED CITY & THE ANANDA

Tharaba Gate

Anawrahta

Mahabodhi

Ananda Temple Monastery

Pitakat-taik

Gawdaw-palin

Ananda Temple

Shwegu-gyi

Thatbyinnyu

Nga-kywe-nadaung

Museum

Nat-hlaung-kyaung

Pahto-thamya

Loka-hteikpan

Sulamani

Shwe-san-daw

Mingalazedi

Dhammayan-gyi

CENTRAL GROUP

Kubyauk-gyi

SOUTHERN GROUP

Myinkaba

Manuha

Nanpaya

Abeyadana

Nagayon

So-min-gyi

Dhamma

Sein-nyet-ama
Sein-nyet-nyima

Pagan-Chauk Road

NEW PAGAN

N
S ✦ E
W

East and West Hpetleik

BURMA

Mingun

Mandalay
Ava
Amarapura

Salween River

Arakan

Pagan

Irrawaddy River

Pyay (Prome)

Shri Kshetra

Pegu

Rangoon

Thaton

Moulmein